Cruise through History

ITINERARY 02

ROME TO VENICE

Around the Boot, Up the Adriatic, with Islands of the Mediterranean: Sicily, Sardinia, & Corsica

SHERRY HUTT

Copyright © 2014 by Sherry Hutt

All rights reserved. No part of this book may be reproduced or transmitted in any form or by any means, electronic or mechanical, including photocopying, recording, or by any information storage and retrieval system without the written permission of the author, except where permitted by law.

ISBN print 978-1-942153-03-0 | eBook 978-1-942153-02-3

TABLE OF CONTENTS

ITINERARY II. ROME TO VENICE – ISLANDS OF THE MEDITERRANEAN AND ADRIATIC

Preface 5

Acknowledgements 9

Introduction:
Travels through the Greek and Latin World 11

Ports on this Itinerary:

1. Rome, Italy
   - a. Rome to Brindisi: The Appian Way – Queen of the Road 17
   - b. The Original Adventures of Pinocchio 29
   - c. Vatican Library 35

2. Naples, Italy
   - a. Virgil's Egg 45
   - b. At Home in Naples: Herculaneum to Villa Sforza 57

3. Amalfi/Positano, Italy –
   Tale of Sybaris and Her Sister Cities (Paestum) 71

4. Corsica, France – Ajaccio - Napoleon's Mother 85

5. Sardinia, Italy
   - a. Caprera – At Home with Garibaldi 103
   - b. Land of the Giants 113

6. SICILY, ITALY
    a. Palermo – The Original Sicilian Vespers 123
    b. Marsala – Garibaldi and The Thousand Take Sicily 133
    c. Segesta – Salvius Slave Revolt.......................... 147
    d. Agrigento/Etna – The Elements of Empedocles 155
    e. Taormina – The Fleeing Women of Sicily................................ 169
    f. Syracuse –
        a. Archimedes' Eureka Moment 181
        b. Dionysius Ear 189

7. CEPHALONIÁ, GREECE –
   CAVE NYMPHS AND THE END OF THE ODYSSEY 197

8. CORFU, GREECE – ELISABETH'S ACHILLEION PALACE......................... 205

9. BARI, ITALY
    a. Frederick II and His Castles: Stupor Mundi............................. 215
    b. The Real St. Nicholas 229
    c. Counting Zimbalo's Angels in Lecce 239

10. DUBROVNIK, CROATIA
    a. Walk the Wall of Dubrovnik... 249
    b. Where Jewish Doctors Made House Calls 261

11. SPLIT, CROATIA –
    RETIREMENT HOME OF ROMAN EMPEROR DIOCLETIAN 269

12. RAVENNA, ITALY –
    GALLA PLACIDIA: MOTHER OF THE WESTERN WORLD 283

13. TRIESTE, ITALY – LAKE BLED: PERFECT DESTINATION WEDDINGS... 301

14. VENICE, ITALY – THE WELL-TRAVELED HORSES OF SAINT MARKS.... 309

INDEX 322

PREFACE TO SERIES

Cruise through History is a collection of short stories grouped by the sequence of many popular cruise itineraries, rather than by country, or period of history. The stories are all true. As the stories move from port to port, they randomly move through time. They are offered not for knowledge alone, but to augment the joy of travel.

It is not necessary for the cruise passenger to peruse several volumes assembling information for the several countries that can be visited on a single cruise. The assemblage is complete in one place. At each port there is a person, a site, an event, or a community of customs, which serves as emblematic of the times and allows the history of place to be drawn together in a fascinating context for the short-term visitor.

No apology is made for the choice of subjects. They have been chosen in an arbitrary manner on the whim of the author, accumulated from past travels, for your enjoyment. The desire is that the reader will share the fun. No attempt is made to be politically correct, or give a chamber of commerce gloss to the stories evident in the remnants of the past. Knowledge of history can teach us a great deal about ourselves, and the human condition, but only if it is honest and fairly told. No doubt it is the quest for "real" that draws adults to travel as often and for as long as they are able.

No effort is made to fully educate those who slept through world history in school, but rather to tell the bits the teachers left out, perhaps intentionally. History in all its glory and warts is fascinating. It easily could be a favorite subject of all students, were the full extent of human folly allowed in the classroom, prior to graduate school. In fairness to history teachers of pre-graduate-college students, so much of the lust, greed, and family blood, that drive the events of history, would be lost on those too young to appreciate imperfection as a natural consequence of adulthood.

The desire to seek knowledge, about distant places and times, fuels international tourism. Many travelers who found history in school to be dull, later in life seek to fill in the gaps in their knowledge, with personal experience. This is the opportunity for the events of one's life to give rich meaning to the human condition and to enjoy stories of fact for which fiction is no rival.

Praise is due to the many historians and other scholars who have delved deeply into source data to ponder the minute details of history for pedagogical pursuits. Such information has been mined here, with attribution, for the lively details, which will heighten the traveler's enjoyment of the past. History is a public good. The more it is found to be enjoyable, the more it will be valued.

Apology is due to those who hoped to foster disciplined scholarship in the author. This is reading for an out-of-the classroom experience. Endnotes are inserted to give due credit to the scholars who have provided valuable information and to remind the reader that these stories are true. The presence of source notes is not to feign an academic appearance. Editorial sidebars and fun bits are in the endnotes.

Where interesting facts exist they are assembled in a story to enhance a port visit on the itinerary. When there are gaps in the facts, or mysteries remain, they are not supplemented by fiction. Rather, an effort is made to look at the known as a guide to the unknown. The reader can draw their own conclusions, daydream through the gaps, and enjoy the reason that so much popular fiction and movies are drawn from historical facts.

As the reader travels to distant ports, the available on-site tour guides will likely give an approved history and, if the traveler is fortunate, an archaeological understanding of distant places. Guidebooks and cruise directors will furnish current local information of where to eat and stay, or what to purchase in the area. This series does not attempt to furnish those resources. These stories are offered to give historical context to the sites often visited as cruise destinations. The stories highlight individuals and their impacts to the landscape that can still be seen.

The stories that traverse the landscape in a Cruise Through History introduce local personalities, sometimes reacquainting the traveler with an historic figure in unexpected circumstances. They prompt a look at not just what exists and the technology of how, but also why events occurred, or why the remnants of human effort look as they do. Where did the missing pieces on the landscape go, as conquests by subsequent cultures altered, evolved, and incorporated the past into their times? What were the intended and unintended consequences that have become the fabric of complex history? These stories take travelers beyond the castle ruins to the people who built them and lived there.

The itineraries in this series have stories at each port that seek to inspire cruise travelers to rise out of their deck chairs and investigate a destination with honesty and irreverence, or the potential traveler to rise from the sofa and embark on a Cruise through History. There is no stigma of a school assignment. Earn an "E" for enjoyment.

Itinerary Series forthcoming-

I. London to Rome - Along the Coasts of France, Iberia, and Northern Italy (September 2014)

II. Rome to Venice – Around the Boot, Up the Adriatic, with Islands of the Mediterranean (Sicily, Sardinia, Corsica) (November2014)

III. Athens to Cairo – Greek Islands, Turkey and the Eastern Mediterranean

IV. Ports of the Black Sea

V. Agadir to Alexandria - Southern Mediterranean, North Africa, and the Atlantic Islands

VI. Miami to Montreal - East Coast of North America

VII. San Diego to Sitka - West Coast of North America

VIII. Mexico, Central America, and the Caribbean Islands (Spring 2015)

IX. Ports of South America

X. Around the British Iles - England, Ireland, Wales and Scotland

XI. Ports of the Baltic Sea

XII. Ports of the North Sea - Hanseatic League, Iceland, and Greenland
XIII. Cape Town to Beijing – Africa, India, and the Far East
XIV. Australia, New Zealand, and the Pacific Islands

ACKNOWLEDGEMENTS

Writing short stories began as therapy from the world of Washington, D.C. Special thanks are due to Lesa Koscielski for an edit of Itinerary II, and to Diana Smoltz for sharing her pictures of Cefalonia. Much appreciation is also due to those who fostered my education in archaeology and cultural property: The Ladies Society of the Smithsonian Institution, who supported my post-doctorate fellowship; the Lawyers' Committee for Cultural Property Protection, where lawyers donate their skill to preservation and protection of heritage in the United States and around the world; the archaeological resources protection expert squad of David Tarler, Martin McAllister, George Smith, Todd Swain, Tim Canaday, Mike Marous, Larry Mackey, Guy Prentice, Alise Foster, Caroline Blanco, Ole Varmer, and the legendary Don and Catherine Fowler. These stories would not be possible without the treasure trove of material in libraries and used bookshops. I am indebted to the Grove Park Book Exchange, Asheville NC, the Bienecke Library, Yale University, the Lanier Library, Tryon, NC, and the Library of Congress. In this increasingly paperless world, bookstores and libraries provide solace and an opportunity to revive our humanity. The greatest thanks go to my husband, Guy Rouse, who has lugged my camera equipment all over the world for more than 25 years.

Itinerary II is dedicated to our children, Lisa, Alexander, and Elizabeth, for whom traveling the world is an indispensible part of their professional and leisure lives.

INTRODUCTION

Travels through the Greek and Latin World

Almost a thousand years before the birth of Christ, Greeks rowed west on the Adriatic Sea, landed near what is now Brindisi, and ran from the heel of the boot of Italy to the place where Rome stands today. They did this for fun and games. Hundreds of years later, Romans paved the road from Rome to Brindisi. They did this to support military and commercial needs. In the current era, roads connected the three capitals of the Christian world: Rome, Ravenna, and Constantinople. Later Roman paving stones became the material for early Christian churches such as in the Square of Miracles in Pisa.

The Greeks and then the Latins were not the only, or the first, inhabitants of the seaside around Italy, the east of the Adriatic, and the islands off the shores. Greeks and later Romans found themselves depleted by warfare with northern Italian Etruscans, tribes from the north of the mountains, and civilizations from northern Africa. Warfare had benefits. The vanquished were a source of slaves needed to sustain the economy of the growing upper class. In the most recent 800 years, as kingdoms grew powerful in Europe, French, Spanish, German and Austrian kings sent their legions to control the mainland of Italy and the islands. Italy was late to expel external forces and unify. Despite the early conquests and the dominance of Rome until several centuries into the current era, Italy remained fragmented from the decline of Rome to the 1860s. In modern times there was much infighting to overcome.

Italy and its surrounding islands were well positioned in the world trade arena. Sitting at the base of Europe, poised to receive and distribute goods from and to the northlands, and as a transition point for ships to the Far East, the kings of Italy from the tenth century forward were the merchants. The Adriatic side of Italy was controlled by Venetian traders and the Mediterranean side by Genoese. Genoa controlled Corsica. Venice controlled Corfu, Dubrovnik, and other growing ports on the Adriatic. It was a symbiotic relationship. Seamen from large trading hubs needed ports to replenish stocks of food and fresh water, and to provide safe haven in storms. Small, but growing, port cities looked to Genoa and Venice for their economic growth.

The stories on this itinerary include tales of personalities and events from 1700 BCE to the nineteenth century of the current era. Some of the stories include familiar names and others introduce new names worth knowing. Italy and the surrounding islands provided fresh space for Greeks to leave their crowed homelands and think new thoughts. The stories on this itinerary include those of Archimedes, Dionysius, Empedocles and Saint Nicholas, all men with roots in Greece, while they lived in Italy. Italy produced a new crop of thinkers, poets, engineers and architects in Virgil, Appia, Onofrio and Zimbalo.

There is no shortage of heroes on this itinerary, real and fictional, well known and those who should be well known: Odysseus, Pinocchio, Garibaldi, Canova, Frederick II, and the slave who led a revolt much before Spartacus, Salvius. There are also stories of those who joined movements that changed the course of history, unnamed heroes in their actions: the leaders of the first Sicilian Vespers, the Papal librarians of the Vatican, and the Jewish doctors, expelled from Venice, who kept Dubrovnik healthy.

Most of the existing literature preserves the deeds of men who shaped the world. As always, the stories on a Cruise through History are arbitrarily chosen, but are ecumenical. On this itinerary the traveler will visit ports where the leadership, strength, and wisdom of women leaders were of major impact. Živa chose to be married in the middle of Lake Bled in ancient times, in what has become a continual ideal place for destination weddings today. Galla Placidia, mother of the western Christian world, financed commissions for mosaics of lasting beauty in the fifth century, while also finding time to establish a papacy in Rome and protect Rome from barbarians.

The fleeing women of Sicily asserted their independence, just as Elisabeth, empress of Austria, expressed her need for solace and independence when she built her Achílleion Palace in Corfu. Letizia Buonaparte raised an emperor and, as she said of herself, diapered and disciplined more future emperors and princes than anyone else. Letizia is almost unheard of except when connected with her famous son, Napoleone Bounaparte. He left Corsica and dropped vowels from his name as he learned French and gained territories.

The women on this itinerary share their homes with you. The nymphs of the caves of Cephalonia greet travelers today as they did Odysseus coming home from the Trojan War. Justa, the child of Herculaneum, holds continual open house of the home her freedwoman mother built, as she waits for her court case to be decided and her freedom established. Elegant women of the Renaissance built homes eighty feet above the mud-entombed Herculaneum, outside of Naples, such as the Sforza palace, now a hotel. The Nuraghe nation invites you to discover it in Sardinia.

Whether enjoyed as a book of history, or read by the traveler port-to-port as their itinerary unfolds, the characters in these stories will become new acquaintances. They are assembled here as a Cruise through History to add meaning and delight to travels.

CTH

14 | CRUISE THROUGH HISTORY – ITINERARY II. – ROME TO VENICE

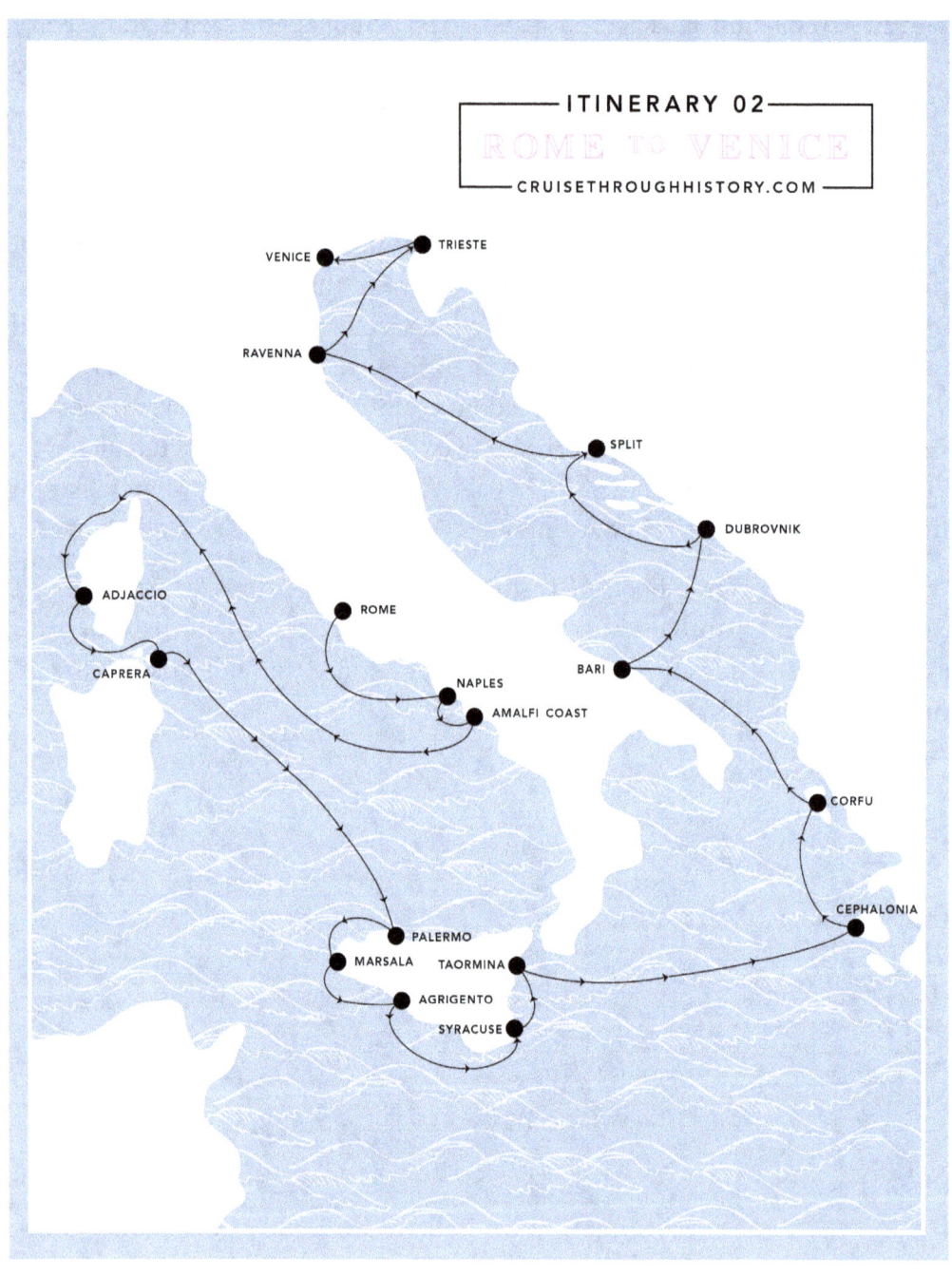

Cruise Through History
ITINERARY II

Timeline | cruisethroughhistory.com

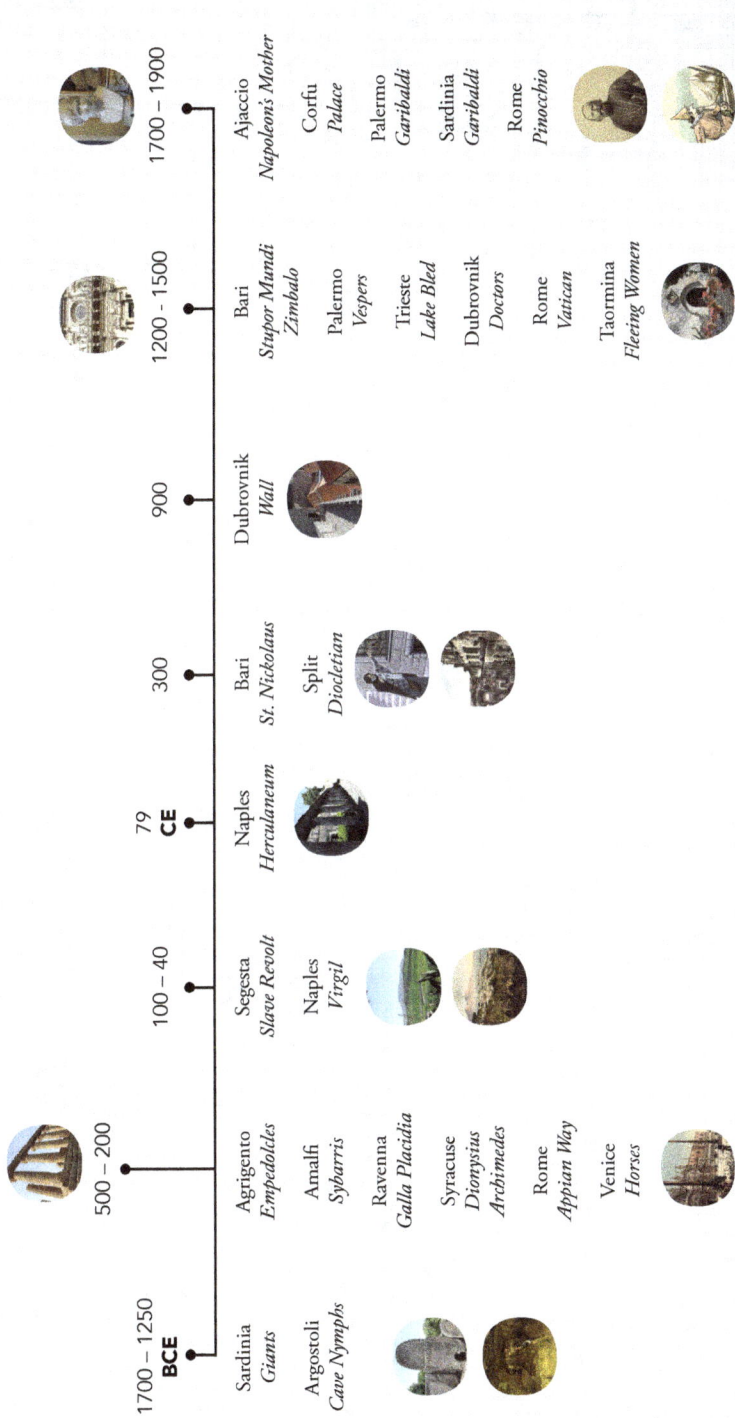

1700 – 1250 BCE	500 – 200	100 – 40	79 CE	300	900	1200 – 1500	1700 – 1900
Sardinia *Giants*	Agrigento *Empedocles*	Segesta *Slave Revolt*	Naples *Herculaneum*	Bari *St. Nickolaus*	Dubrovnik *Wall*	Bari *Stupor Mundi Zimbalo*	Ajaccio *Napoleon's Mother*
Argostoli *Cave Nymphs*	Amalfi *Sybarris*	Naples *Virgil*		Split *Diocletian*		Palermo *Vespers*	Corfu *Palace*
	Ravenna *Galla Placidia*					Trieste *Lake Bled*	Palermo *Garibaldi*
	Syracuse *Dionysius Archimedes*					Dubrovnik *Doctors*	Sardinia *Garibaldi*
	Rome *Appian Way*					Rome *Vatican*	Rome *Pinocchio*
	Venice *Horses*					Taormina *Fleeing Women*	

ROME
The Appian Way – Queen of the Roads

A good road can make the difference for a nation seeking to defends its territory and build its economy. This was obvious to Appius Claudius in 312 BCE, when he began to build a road from Rome to distant territories.[1] That road became known as the Appian Way (Via Appia).

The novel idea of Appius became popular as an alternative to moving armies and grain by sea. It was quickly replicated throughout the Roman territory. No longer would Roman generals need to stop to ask directions to avoid getting lost. Roman chariots could travel at great speed outside of the circus, that is, the sports arena. Collection of taxes, to finance the road, could be facilitated. Appius could imagine all sorts of possibilities.

This is the short story of the first, and for a long time the longest, road in the history of travel. The Appian Way instigated a critical shift in the way goods and armies could move. Empire building was no longer dependent upon the sea. For these reasons the Appian Way was known in ancient times as "regina viarum," the "Queen of the Roads."

Before Via Appia

The Appian Way covers 350 miles from Rome to Brindisi, but the story of the road goes back further in time. As in many other realms, Greek ingenuity preceded that of the Romans. The Greeks found they needed more than a

---

[1] Appius was well aware of what people needed as he was the head of the city public works department. He also knew what people should do, as he was the chief sensor in charge of public morals. Irene M. Franck and David M. Brownstone, The European Overland Routes, Facts on File, New York, 1990, p. 37.

goat path to transport items between Greek cities and Troy. Rather than be dependent upon boat travel across the Aegean Sea in inclement weather, they sought a land route across northern Greece to ports on the Adriatic, such as Apollonia and Dyrrhachium.[2]

The road begun prior to Via Appia was known as the Via Egnatia. It ran from Troy west to the Adriatic coast, where the route connected from across the sea at Brindisi on the Italian side. Eventually, Via Egnatia was extended eastward to Constantinople. With the completion of Via Appia from Rome to Brindisi and the extension of Via Egnatia, there was a direct highway from Rome to Constantinople, connecting the capitals of the Christian world by land, with only a short section across the sea. All of this was completed hundreds of years after Appius, but it was his vision that made it possible.

The early Via Egnatia had turf issues. The road passed through the lands of the ancient rulers of Macedonia, Bulgaria, and Yugoslavia. Greece and Persia coveted the road. The Via Egnatia was a commerce route without a single military protector, that is, until the arrival of the Romans.

Appius Claudius knew the value of the road for commerce. He also learned from the Via Egnatia experience that the road must be suitable for armies to sustain continuity of use. He achieved his goals with the Appian Way. By terminating his road at Brindisi, he allowed for Roman troops to cross the Adriatic at its most narrow point. From there Roman legions could move east along the Via Egnatia, unifying control of the road as they went. They could send the spoils of war home and keep their supply lines open with the established road.

Road Building with Appius

To the extent that he could, Appius utilized the centuries old Greek footpath from Brindisi to Rome. Greek Olympic hopefuls had often run from the area that became Rome to Brindisi, where they would take ships back to their

---

[2] Much to the disappointment of present-day Greeks, these ports are now within Albania. Apollonia, also known as Epiamnus, is on the bay of Vlora, and Dyrrhachium is also known as Durazzo, or Durresi.

homeland. Runners travel light. Appius needed to create wide roadbeds that could carry heavy wagons and would not flood out at the bottom of valleys in the rainy season.

Then, as now, the key to a good road is the drainage. Appius laid out roadbeds that were slightly raised in the middle to encourage drainage. He instituted the roadside gutter to carry away the runoff. Roads that ran along flat terrain or mountainsides were easy to keep level and drained. The challenge for Appius was in engineering level roadbeds in valleys and across streams.

The Romans used aqueducts to move water to cities. They had developed the technology to carry the substantial weight of water high above ground, to achieve the required slope, supported by stone or brick arches.[3] Appius used the arch-supported roadbeds to level out those places where the road would traverse marshes or low-lying terrain. These he called "viaducts."

---

[3] One of the early aqueducts is named Aqua Appia.

The roads built by Appius were 10 to 15 feet wide to accommodate large wagons and oncoming traffic. The width of a road was especially important in the high mountains. Troops could march several abreast on the Appian Way. Wide roads helped with navigating curves. Appius developed solutions to address road-building problems, which are still in use today.

Appius experimented with road paving. A dirt roadbed might suffice in dry areas, but for damp areas and in areas of heavy traffic, such as in cities, something more was required. Appius at first tried gravel and later used cut stone to pave the roads. Decades later the road builders used silex, cut sheets of volcanic rock.[4] The cut rock was so well fitted that mortar was often not needed. In some places the stones were fixed with lime cement. When new, the roads were smooth. When the road route went through a city, such as Pompeii, steppingstones were placed across the roadbed at a distance that permitted people to walk across, while still allowing wagons to traverse the road and water to drain. There were also sidewalks for pedestrians in the cities.

Appius did not need to consider traffic control signs. If there were directional signs they would have been simple, Rome this way and Constantinople that way. There are very old mile-markers along the Via Appia and the Via Egnatia, initially placed when the roads were new. There were also markers indicating the builder or sponsor of a section of road. Lessons learned on the Via Egnatia were employed on the Via Appia. Then the Via Egnatia was improved with updated technology from the Via Appia experience. Where wood was initially used for bridges or road support, stone or brick was eventually inserted as a replacement.

Appius and his civic works department had employment security for life. By 117 CE, there was a network of roads across all areas of the Roman Empire.[5] To the credit of Roman road engineers, many of their efforts are still visible or in use two millennia later.

---

4   Franck & Brownstone, p. 39.
5   Builders of the Ancient World, National Geographic Society, Washington, DC, 1986, p. 41.

The Appian Route

The Appian Way begins in Rome at the Forum. It traveled out of town along the Via Latina, passing through a gate in the wall. When the walls were later rebuilt, a gate was specially constructed for the road at Port Appia. Then, as now, beyond the city walls the road went through affluent neighborhoods.

Once the Appian Way left the vicinity of Rome, the road went straight down to the coastal city of Anxur, now known as Terracina. Today there is a seaside resort at Terracina, but back in the day of road building it was a port city capable of receiving supplies for an army. The road then hugged the bay south of Terracina, until it veered east to Capua.

By going east to Capua, north of Naples, the Appian Way went north of Mount Vesuvius. Although it would be several centuries until the fateful eruption, there were enough minor eruptions during the life of Appius to put the road builders on alert. Getting to the port of Naples was not a concern for Appius. His superiors were more focused upon battles with the remaining tribe of Sammites, living in the hills north of Capua. Capua sought the help of Rome to dispel the enemy, forging bonds between Rome and Capua. The Appian Way was a sign of support and a practical necessity for the Roman army. It was 132 miles from Rome to Capua on the Via Appia.

In 295 BCE the road builders were at work extending Via Appia beyond Capua. By 290, the road extended to Tarentum, in the heel of the boot of Italy. The southeastern area of Italy was at the time still Greek in culture and loyalty. The citizens of Tarentum appealed to a Greek king, King Pyrrhus, to repel the Romans. The ensuing battle was a grizzly affair. Although King Pyrrhus was the acknowledged victor, he was recorded as saying, "One more such victory and I am lost." It was the original Pyrrhic victory.

By 272 BCE the Romans resolved the issue with Tarentum by controlling the Puglia region. Appius Claudius died in 273 BCE, without seeing his road finished. In his name, the road continued across the heel of the boot of Italy to Brindisi, on the western shore of the Adriatic Sea. The smooth highway from Rome to Brindisi was 350 miles long when complete.

To commemorate the end of the road, two columns were constructed at the wharf in Brindisi. From that wharf, ships would go to the Greek ports on the other side of the Adriatic. Travelers would continue from there on their journey on the Via Egnatia.

Today there is only one column at the top of the stairs that lead to the water in Brindisi. The other column is now in Lecce, the lovely little town inland from Brindisi. In 1528, Brindisi made a gift of the column to Lecce in thanks for the efforts of the Lecce town saint, whose prayers spared the people of Brindisi from a plague.[6]

---

[6] See Counting Zimbalo's Angels in Lecce, this itinerary.

The Appian Way in History

Any child with a chariot could use the road. There were no speed limits, such as limiting chariots to one horse only near residential areas. In cities, the roads were widened by as much as three or four times the typical width of a chariot in order to accommodate substantial two-way traffic.

The roads were not controlled to collect tolls. All citizens were taxed. If the taxes were not paid, the taxpayer could be put in prison and/or sold as a slave. Slaves could be used to build and repair roads. They could also revolt against a system they felt was unjust. The slave Spartacus led the most famous slave revolt in Roman times.

The slave revolt led by Spartacus was from 73 to 71 BCE. It is famous as it was large in scope and well documented. Spartacus led a group of trained gladiators out of the coliseum arena to terrorize Roman civilization. Rome never recovered.[7] The slave mob used the Appian Way to leave Rome. The Roman soldiers, with fast chariots, used the road to apprehend them. In the end, the roadside of the Appian Way became dotted with 6,000 crucifixions of captured former slaves.

There is also a legend that Saint Peter walked the Appian Way from Rome. He was anxious to get out of town to avoid persecution by Emperor Nero. The legend holds that Jesus Christ appeared to Saint Peter and implored him to return to Rome to seek the understanding of the Romans in his word. Saint Peter asked, "Domine, quo vadis?" That is, "Lord, where are you going?" Jesus answered, "To Rome, to be crucified anew." Peter was instantly ashamed of his weakness and returned to Rome. Today the site of the interaction of Saint Peter and Jesus, about two miles outside of Rome, is marked with the Church of Santa Maria in Palmis, also known as the Domine Quo Vadis church.[8]

---

[7] See Slave Revolts of Segesta, this Itinerary. Also, Theresa Urbainczyk, Slave Revolts in Antiquity, University of California Press, Berkeley, 2008.
[8] Some believe the footprint preserved and framed inside the church is that of Christ.

Later legend placed the crypt of Saint Peter in one of the mausoleums along the Appian Way, in the Catacombs of St. Sebastian.

It was forbidden to bury people in the city limits of Rome. Instead wealthy families carved catacombs out of the rock under and along the Appian Way, just outside of the city. Christians and pagans were laid to rest in close proximity in the catacombs. Later, the remains of those identified as Christian martyrs were removed to various churches. Today those catacombs are a major tourist destination.

The Appian Way Today

In 1784, a new Appian Way was constructed, parallel to the older road. The new road is the Via Appia Nuova. The original road is designated the Via Appia Antica. The catacombs are along the Antica road.

In 1960, the Appian Way Antica was used as part of the men's marathon in the Summer Olympics. There are portions of the road off limits to cars, where people can walk unobstructed for about ten miles. Other parts of the original road are still open to vehicle traffic. The Appian Way Antica just outside of the city of Rome is open to cars. The road is in constant use and traffic jams are frequent. It is the only means for tour buses to access the catacombs.

The Appian Way is no longer a road of military significance. Cargo now travels the network of superhighways through Italy. However, several of the road building technologies first used by Appius Claudius are in use today. That people from the provinces were able to easily travel to Rome helped to build its status and economy, which have endured. If a good road enables a community to flourish, then the Appian Way deserves its title of "Queen of the Roads."

The Original Adventures of Pinocchio

At cruise stops along the northern coast of Italy running from Florence to Rome, the ubiquitous curio stands all have red puppets, with conical bodies and long wooden noses. Although the puppet may not be familiar to Americans, it is easily recognized as Pinocchio. The reason why Italians sell the puppet, seen as often as Italian ices, is not readily apparent to foreigners. There is no Disneyland in Italy.

Fifty-seven years before the Disney version, Pinocchio appeared in the children's literature of Italy. He was a comic star in Europe prior to making his film debut in America. For over 100 years, Pinocchio has been an icon of fable and fantasy. This is his story.

Naming Pinocchio

Identifying Pinocchio is easier than explaining the origin of his name. Northern Italians, particularly in the area of Pisa, where the pinion pine tree is harvested for its pine nuts, will tell you that the name "Pinocchio" must come from that area as "Pinocchio" means pine or pine nut. However, in the original Italian story, Pinocchio is made of cherry wood.

Another explanation for Pinocchio's name is that the folk tale of a puppet that became a boy was well known throughout Italy. The Italian word for a knot in wood is "nocchio." So a knotty pine puppet could be logically named "Pinocchio." Another option would be to suspend reality, since Pinocchio is a puppet after all, and just accept the name given to the handiwork of the woodcarver Geppetto.

The Man Behind the Puppet

Pinocchio was the creation of Carlo Collodi in 1883. Collodi was not a woodcarver. Carlo Collodi is the pseudonym of Carlo Lorenzini (1826-1890). Collodi is a village in Tuscany, the birthplace of Carlo's mother. Perhaps Lorenzini, a former soldier and then a newspaperman, was skittish about being known as the author of morality tales for children wherein the central character is a puppet.

Lorenzini grew up in Florence. He gained much of his education on the streets, while his parents worked as domestic staff. After trying to establish himself as a satirical journalist, he took as a job as a government bureaucrat in the education department. Frustrated by an inability to accomplish reforms in childhood education, he turned to writing. No doubt his youthful experiences informed his later stories.

In his mid to late twenties, Lorenzini wrote fiction and non-fiction books for adults. Some were published. None were widely successful. To add to his income, he translated French fairy tales. Thus began his interest in writing for children.

Lorenzini's first success as a writer was the fairy tale of Giannettino. It was a tame story that promoted education. Encouraged by his success, Lorenzini wrote to a friend who edited a newspaper in Rome, which was geared to children.[9] *The Adventures of Pinocchio* first appeared in Rome as a weekly-serialized story of the life of a wooden puppet. The installments appeared in 1881 through 1882. They were so well received that Lorenzini published the collection as a book in 1883. The book was an instant success. It was first available in the English version in 1892.[10]

Lorenzini did not write for his children. He never had children. It is said that he did not like children.[11] Pinocchio was written as a warning to children that if they were bad, then bad things would happen.

---

[9] The newspaper in Rome: *Giornale del bambini*.
[10] *Your way to Florence*, http://www.yourwaytoflorence.com/db/pinocchio/pinocchio.htm. Last visited 4/16/12.
[11] Nathaniel Rich, "Bad Things Happen to Bad Children," *The Slate Book Review*, posted Oct. 24, 2011, http://www.slate.com/articles/arts/books/2011/10/carlo_collodi_s_pinocchio Last visited 4/16/2012.

In some of the installments Pinocchio is beaten. Finally, his enemies, the Fox and the Cat, hang him. He dies. The weekly readers were outraged. Pinocchio could not end in death. So Lorenzini added installments where the Blue Fairy, his mother figure, came along to revive him. Readers received an unintended happy ending.

The Original Story

In all derivations of the story since its inception, Pinocchio is a wooden puppet that desires to become a real boy. The adventures vary with the telling. Regardless of when and where the story is told, Pinocchio cannot tell a lie without his nose growing longer.

The original Pinocchio was made of wood. His clothes were made of flower-printed paper. His hat was made of bread. Consistent in every Pinocchio story is the tendency for his nose to grow longer as a telltale sign that he is under stress and is about to tell a lie.

In the original story, before there was a puppet, there was a block of cherry wood. An old carpenter spotted the brick of wood as too fine to throw on the fire and decided to make it into a table leg. When he tried to cut the wood, a little voice called out in pain. When he tried to shape the wood, a little voice giggled as though he was being tickled. The carpenter was perplexed. He could not find the source of the voice. He could not work with the wood without hearing the voice. So he gave up and made a gift of the wood to his friend, Geppetto, who made marionettes. If the wood could talk perhaps it could dance. It was meant to be a puppet.

From the moment Geppetto gave Pinocchio a mouth, the puppet was insolent. When Geppetto gave him hands, Pinocchio snatched the carver's wig. The first thing Pinocchio did when he had legs and feet was to kick Geppetto. Then he ran out of the house. Geppetto realized that Pinocchio could not hear, as he had no ears.

Geppetto sold his winter coat to buy schoolbooks so that Pinocchio could go to school. Both had intentions that Pinocchio would learn to read and write to become a productive member of the household. However, Pinocchio was easily distracted.

Pinocchio sold the schoolbooks on the way to school in order to buy entrance to a puppet show. He upset the show by getting up on the stage. The puppet master grabbed Pinocchio and threatened to put him in the fire to cook his dinner. Frantically, Pinocchio told his tale of the poor Geppetto. The puppet master gave Pinocchio gold pieces to buy Geppetto a new coat and replace the schoolbooks. Instead of returning to Geppetto, Pinocchio headed out to his next adventure.

When the Fox and the Cat saw the gold coins, they created a scam to use against Pinocchio. They told him of a magic meadow where he could plant his coins and enlarge his holdings. Before going to this magic meadow Pinocchio took a nap. When he awoke it was dark. Fox and Cat were gone. He tried to find his way to the meadow alone. Two robbers, who looked like Fox and Cat, appeared and demanded his coins. Pinocchio could not talk as the coins were under his tongue. So the Fox and Cat hung Pinocchio and left him to die. That was the intended end to the story at chapter 16. Fortunately for Pinocchio, his creator was encouraged to keep writing 20 more chapters.

Pinocchio was a very lucky little puppet. The Blue Fairy saw his predicament. She clapped her hands and the Dog and Hawk appeared to rescue him, put him in a carriage, and deliver him safely to a nice little bed in a fairy castle. The sarcasm of the author is evident as he wrote to please his young readers and their parents.

While Pinocchio rested in the fairy castle, the Blue Fairy called in three famous doctors: Crow, Owl and Cricket. They prescribed bitter medicine. As Pinocchio drank his medicine he was cured. Once he was feeling better, Pinocchio began to lie about losing his money. The coins were in his pocket. His nose began to grow. The Blue Fairy told him that when he tells lies, his nose would grow. He promised to be good, so the Blue Fairy called in woodpeckers to bring his nose down to size.

Pinocchio left the Blue Fairy and started on his way home to Geppetto. Before he arrived home he ran into Fox and Cat. This time they took him to the magic meadow where he buried the coins. In the morning when he looked, the coins were gone. He trudged home to Geppetto without schoolbooks or gold coins. Despite all, the woodcarver was grateful just to see him.

On his way once again to school, Pinocchio met the lazy boy of the class, Carlo. Together they decided to go to Toyland instead of class. Toyland was heavenly. Pinocchio and Carlo played together endlessly. Each day as they played, Pinocchio noticed that his ears were growing longer and were hairy. Then he noticed his friend was walking on all fours. He laughed, but it sounded like a braying donkey. They had both turned into donkeys.

Carlo the donkey was sold to a farmer. Pinocchio the donkey was sold to a circus. He was beaten and made to do tricks. He was fed straw. As a performer, Pinocchio was useless. His new owner sold him to a man to be skinned. The muleskinner tied a rope around Pinocchio's neck. The other end of the rope was tied to a large rock. The man threw Pinocchio into the ocean to drown him so he could be skinned.

At the bottom of the sea, fighting to breathe, Pinocchio called out to the Blue Fairy. She sent a fish to save him. The fish ate away the donkey flesh, leaving the little wooden boy exposed. When the muleskinner pulled on the rope he had a puppet looking at him instead of a dead donkey. The man was enraged. He decided to sell Pinocchio for firewood to recoup his investment. Pinocchio slipped out of the rope and jumped into the sea. He swam away.

Imagine Pinocchio happily swimming along in the sea. He was no longer a donkey. Just then a shark appeared. The shark opened his mouth and Pinocchio was swept into the cavernous belly of the fish.

Pinocchio was in a predicament, but as usual, he was in luck. He was lucky that his story was serialized. In a previous episode, the shark that swallowed him had swallowed Geppetto. Geppetto had been fishing when his boat capsized in a storm. Geppetto was swallowed with bits of boat. He had managed to hang onto a candle and some dry matches. Together the woodcarver and his puppet used the lighted candle to find their way out of the shark stomach and up to its mouth. It was there that they realized that this particular shark suffered from asthma. It snored. The shark slept with its mouth open. It also slept near a beach. Geppetto and Pinocchio walked out of the shark and up to the beach. They were saved.

While sitting alone in the belly of the shark, Pinocchio had an epiphany. He decided to be a good boy. Once they were safe, and while Geppetto sat on the beach, Pinocchio went to a farmer and worked hard each day to buy food for Geppetto so that the old woodcarver could regain his strength. Then Pinocchio worked at night weaving reed into baskets to sell. He used the basket money to buy new clothes. When Pinocchio learned that the Blue Fairy was having hard times, he used some of his basket money to buy things she needed. In return for his generosity, the Blue Fairy turned Pinocchio into a real boy. Happily the fairy said, "When bad boys become good, their looks change along with their lives!"[12]

International Stardom

After the serialized story was released in a book, Pinocchio became a big star throughout Europe in various comic books. In the United States, he appeared in his own Disney movie, made originally in 1940. In 2004, Pinocchio made a cameo appearance in the animated movie Shrek. Pinocchio became a favorite character in Japan in the 1970s. Whenever Pinocchio appears, in any format and in any language, there is a universal understanding that his nose will lengthen when he tells a lie.

Most people know Pinocchio through the Disney movie version. That version has a cricket that sings. The Disney cricket dispenses good advice, not foul-tasting medicine. Just as Pinocchio evolved from a wooden puppet to a real boy, his story has evolved from a harsh morality tale to one of delightful entertainment.

---

[12] Chapter 36. http://www.literaturepage.com/read/pinocchio.html. Last visited 4/16/12.

THE VATICAN LIBRARY

Libraries make wonderful visitor destinations. Among libraries of the world the Vatican Library in Rome is a fascinating place, often overlooked by travelers to Vatican City. The Vatican would remind us that, "The popes always had a library."[13] One common misconception would be that the library is full of dusty liturgical tomes. In reality, the Vatican Library is full of gems of history that reveal the evolution of politics and the foundation of Renaissance secular literature, which includes some tantalizing royal love letters.

The Vatican Library was not always in Rome. Prior to the Renaissance, Rome was not an attractive residence for people or books. As a result of war and plague, the population of Rome had dwindled to about 20,000 inhabitants early in the fourteenth century. Not even the popes wanted to stay in Rome. Several popes found the air much better in Avignon, France. They brought their reading material with them.

When Pope Nicholas V made the decision to consolidate the Vatican library collection in a new facility in Rome, he may have been thinking that the move made practical sense. He may have secretly hoped that his public library for the "Court of Rome" would be an international success. If so, the library exceeded his most saintly dreams.

After several years of restoration, the Vatican Library reopened to the public in September 2010. It is now possible for visitors to Rome to experience the site that brought the popes back to Rome and fostered the Renaissance in literature and art. This is the story of the history of the Vatican Library and the treats that await its present-day visitors.

---

[13] http://www.ibiblio.org/expo/vatican.exhibit/exhibit/a-vatican_lib/Vatican_lib.html. Last visited March 20, 2012. Very little of the collection prior to the thirteenth century has survived.

The Vatican Library in History

Before he died in 1455, Pope Nicholas V created a single Vatican Library in Rome to house the far-flung volumes of the papacy. Reading books and collecting books had been the passion of Nicholas. He knew their value as fonts of knowledge and as historic resources to be protected in perpetuity for the bits of history represented within the fine bindings. Nicholas believed that books were to be kept in circulation and not preserved in vaults away from fresh minds.

As a child of the Catholic Reformation, Nicholas was ecumenical in his book collecting. One hundred years later, the Counter-Reformation would take hold of the Catholic Church and instill censorship. Not all of the early collections of Pope Nicholas would be appreciated. As long as the policies of Nicholas could outlive him, however, the library would grow to become the largest collection of classical-secular literature in the world. It would also provide a safe home to religious texts.

The Vatican Library was given a new home by Nicholas. He provided a lovely, decorated suite of rooms in the Vatican complex with large windows for ample light for reading. From 1455 to 1481, the collection grew from 1.200 to 3,500 volumes. Physically and intellectually, the Vatican Library became the center of the Renaissance in art, scholarship, science and philosophical thought.[14]

The Vatican Library did not sit in a vacuum at the Vatican complex as the sole bright spot. Nicholas prompted construction on the Basilica of St. Peter, which became the palace of the popes in Rome, and he enlarged the fortress of Vatican City.[15] Throughout Rome, Nicholas undertook to repair the streets, bridges, and the water system. In full, the civic improvements to Vatican City under Nicholas touched off a building spree in Rome that became a marvel of urban renewal.

---

[14] Nicholas included the works of Herodotus, Thucydides and other classical Greek compositions in the collection.

[15] The improvements to St. Peters were not universally appreciated. Nicholas tempered some of his plans to pacify historic preservationists of the time. He allowed, with some restorations, the former home of the popes at the Basilica of San Paolo to remain open in the city. The church burned in 1823. http://www.newadvent.org/cathen/11058a.html. Last visited March 20, 2012.

Ecclesiastics and merchants followed the lead of Nicholas and built beautiful estates in Rome and in the immediate area. The structures instigated by Nicholas, as well as those he inspired, exist today in the beauty that is Rome. His efforts caused the city to become repopulated after so many years of decline.

Pope Sixtus IV completed the work that was begun by Nicholas. Sixtus is credited with building the Sistine Chapel and the Sistine Bridge across the Tiber.[16] He is regarded as the second founder of the Vatican Library. It is due to his efforts that water runs in the Trevi Fountain.[17] A tireless reformer, Sixtus straightened the streets of Rome by day, so that the city was habitable

---

[16] The earlier bridge collapsed during the time of Nicholas when there was a solid mass of the faithful crossing the river. There was great loss of life.

[17] A pope had multiple duties as religious icon, city administrator, and commander-in-chief of papal troops. As the military prowess of the Vatican waned over the Renaissance and beyond, the popes maintained their position as guardian of the faithful and able city administrator.

again and could be easily traversed. Then he made every effort to rid the streets of thousands of prostitutes. By night, in his study, Sixtus cut excesses from liturgical texts. He also tangled with the Medici, which was his undoing. It was not possible for one pope to reform the physical structures of Rome and the political infrastructure of the Vatican in the same lifetime. He was pope for less than fifteen years and died in 1484.

Next to being pope, the most prestigious job at the Vatican was librarian of the Vatican Library. The librarian, as distinguished scholar in residence, was host to eminent historians, philosophers, clerics and even magicians.[18] Late sixteenth-century travelers considered the Vatican Library a must-see stop in a cultured itinerary.

Historically, books were received into the library collection by gift, purchase, and conscription. In 1623, at the close of the Thirty Years War, the long-

---

[18] Yes, magicians, see n. 13.

standing Palatine Library collection in Heidelberg was carved up as spoils of the war. Much of that collection came to the Vatican immediately, or as part of the estate of a later deceased benefactor. In 1815, a few dozen volumes of the Palatine collection were returned to Heidelberg as a token of the spirit of the Peace of Paris. A year later, Pope Pius VII sent 852 volumes of the collection to the University of Heidelberg. The remainder of the collection is in the Vatican Library.

Part of the Palatine collection that eventually came to the Vatican as a result of the Thirty Years War was included in the large library collection of Queen Christina of Sweden. The Swedish monarchy obtained its piece of the German collection in the early 1620s at the end of the war. It was retained in Sweden until Pope Alexander VIII purchased the royal collection in 1689 upon the Queen's death. It arrived just before his death in 1691.

No one can argue about the quality of care afforded the Vatican Library collection. Books that would have been lost in war or fire have been safe in its walls for centuries. The collection has remained open and available to scholars to support their needs unattainable anywhere else.

Some of the early business practices contributed to the long tenure of the collection. Books were assembled by topic on benches. Each bench of books was catalogued in chronological order, so that new books were added to the end of the row. A chain secured the bench of books, to which each book was also separately chained. If a book was checked out of the collection, the individual chain remained in place on the book, providing a constant reminder of the need for eventual return to the library.

Treats in the Collection

Beyond the beauty of the library environs and the aura of a great world stature library, there is a wonderful collection to be enjoyed. Even the seeker of light historical fare, rather than pedantic research pursuits, will find much to enjoy in the Vatican Library.

The Vatican Library holds the love letters of Henry VIII to Anne Boleyn.[19] The letters are in English and French. They exemplify the breadth of the secular collection. Henry was, after all, seeking a divorce from Catherine, so that he could marry the pregnant Anne. Henry obtained his heart's desire. He and Anne were married in 1533. The letters meant little to Henry once Anne lost her head. For the Vatican archives the letters were proof of the fickle nature of royal love.

King Henry VIII of England is best known for his domestic affairs. He was also a classical scholar. In the Vatican collection is another, more pious view of Henry. In 1521, Henry wrote a treatise in Latin against Martin Luther. The volume was quickly received as a popular lending item. It would be interesting to see who checked out the book.

---

[19] http://www.loc.gov/exhibits/vatican/vatican.html. The list of items in this story is taken in part from the exhibition collection notes of the United States, Library of Congress, in Washington, D.C., where part of the Vatican Library Collection was on display while the premises in Rome were in the midst of renovation until 2010. Note that the Library of Congress, in the Jefferson Building behind the U.S. Capital, is another exciting library, where the housing rivals the collection in fascinating opportunities for the visitor's enjoyment.

Lovers of ancient maps will find the Rome street plan from 1330 in the Vatican Library, as well as the more recent view of Rome in 1593, brought about by the urban renewal of Pope Sixtus. There are the pages of the original sunspot observations of Galileo Galilei from 1612. Lovers of poetry, who also remember their parochial school Latin, can read the original poems of the great Italian poet of the fourteenth century, Petrarch. Petrarch's book was self-scribed onto the parchment from 1357 to 1362.

Each book in the library has its own story. The borrower cards tell of the now famous people who read the texts. If the name on the borrower card has no line through it that means that the borrower never returned the book. There was a handwritten index of books that served as the inventory of the library until 1620. Some of the books were later crossed off as removed during the Counter-Reformation in the 1530s, when censorship was in flower. At that time there was also an index of forbidden books. Other books simply had the offending pages removed for burning.

Valuable information for researchers is found in the margins of the pages. Some of the books have arguments to the text inserted in the margins. In some, the author responds and defends his position. In one instance, a librarian of the late 1500s went through a liturgical text and gave it some edits and side notes. The annotations read like an early form of blog posting.

The Vatican library is an ongoing testament to the broad impact of popes as leaders of the western world. The popes were guardians, and in part censors, of the preservation of secular literature as well as liturgical texts for the Christian world. They were the mayors of Rome, in charge of all civic works and urban renewal. Until 1860, the popes were the military and governmental leaders of the Papal States, the nation-state region that occupied a large swath of the middle of present-day Italy. In their religious and secular roles, the Vatican Library is their legacy archive.

Today the pope remains a world leader of spiritual thought, relieved of most political duties. Rome is an independent city within an independent nation. The present-day visitor need not be concerned with the political evolution of papal power. It is enough to know that when the lines are long for entrance to the Sistine Chapel, there are other wonderful and significant sights to see in the Vatican.

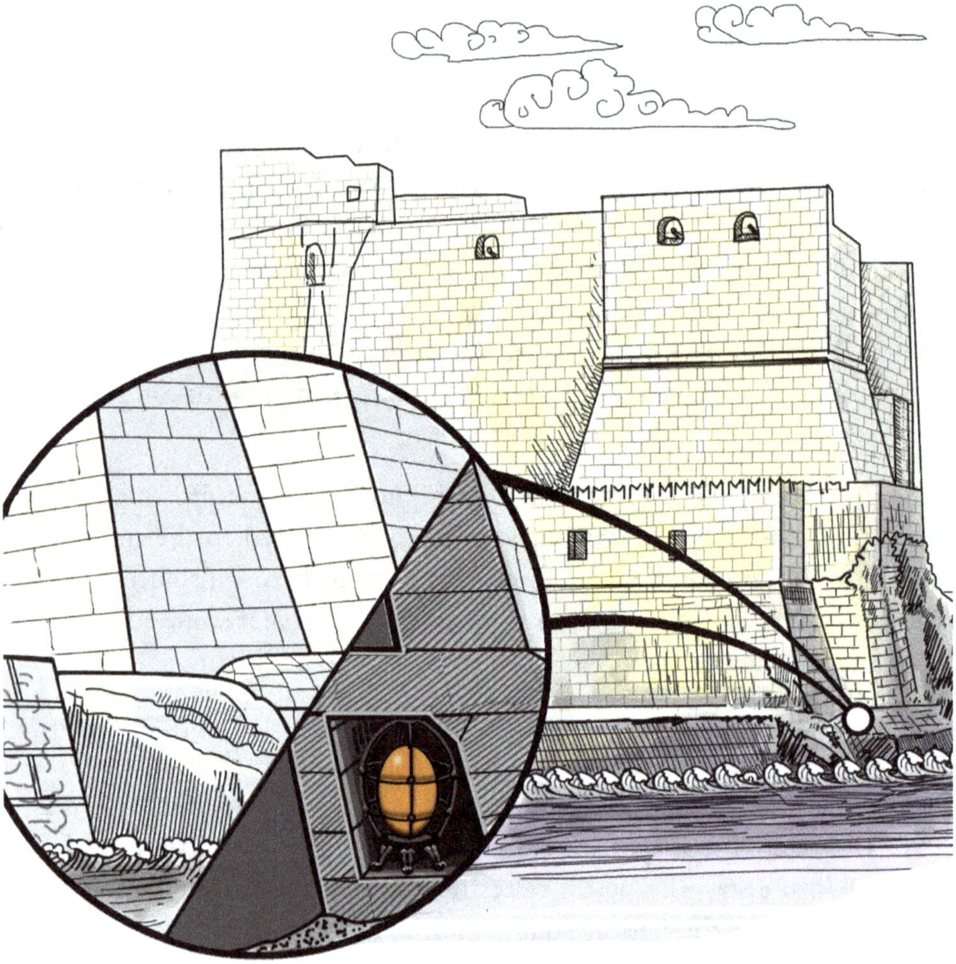

CRUISE THROUGH HISTORY

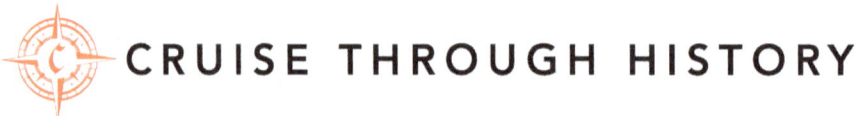

NAPLES
VIRGIL'S GOLDEN EGG PROTECTS NAPLES

Publius Vergilius Marco, known to the world as Virgil, lived from 70 to 19 BCE. He was appreciated during his lifetime as a great writer. Virgil spent the last ten years of his life in Naples, writing an ode to the city, one of his most famous works, the "Aeneid."

One thousand years after his death, the citizens of Naples raised his memory to cult worship as though Virgil was a mystic seer of the ages. In a work written 40 years before the birth of Christ, Virgil predicted that a child would be born and through him the world would experience peace. To the citizens of Naples at the turn of the first millennium of the current era, Virgil was more than wise. He marked the end of the pagan era. He was deified as a Christian before the time of Christianity. The setting for his divine transition to peace and Christianity was, of course, Naples.

Mythology surrounding the life of Virgil in Naples grew as a means to explain the miraculous existence of the city. As earthquakes and volcanic ash devastated nearby cities, and as plagues ravaged the citizenry of other cities, Naples stood unharmed and healthy. As the story goes, Virgil crafted a golden egg and buried it in the foundation of the building where the Castel dell'Ovo now stands. As long as the egg is not stolen or broken, Naples will stand protected from all harm. Naples owes its good fortune to Virgil.

This is the story of the man, the myth, and the golden egg. Although Virgil's tomb can be found in Naples, it is his impact upon the city during his lifetime that the visitor to Naples today can enjoy. After all, many myths are built upon a kernel of truth.

The Mortal Virgil

There are few facts known about the early life of Virgil. Such mystery enabled the later mythmakers who filled in the gaps. Since Virgil was famous for his poetry during his lifetime, his contemporaries often wrote of him and of their association with him. It is from these surviving works that the life story of the mortal man can be pieced together.[20]

Most historians believe that Virgil was born in a small village in northern Italy near Mantua. His family may not have been wealthy, but they had sufficient means to provide for his education. Young men of the time possessing his intelligence and background would tend toward a career in law, or letters, and oratory. Virgil preferred poetry.

Virgil may have started school when he was only five years old. His education included time in Milan and Rome, where his curriculum included rhetoric, medicine, and astronomy. His classmates regarded him as shy. That Virgil had bad health beginning in his childhood added to his reputation for being aloof or withdrawn. In poetry he found a means for expression.

Virgil lived during turbulent times in Rome. The slave rebellion of Spartacus raged while Virgil was a young child. Rome was then thrust into civil war. The assassination of Julius Caesar in 44 BCE had an impact on the twenty-six-year-old Virgil, as did the civil unrest that followed. The emperor Octavian, who would become a long-time friend and patron of Virgil, led the victorious battle against Caesar's assassins. Octavian paid his veteran generals for their service by giving gifts of land; much of it in northern Italy, and some of it expropriated farmland formerly owned by Virgil's family. Octavian and Virgil maintained their friendship despite this fact. Octavian was never known to be apologetic. In all of Virgil's poetry, in some of which he praises Octavian, he never criticizes the actions of Octavian.

---

[20] Historians have also searched Virgil's poetry for autobiographical clues. Taken as a whole, there is more conjecture than fact upon which to base a story of Virgil's early life.

In contrast to the angry world around him, Virgil's first confirmed poetry was bucolic. The "Eclogues," written around 42 to 38 BCE, start with a pastoral theme. There are references to land seizures, but there are no diatribes or obvious autobiographical references. Rather, the poetry describes the change of life in the countryside. The "Eclogues" describe an Arcadia; that is, an ideal life in a rural setting. The Arcadia image would resonate through Western literature for the next two thousand years.

It is in part four of the "Eclogues" that Virgil developed the image of a coming golden age for Italy. The golden age is ushered in with the birth of a child. The child is not described. For the mythmakers of the eleventh century, it was certain that the "Messianic Eclogue" foretold the coming of Christ.

Virgil's poetry followed the epic tale form familiar to him as employed by the Greek Homer, hundreds of years earlier, in the "Iliad." As Homer told the tales of Greek heroes, Virgil sought to record the stories of Roman life in verse. However, Virgil's style was new and instantly appealing to his contemporaries, such as Horace. In the early years of the medieval times, Dante chose Virgil as his guide through Purgatory in the "Inferno." Much of Virgil's poetry has survived as it has been referenced through time in the work of others.

The second major collection of Virgil's work was the "Georgics." Again, Virgil looked to the Greeks for his poetic structure. The poem, which was written between 37 and 29 BCE, details farm life. There are tips on planting crops and tending livestock. The final book of the work includes a story of the invention of bee keeping, as a gift from the gods. It was this poem that Virgil read to Octavian, to help the emperor relax upon his return from defeating Caesar's enemy Antony and the woman who gave him a safe haven, Cleopatra, in 31 BCE.

The "Aeneid" as Capstone of Roman History

Virgil wrote the "Aeneid," while in Naples, from 29 BCE until his death in 19 BCE. Friends of Virgil then finished the work. The "Aeneid" is the epic tale of the travels home to Italy from Troy of the prince Aeneas. Virgil expanded upon the epic storytelling style of Homer to add poetic sidelights and further tales of tragedy.

The "Aeneid" has two parts, not unlike the "Iliad" and "Odyssey" of Homer, only in reverse. In Homer the war in Troy is the first part and the voyage home the second part. In the "Aeneid" the travels from Troy to Italy comprises the first part. The second part is the founding of Rome and the glory of Roman emperors to Augustus.

On his way home from Troy, a storm causes Aeneas to be washed up on the beaches at Carthage. The Carthaginians become his audience for the story of his battle in Troy, loss of his wife, and wanderings on the way home, prior to landing in Carthage. The Carthaginian queen, Dido, is smitten by Aeneas. When he leaves suddenly to continue to his travels and rise to the occasion to find a site for Rome, Dido is left angry. She vows that Carthage will become an enemy of any new city that is founded by Aeneas. Indeed, Dido predicts the rivalry between Rome and Carthage over the ensuing centuries.

In the second half of the "Aeneid," Aeneas marries again, engages in several battles, and eventually secures a site for Rome. He is a character with emotions and personality. Aeneas constantly reconciles his inner turmoil to give care to his aging father and young son, while moving forward toward his duty to Rome.

Virgil was a poet of the court. His long-time friend Octavius became the Roman emperor Caesar Augustus, who ruled at the time the "Aeneid" was being written. Virgil cast Aeneas as the founder of initial Rome and Augustus as the new founder of the greater Rome. In the "Aeneid," Aeneas even foretells of the coming great rulers of Rome, who would vanquish the Carthaginians and prevail over Anthony and Cleopatra.

Virgil was known to have read complimentary parts of his poem to the appreciative ruler. The "Aeneid" captured so many of the high points of Roman civilization, that it became the descriptive history of the day. It was an immediate success in Rome, even though it was unfinished and unpolished by Virgil at the time of his death in 19 BCE.

Virgil was working on the "Aeneid" when he contracted a fever. He had gone by boat to Greece, as if to experience the travels in his story. Fearing the worst, Virgil sailed back to Italy. He never left the ship as he died in the harbor.

Virgil had ordered that the "Aeneid" be burned should he die prior to finishing the poem. Augustus would not allow that to happen. He ordered two of Virgil's literary colleagues to finish the poem. Their additions and edits have added to the mystique of the meanings sought within the lines.

The "Aeneid" was immediately regarded as Virgil's greatest work. Students of Latin and Greek began to study Virgil with their Homer from the time it was written. They still do today. Poets of the classical tradition refer back to Virgil as the wellspring of all poetry. Even Ovid, the Roman poet, exiled to Constanta thirty years after Virgil's death, parodied the "Aeneid" in one of his love sonnets.[21]

The Mythical Virgil

Virgil's body was entombed in Naples, in a tunnel built by Augustus. The citizens of Naples immediately venerated the site. Over time stories of the feats of Virgil grew until he became a deity. The preservation of his memory achieved cult status.

By the eleventh century Virgil had evolved into an ancient sorcerer with special gifts. There were stories of his miraculous birth, his feats, and his special gifts to Naples. Any idea that he was conceived and born in the usual manner, or that his poetic gifts began with an advantaged education, fell away from the popular local memory, to be replaced by mythical legends.

The mythical Virgil was born to Stimichon, the astrologer, magician, and physician, and the very beautiful Maia. Maia's father knew her beauty would attract many suitors, so he kept her locked up in a tower. Stimichon, who was the family doctor, loved Maia so he devised a plan to breech her cell.

---

[21] See Ovid's story in Itinerary IV. The Black Sea, at the port of Constanta.

Stimichon changed himself into flakes of gold leaf. The light flakes blew through the open window in the tower and landed in a glass of wine, just before Maia took a drink. Maia saw the gold in her glass and thought it was a good omen. She knew that drinkable gold could transform one's life. She drank quickly and deeply.

The effect upon Maia was immediate. She felt a sensation in her womb. Darts of heat pulsed throughout her body. The pleasure and agony was so intense that Maia became exhausted and fell asleep.

When Maia awoke she instantly knew she was pregnant. When the family doctor arrived, Maia confided in Stimichon. He told her that a miracle had occurred. To preserve her honor, Stimichon convinced Maia's father that Maia and Stimichon should be married. The father agreed.

During the pregnancy Maia experienced many strange dreams. Stimichon would interpret them for her. The dreams foretold that the child would be special. In one dream Maia gave birth to a laurel twig, in Latin a virgule laurea. The tree quickly sunk roots and grew strong. They decided to name the child Virgil after the laurel branch.

One day when Maia and Stimichon were traveling, Maia felt the child ready to be born. Leaning on a tree by the side of the road, Maia gave birth to Virgil. He came forth and walked as soon as his feet touched the ground. He had teeth and hair at birth. He could talk. The site of the birth burst forth with blooming flowers. The parents knew their son was special.

Virgil and the Golden Egg

The citizens of Naples have long regarded their city as a magical place. In the eleventh century the reason for their special status could be traced to Virgil. Several Virgil myths explain their reasoning.

One myth tells how Virgil became the lord of the flies. He was sleeping in a field when a gnat awakened him. Once awake he could see a snake poised to strike. Tragedy was averted. From that time forward Virgil had a way with

flies. He used his mystical knowledge to keep flies out of churches in Naples and from spoiling meat in the market.

Virgil's greatest gift to Naples was the golden egg. In Virgil's time great plagues swept large cities. The area was subjected to earthquakes and the nearby volcano, Mount Vesuvius, threatened to explode. Although catastrophes struck other cities, Naples persevered unharmed. The citizens of Naples knew they were blessed and searched for a reason.

The reason for the great success and long life of Naples was assigned to Virgil. They believed that he was using his mystical powers to protect them. The means is explained in the story of the golden egg.

Virgil gilded an ostrich egg and then placed the egg in a crystal sphere. The treasure was then locked in an iron cage. The cage was buried in the foundations of a castle. As long as the egg remained intact and in place, no harm would come to the castle or to Naples. If a treasure seeker were to remove the egg, or harm it during removal, the castle would sink into the ocean. Naples would fall into ruin. That the castle stands today and that Naples remains a vibrant city is testimony to the miracle of Virgil's egg.[22]

Naples and Its Castel dell'Ovo

Visitors to Naples today can still walk on the causeway where Virgil roamed as he gathered inspiration for his poetry. The villa in existence in the first century BCE, when Virgil buried his egg, is long gone. In the twelfth century a castle was erected on the ancient site. The castle is called Castel dell'Ovo, or Egg Castle.[23] It is this castle that is referred to in the stories of the buried egg. That Virgil's death preceded the erection of this castle by over a thousand years is just part of the mythology.

---

[22] The twelfth century castle did not exist at the time of Virgil. There was an occupation of the site by Greeks in the sixth century. At the time of Virgil there was a villa on the site of the buried egg.

[23] The castle is open for visitors every day. The Roman foundations are still visible.

Across from the Mergellina railway station and in back of the church of Santa Maria di Piedigrotta is a tunnel in which the tomb of Virgil is believed to be located. Local mythology holds that a tree at the site, planted at the death of Virgil, died when Dante died. Then Italian poet and historian, Petrarch, planted another tree. Souvenir seekers dismembered that tree.

Unfortunately for Naples, it has become infamous for pickpockets, which often deters tourists from experiencing its rich history. One twenty-first century author reminds potential visitors that creativity and Naples are long-standing partners.[24] The city has much to offer. Virgil refers to the invention of pizza in Naples in his "Aeneid."

> …thin cakes … (they) gnaw the fated circles of their crusts …
> the quartered surfaces of their flat loaves.[25]

Gennaro Lombardi brought Neapolitan pizza to New York City in 1906. Today visitors can travel to his city to taste the original and bask under Virgil's protective aura.

---

[24] Michael A. Ledeen, Virgil's Golden Egg and other Neapolitan Miracles, Transaction Publishers, New Brunswick, 2011.
[25] Ledeen, p. 1, Aeneid, Book VII.

AT HOME IN NAPLES: HERCULANEUM TO VILLA SFORZA

On the afternoon of August 24, 79 CE, the day became prematurely dark. With a velocity that precluded any hope of escape, a river of mud swept through the coastal resort town of Herculaneum. Street venders, artisans in their studios, and townspeople at leisure were all swept away or buried by the brown wave of mud.

At the first sign of sparks rising from nearby Mount Vesuvius, some of the more cautious residents of this Roman suburb of Naples left the city, traveling south. Others boarded ships moored in the harbor. Captains of those ships, who delayed too long over their lunch, did so at their peril and that of their passengers and crew. Failure to take advantage of the warning sparks proved fatal.

While nearby Pompeii was being covered in ash, Herculaneum was buried in volcanic mud. So complete and so deep was the coverage, that Herculaneum was forgotten for the next 1,700 years. As if to guard the secret city, Mount Vesuvius erupted again in 1759, just as discovery was imminent.

During the period that Herculaneum lay hidden, a new population of beach-loving residents moved into the area. They were oblivious as to what lay beneath their homes. A road was built that ran from the foothills of Vesuvius to the area of the old and buried gates of Herculaneum, and then along the ocean. This was prime real estate. Just as the area was prized in ancient times as the site for vacation homes of the well-to-do, in the eighteenth century the boulevard became the location for a royal palace and the lavish homes and gardens of wealthy families.

Over time the villas evolved into multi-family housing and then some became hotels. One of the eighteenth century villas that became a hotel is the present-day Villa Miglio d'Oro. The owner has retained all of the period charm. From the suite windows, guests have a perfect view of the excavated portion of ancient Herculaneum and the ocean beyond.

This is the story of city life in Herculaneum, then and now. The setting for the complete story, that now spans two millennia in time, can be traversed in just a few hundred yards. Whether visiting for a few hours or an overnight stay, Herculaneum is a wonderful excursion when visiting the port of Naples.

Herculaneum – Until August 23, 79 CE

Herculaneum is an ancient city originally settled by Greeks in the eighth century BCE. As the major city to the north, Naples, developed as a major port city, Herculaneum remained a quaint retreat for its wealthy merchants. The Herculaneum harbor accommodated pleasure craft. Its streets were lined with the villas of the wealthy.

The popularity of Herculaneum was in part due to its beachside location. The main economy was centered on pleasure. There was a theater and the baths of a Roman city. There were also craft shops, artisans, and wine bars. There was no brothel and no temple in early Herculaneum. Pleasure was pervasive and there was no need for contained buildings for fun or penance. There was no military or political presence. Residents had no appetite for hostility or political argument amid their relaxation.

Herculaneum was culturally aligned with Pompeii, another resort town for wealthy citizens of leisure. These were not Roman towns and they resisted Roman control. Herculaneum had an ecumenical mix of ancient Oscan, Sammite, and Greek people. The language was Oscan, similar to Latin. The graffiti of young boys in Herculaneum, found on recently excavated walls, are evidence of a cultural mix of pagans and Jews, named Florus, Manius, and David.

The patron god of the city was Hercules. It was not the style of citizens to take anything seriously. A drinking establishment prominently displayed a portly and intoxicated Hercules as its business moniker.

The main street of Herculaneum is 40 feet wide. It was a pedestrian mall, wide enough to allow large wagons to pass. The streets were kept clean and litter free. Littering was punishable by a fine, a beating, or both.

The best street in town allowed its residences to face the water and to receive sea breezes. Along the ocean view street are the most elegant homes, with lovely courtyards, fountains and pools. These homes had elaborate interior decoration. The homes were decorated with statues, of which only the bases remain. The bodies of a marble population were carried out to sea by the river of volcanic mud.

One of the homes of the elite had a sundial and a water clock. In the peak of summer there were 12 hours of daylight in the warm, sunny, climate. Days were, of course, shorter and cooler in the winter.

Residents of Herculaneum had house slaves. They ate a diet rich in fresh fish. They bathed regularly to be clean and as a social occasion.[26] They decorated their homes with the art of mosaics, carvings, and gilt metal sculptures. Their household furnishings included elegantly and delicately sculpted wood tables, of the type seen in eighteenth century Early American and French provincial furniture. The later furniture was styled after the archaeological excavations of Herculaneum inspired world fashion.[27]

Herculaneum may have been a small outpost, but it was well known around the Mediterranean. In 61 CE, the Apostle Paul came ashore near the city. Evidence of the effect his preaching had on some of the locals can be seen in

---

[26] Residents enjoyed their baths. Bathhouses were clean, elegant, and well run. They allowed men and women to bathe in the same facilities. With Christianity came the end of frequent and public baths. Roman Emperor Hadrian in 111 CE outlawed mixed bathing.

[27] The popular Early American style four-poster bed, where each post is topped with a pinecone, is actually a style copied from the Greco-Roman furniture at Herculaneum. The pinecone motif on furniture was a favorite Dionysius era fertility symbol. In the eighteenth century in America, the pinecone became the symbol of hospitality.

a shrine with a simple crucifix found in a small, upper-floor room of a home. Twelve years later the leader of the slave revolt of Rome, Spartacus, made a less auspicious tour through the area.

For 3,000 years Vesuvius slumbered, only occasionally throwing forth embers. Then in 62 CE, the mighty volcano rumbled through the valley with such force that earthquakes were widely felt. Herculaneum was severely damaged.

The very wealthy living in Herculaneum had other options to enjoy seaside living than to be in constant threat of the volcano. They moved away from the quake zone or simply gave up their second homes. Damaged homes fell into disrepair. The population declined. The fine craftspeople who serviced the wealthy cliental moved to be near their patrons.

The people who remained in Herculaneum remodeled former grand villas into shops and multi-family living quarters. The area remained a popular seaside vacation spot available to people of lesser means. Artists found the light and rent attractive for their studios. Snack shops opened along the once elegant boulevard, to service the new class of residents. The city became a Roman protectorate. Life went on happily although more modestly.

A Civil Action – No Justice for Justa

In the written records of daily life in Herculaneum that have survived is a court case involving child custody. The child's name was Justa. Her father was a man of property and her mother was his slave at the time of her birth. The case gives great insight to life in Herculaneum in the first century of the current era.

When the earthquake of 62 CE shook Herculaneum, the opportunistic merchant Gaius Petronius seized on vacant real estate to better his living standard. He moved into a nice house with his wife, the former slave, Calatorius. Petronius was able to buy his wife's freedom, but the couple was unable to have children. He turned to his slave, Vitalis, who gave birth to a girl in the year following the earthquake. Their daughter was named Justa.

Over time Vitalis was able to buy her freedom from Petronius. They remained in the home as parents to Justa, with Calatorius. Life at home was at least amiable until Calatorius gave birth to a child. Calatorius wanted Vitalis out of the household as much as Vitalis wanted a home of her own. The catch was that Petronius did not want Justa to leave. Vitalis left the home without Justa.

In the capacity of a freedwoman Vitalis brought a legal action to receive custody of Justa, who was technically the property of Petronius, because she was born as a slave to a slave. In an out-of-court settlement, Vitalis paid Petronius for his costs of care for Justa. Justa then went to live with her mother. By all accounts mother and daughter lived a happy and prosperous life.

Happiness was cut short for Justa. When she was in her early teens, her mother died. Petronius would have been a suitable guardian, but he died shortly after Vitalis. Fortunately, Justa was able to continue her mother's business and take care of herself.

Calatorius had never shown maternal concern for Justa. She was, however, attracted to Justa's increasing assets. Calatorius brought a court action to receive Justa as property of the Petronius household and to assume control of all of Justa's assets. Her theory was that Justa was a slave, who went to live with her mother while a child, and thus was still property of Calatorius, the heir to her husband's estate.

Justa fought back, claiming to be a freedwoman prior to the death of her mother. Paperwork that would have disposed of the matter could not be found. At the time of a court hearing a surprise witness came forward. He claimed to be the man who acted as the negotiator in the resolution of the earlier custody battle in which Vitalis paid Petronius for Justa. The witness was a freeman in the Petronius household at the time of the custody battle.[28]

A judge in Rome heard the case. He took the matter under advisement in 75 CE. The case was still pending a decision in 79 CE when all the parties to the case in Herculaneum were swept up in the volcanic mud.

---

[28] Some researchers offer the theory that the witness was Justa's actual father, living in the same household. A crucifix in an upper room of the house begs the question of whether Calatorius rented rooms to Christians. Joseph Jay Deiss, Herculaneum, Thomas Y. Crowell Co., New York, 166, p. 79.

August 24, 79 CE

August 24, 79 CE began as any glorious summer day at the beach. Then the earth shook the entire Vesuvius plain from the mountain to Herculaneum. The shaking was felt in Naples. The horror of the events of that day were recorded by a brave ship's commander for the Emperor Titus, Pliny, and by his nephew, Gaius Plinius Caecilius Secundus, better known as Pliny the Younger.

The elder Pliny left the harbor in Naples with a ship intended for Herculaneum to rescue its inhabitants. Sensing the importance of his mission, the commander kept writing throughout the day. When he arrived in Herculaneum rocks were strewn on the beach, but he felt no sense of imminent danger. He enjoyed a late lunch and then took a nap. He would sail when the wind shifted.

As Pliny slept, the ship and the beach filled with cinder and ash. The sky turned dark. A rain of pumice stones awaked him. The sea became too rough to sail. As the commander pondered his next move, sulpher gas permeated his lungs. He, his crew, and his intended passengers choked to death.

Meanwhile, in Naples, Pliny the Younger and his mother attempted to leave the city to avoid falling debris. They began their departure in a cart, but the ground was shaking so violently that the cart was useless. A cloud of ash descended upon them from the sea. They ran away from the water into a field of tall grasses. The world around them was in total darkness, except when falling ash ignited the grass as they ran.

Just when Pliny the Younger felt that the world as he knew it had ended, daylight appeared. Shapes of other survivors appeared from the seascape of ash amid grass. By August 26, the inhabitants of Naples began to return home. Pliny the Younger learned that the intact body of his uncle had been recovered. It was as though the elder man was merely asleep next to his notes of the day.

Although Naples remained intact, Pompeii was covered in hot, molten stone. Herculaneum was covered in mud. Under the weight of the mud the beautiful mosaics in the homes of wealthy beach residents buckled like paper. Across the city, the mud was 65 to 85 feet deep. The mud was left to harden for the next 1,630 years.

Reclaiming Herculaneum

From 80 to 1630 CE, battles of various eras occurred by those oblivious that beneath them lay Herculaneum. In 1631, Vesuvius erupted with the same might to send more rivers of mud down to increase the depth of the buried city. Then in 1709, a monk found that slabs of marble were impeding his ability to dig a well. He had no idea that he had struck upon the upper seats of the theater in Herculaneum. He sold the marble to an Austrian prince for his villa. It apparently never dawned upon the prince that perfectly cut marble is not a feat of nature, regardless of the divinity of the benefactor. The city remained hidden.

Fifty years later, after the Spanish drove the Austrians from Naples, a general directed his troops to dig at the site of the monk's well. They worked quickly, without keeping records. They were on a hunt for treasure. They found very little, but created a mess.

Pompeii was discovered in 1763. That changed the focus of all inquiry in the area. A Swiss archaeologist, Karl Webber, was able to impress the authorities with the importance of a dig at Herculaneum. He mounted an organized excavation.

For the next hundred years, Herculaneum became a world famous phenomenon. Thomas Jefferson included Herculaneum and Pompeii on his world tour. French King Francis I kept the excavations going at Herculaneum, when in 1828, the French replaced the Spanish as overlords. Work came to a halt in 1875, when slumlords objected to the tunnels under the tenement housing they had developed out of the once lovely neighborhood.

The Italian government took control of the excavations at Herculaneum in 1927. They appointed talented archaeologists to direct scientific, orderly excavations. Instead of gracing private homes, objects found at the site were recorded and housed in museums, which later were open to the public. Although war interrupted the excavation and economic downturns have hampered government support, excavation has continued at Herculaneum.

Urban Renewal and the Villa Aprile

Before the newcomers knew the importance of that which lay almost 100 feet beneath the street, the early eighteenth century brought another wave of population to enjoy the seaside ambiance, south of Naples. Emerging Italian royalty came to the area to build palaces. The Bourbon King Carlo and his Queen Amalia built a palace at the foot of the Vesuvius plain in 1738. Their estate became the beginning of the Royal Road of Calabrie, a lengthy boulevard of stately homes of minor royals and those who could afford to live like royals.[29] The road came down to what would soon be exposed as the gates to Herculaneum, before it ran along the sea.

Within a few years there was a proliferation of villas along the Royal Road. Over 220 villas were built by the middle of the eighteenth century. They were built in the Baroque and Rocco style, by a bevy of Italian architects.[30] The villas had in common the use of Vesuvius and the sea as backdrops for their gardens. Villas were designed almost as fortresses from the street, with open windows to the gardens. The gardens had classical accents, such as grottos, Greek statuary, fruit trees, and meandering paths leading to fountains and pools.[31]

One of the villas of the period is the Villa Aprile, built almost directly across from the now excavated gates to Herculaneum. It was built around 1730 in the Baroque style with a large central garden of ponds, marble sculptures, and fruit trees. Almost one hundred years later this villa was fortunate to fall into the hands of a notable who could appreciate its history and who could afford to restore its original beauty.

Villa Aprile became the Villa Cardinal Sisto Riario Sforza around 1840. Cardinal Sforza had a family pedigree almost as old as the villa he acquired. Born in 1810, he was a descendent of the bold Catarina Sforza and her

---

[29] The original palace is now the residence of the agriculture faculty at Naples University.
[30] Fernando Sanfelice (1675-1748); Dominica Antonio Vaccaro (1678-1745); Giovan Antonio Medrano (1703- unk); Fernando Fuga (1699-1781); Luigi Vanvitelli (1700-1773).
[31] J. Paul Getty used one of the villas as the inspiration for his Malibu California museum.

first husband Girolamo Riaro. Catarina was twenty-one and seven months pregnant in 1484, when she stormed the Castel Saint Angelo in Rome amid a squabble between cardinals for control of the papacy.[32]

Cardinal Sforza led a more sanguine existence than his ancestor. He became the private secretary to Pope Gregory XVI in 1841. As a cardinal, his most bold step was to speak out against the Dogma of Papal Infallibility. The villa must have provided quiet sanctuary from life at the Vatican. Cardinal Sforza took good care of his historic treasure. Unfortunately, the Cardinal had only 20 years to enjoy his home. In 1860, he was exiled during the collapse of the Kingdom of the Two Sicilies during the unification of Italy.

---

[32] See Itinerary I. Florence – Princess Sisters of the Renaissance.

Today in Herculaneum

Today visitors to Herculaneum can walk the broad main street and peer into the villas of the wealthy, the shopkeepers, and the artisan studios. The mud in Herculaneum preserved that which the hot ash destroyed in Pompeii. In Herculaneum, furniture remained in place, as did food in the cupboards and the tools of tradesmen and artists. Items recovered from the site can be viewed in the Herculaneum museum just a few blocks from the excavated city.

Across the street from the main gate to Herculaneum is the Villa Miglio D'Ora. Formerly the Villa Aprile and the Villa Sforza, the Miglio D'Ora has once again been restored to retain the original beauty in its new function as a hotel. Whether enjoying a cool drink in the bar that opens to the garden, or staying overnight, the visitor can enjoy the ambiance enjoyed by Cardinal Sforza. There the archaeological features, the hidden pools and grottos, the elegant statues, all coexist with the modern swimming pool. From the suite windows are the everlasting views of Herculaneum and the sea beyond.[33]

---

[33] The museum of artifacts from Herculaneum goes back to 1860, when the unifier of Italy, Garibaldi, appointed his biographer Alexandre Dumas as the museum director, based in Naples. The appointment did not last long. The first scientific director was Giuseppe Fiorelli.

AMALFI COAST FROM SYBARIS

ON THE IONIAN SEA TO PAESTUM ON THE TYRRHENIAN SEA

A Tale of Sybaris and Her Sister City, Paestum 510 BC

This is the story of the ill-fated city with one economic class of people – an upper class. In this haven of extensive wealth, without business competition, natural hazards or enemies, the city managed to self-impose its destruction. In this tale, the leading character is the city of Sybaris, on the southern coast of Italy, at the arch of the boot. The city possessed such wealth that it founded an extension of itself, in an ideal setting. The master-planned city was Paestum, accessed in 500 BCE overland from Sybaris and today from ports on the Amalfi Coast, or Naples.

Sybaris eclipsed its dowdy Sicilian competitor, Syracuse, in trade with Greece. At the height of Sybaris civilization it created its sister city Paestum, an expression of the best that sixth-century wealth of a Greek city could create.[34] Paestum enabled Sybaris to control trade all through what is now Italy, by moving trade goods overland from Sybaris to Paestum, from which ships could sail north and south to control trade on the west coast of Italy. Despite its success, Sybaris orchestrated its own downfall by enraging the otherwise peaceful city of Croton, its Ionian coastal neighbor to the west.

---

[34] All dates in this story are Before the Common Era, BCE, unless otherwise noted.

The story of these ancient cities comes to the modern day through familiar names. The ancient Greek author Herodotus wrote of Sybaris in tales that were best sellers during his time in Athens. Pythagoras, who relocated from Samos in Greece to Croton, an outpost Grecian territory on the Ionian Sea, in 529 BCE, lived to recount a cautionary tale. Details of the Sybaris story are also available from the biographers of later tourists to the area, Hannibal and Spartacus.

Some of the names in this story may be familiar. The themes of greed, self-promotion and power are present here. The term "sybarite," for a greedy person is commonly used in the twentieth century, although the story of its origination is not usual classroom fare. The excavation of Sybaris in the later part of the twentieth century spurred new interest in the original sybarites. For the traveler to southern Italy, or the Amalfi Coast, the story of Sybaris and its sister city of Paestum sets the stage for more than two millennium of opulent living in the area.

Greeks Seek More Space – Sybaris and Syracuse

The Greeks were sometimes victims of their own successes. Athens grew until its population felt crowded. Adding to the congestion in the Athenian-dominated Ionian Peninsula were the Greek-speaking Dorians from Albania, who migrated south to the peninsula in the eighth century BCE. The newcomers were pushed further southward to the Peloponnesian Peninsula where they populated Sparta. Greeks who sought more space and additional business opportunities either settled in what was referred to as Asia Minor,[35] or they sailed west across the Ionian Sea to establish Magna Graecia in Italy. The setting for this story is Magna Graecia, in the area of the arch of the boot of Italy, more properly known as the Gulf of Taranto.

Inland from a shallow bay, midway along the coast of the Gulf of Taranto, the space-seeking Athenians founded the city of Sybaris in 720 BC. The site was attractive as the city sat between the Sybaris and Crati rivers, one of which was navigable most of the year. The rivers provided a harbor lagoon, which became critical to the success of Sybaris as a natural trading port. The fertile plains between the two rivers immediately supplied the residents with crops for export to hungry Athens. In exchange, Athenian tradesmen sent ships with local goods.

The founding citizens of Sybaris quickly became landed gentry as the import/export business replaced farming as the preferred means of income. The Sybarites did not own ships and took no risks. They found it was easier to receive goods from Greece and transport them over the hills to the northwest and the waiting Etruscan ships on the Tyrrhenian Sea at the new port of Paestum. From Paestum, goods from places in the Far East, such as Persia, went north as far as Britain. Ships returning to Paestum held wheat and wool from Britain, as well as tin from the area of Cornwall. Sybaris was a major player in the world economy of the sixth century BCE.

The overland route from Sybaris to Paestum was popular as it was faster than the sea route. It was also safer. Goods could travel in carts in a few days'

---

[35] Asia Minor in this sense is the area surrounding the Black Sea. See Itinerary IV for stories from the Black Sea.

time, rather than the journey of several weeks by boat. Boats were dependent upon good weather. Travel by sea through the Straights of Messina, where the toe of the boot of Italy nears Sicily, was not a good option as reefs that created dangerous currents could cause disaster in the narrow channel.[36] Overland travel meant avoiding tariffs charged to ships that stopped at the port of Syracuse prior to entering the straights. Overland travel avoided risk of capture by Carthaginians, who controlled western Sicily and sea routes in the Tyrrhenian Sea.[37]

The geographical advantage in trade created a wealthy society in Sybaris, at the expense of Syracuse. The economic advantage would not have been notable had the Sybarites not flaunted their great wealth and the Syracusans not adopted a self-effacing, almost Spartan, existence. Fortunately for Sybaris, the citizens of Syracuse were satisfied to suffer in silence.

Herodotus described Sybarites as people who never saw the sun as they went to parties all night and slept all day. It seems the sea-to-sea overland-transport business was self-sustaining. It required no actual effort of the leading citizens of Sybaris who controlled the route.

Women of Sybaris wore gowns from Persia with elaborate beadwork. They wore satin sandals with cork high heels. They dyed their hair blond and wore gold tiaras, with other jewels. The men wore wool tunics with sashes. They had long purple cloaks flowing from their shoulders, of the type reserved for nobility in Athens.

In Sybaris women attended parties with men. Their slaves attended them with chamber pots. Major parties were planned a year in advance to allow citizens to prepare.[38] The Sybarites are credited with inventing the bathtub

---

[36] The reefs between the toe of the boot of Italy and Sicily, which caused whirlpool problems for ancient mariners, were the infamous Charybdis and Scylla of mythology. The whirlpools were destroyed in 1908 by earthquakes, which also destroyed much of Messina in Sicily and the town of Reggio in Italy. Doré Ogrizek, The World in Color: Italy, Whittlesay House, McGraw-Hill, New York, London, 1950, p. 339.

[37] Carthage on the African north coast was part of what was generally referred to as Libya.

[38] Orville H. Bullitt, Search for Sybaris, J. B. Lippincott Co., New York, 1969, p. 60.

and vapor baths of scented herbs. The most celebrated of citizens were the chefs. A well-regarded chef could hold the sole right to a recipe for a year, in what may have been the earliest example of intellectual property rights.

Sybarites rode slowly down tree-lined roads in coaches. Slaves were forbidden to exert themselves in labor in sight of a citizen. When the summer heat came to town, the citizens went to the hills to enjoy cool grottoes. They traveled infrequently to Greece and almost never to Sparta. Even the barely used military cavalry moved in style. The cavalry horses were trained to parade as if dancing to music.[39]

In intentional contrast to Sybaris, it was against the law in Syracuse for women to wear gold or colorful clothing. Men were advised not to look foppish. Women only went out after dark if escorted, and even then, only when necessary. Only ladies of loose morals wore jewelry and went out alone at night. Syracuse was not a party town. It was an amiable sister city to Sparta.

The Growth of Trans-Calabrian Trade – Sybaris and Paestum

Paestum, on the west coast of Italy, was an extension of Sybaris. Since its development responded to an expanding and lucrative trade economy, and since it followed Sybaris in time, Paestum was the recipient of lavish expenditures on infrastructure. As Paestum did not exist as a political center, it did not suffer the repercussions eventually visited upon Sybaris for the hostile actions taken by its city leaders. When Sybaris taunted its neighbors until they obliged it with a sacking, Paestum was spared. Although little can be seen of Sybaris today, Paestum is a three-star Michelin Guide attraction.[40]

From 600 to 400 BCE, Paestum stood as an elegant city of yellow limestone. It was neatly laid out, in traditional Greek style, with parallel streets above a

---

[39] Bullitt, at 64.
[40] Michelin, The Green Guide, Italy, 2002, pages 312-313. Outside the gates to Paestum are five-star hotels. At the crossroads of the archaeological sites of Sybaris there is a solitary bar and pizza pub.

marina. The several temples each have an external sacrificial alter. On the south end of the city is the oldest temple, dedicated to Hera, the sister and wife of Zeus. This temple was built 100 years before the Parthenon in Athens.

On the north end of the city site is the Temple of Ceres, dedicated to Athena. This temple has an internal colonnade of early Ionic columns, surrounded by an outer ring of Doric columns. Next to it there is a newer temple, probably mid-fifth century BCE, dedicated to Poseidon, Zeus, Apollo, or all three for good luck. Known today as the Temple of Neptune, this structure has fluted Doric columns that taper upwards and are slightly convex, an architectural trick on the eye for a pleasing, vaulted effect. Across the road from these temples is a complex of elegant townhouses, homes of the Paestum elite, some with courtyard ponds.[41]

After the loss of its parent city, and with the emergence of competing ports, Paestum fell from dominance. By 400 BCE, the city was controlled by local tribes. They did nothing to enhance the city.

Paestum experienced renewed vigor as a Roman city in the third century BCE. During this time, in the city center, the Romans added their classic touches of a forum, gymnasium, and amphitheater. The city was abandoned due to a malaria epidemic at the beginning of the current era, which spared the city from urban renewal. New building would have caused existing building materials to be repurposed for lesser structures. Well-preserved art and artifacts from the Roman period can be seen today at the museum across from the city site.

Greed Awakens Peaceful Souls – Sybaris and Croton

The legacy of a city with lives too well lived is the barren plain that is Sybaris today. After almost 300 years of enjoyment, the end of Sybaris came swiftly in 510 BCE. It was an act of self-destruction.

---

[41] There is an excellent museum at Paestum. Inside the museum are floor tiles and wall paintings removed from the villas at Paestum, which give great insight to the wealth of the inhabitants.

Seventy-five miles to the west of Sybaris was, and is today, the quiet city of Croton. Croton was also founded by Greeks, but on land not as fertile as the plain of Sybaris. Croton did not experience the trade opportunities of Sybaris. Croton lay between high mountains and the sea, making overland travel to the west coast difficult.

What it lacked in international commerce, Croton made up for in internal pursuits of art, athletics, and schools of medicine and mathematics. Crotonians focused upon their minds not their wardrobes. Pythagoras founded a school in Croton in 529 BCE, where he taught philosophy and astronomy to men and women. He believed in equality of the sexes and in self-improvement.

Sybaris and Croton could have coexisted in their separate spheres indefinitely, had a leading citizen of Sybaris not chosen to expand his power. In 510 BCE, a wealthy merchant of the city named Telys chose to exert further dominance by convincing other Sybarites to exile 500 of its richest men. Hastily driven from their homes, the men went to Croton, where they were given modest shelter. An enraged Telys threatened war on Croton unless they would expel the encamped Sybarites.

Pythagoras stood in front of the people of Croton and urged them to follow a path of statesmanship. Thirty men from Croton were chosen as ambassadors to Sybaris. Upon arriving in Sybaris, Telys mustered a crowd to ambush the ambassadors, murder them, and throw their bodies over the city wall. Fortunately, Pythagoras was not among the delegation.

Men of Sybaris did not engage in physical labor. Dispatching the Croton delegation was delegated to Sybarite slaves. Once gathered together for violence, the slaves chose to revolt rather than return home. Almost overnight, Sybaris experienced unprecedented internal turmoil.

Croton did not have a large standing army. It had not devoted much of its scarce resources to making war. However, Croton did have a large contingent of athletes and intelligent leaders. Sybaris had a lovely cavalry. The cavalry was, as all things in Sybaris, well dressed. As the two cities met on a battlefield, both sides were inexperienced in fighting and apprehensive about making war.

Then a lowly citizen of Croton had a brilliant idea. The Crotonians brought musicians to the front lines and began to play Sybaris parade music for the opposing cavalry. Instinctively, the Sybaris horses began to dance, creating havoc in the Sybaris army. The Crotonians took advantage of the confusion to move in and clobber the Sybarites. This brief war of 510 BCE became the first, and perhaps the only, to be resolved by music.

The Croton army marched on to Sybaris, where it held a siege for 70 days before they were able to enter and sack the city. Former Sybarian slaves may have aided the Crotons. The Crotons took no prisoners as they ravaged the city. They pulled down buildings and set the debris on fire. Then the Crotons opened the Sybaris floodgates and allowed the two rivers to submerge the city.

Postmortem

Sybaris never recovered from the ill-advised aggression of Telys. Survivors tried to return and rebuild, but they were driven from the site by mosquitoes. Eventually, the remainder of the Sybarites moved to higher ground and built Thurii, with the aid of new arrivals from Athens.

Once ensconced in Thurii, the former Sybarites attempted to assert their dominance in city affairs. They chose the best business opportunities and the best real estate for themselves. The newly arrived Athenians took issue with the Sybarites. The newcomers killed the Sybaris survivors and then argued among themselves. To resolve disputes the factions appealed to the Oracle at Delphi. In true ambiguous fashion, the Oracle directed the Thuriians to appeal to the gods as the founder of all cities. The Thuriians returned home, built a temple to Apollo, and lived in relative harmony.[42]

The Thuriians established a democracy. They divided the citizenry into ten tribes, each representing groups that founded the city. The assemblage made friends with Croton and established an alliance with Athens. The new city moved from the aristocracy of Sybaris to democracy, universal suffrage, and private property ownership.[43]

Thurrian men wore long hair and turbans. They covered their bodies in oil and wore wool robes. They went barefoot. The Thurii community was wealthy, but never opulent as Sybaris had been.

During the decline of Athens and the growth of Roman influence in the fourth to third century BCE, Thurii declined. The resilient tribes of Bruttians and Lucenians, which had preceded Sybarites in Magna Graecia, returned to control the area.

---

[42] Justinus wrote that in the Temple of Apollo at Thurii were the arrows that Hercules had in his quiver at Troy. Bullitt, p. 120.

[43] Thurii existed under a code of laws drafted by their leader, Charondas. According to code a man who married twice could not govern, as he would have exhibited a practice of making poor decisions. Busybodies and gossipers were put into the same class as adulterers, all of whom were subject to public ridicule. Bullitt, p. 121.

Around 273 BCE, the Romans took control of Paestum. They plundered the gold of Paestum to finance war against Hannibal. In 218 BCE, Hannibal crossed the Alps and eventually settled in Thurii. Thurii became Hannibal's last stand as a warrior, as he was recalled home to Carthage in 203 BCE. Along the way home, Hannibal plundered as he went, destroying property of allies as well as foes. He is reputed to have killed at least 4,000 horses as he recalled soldiers from Greece and what is now southern Italy and Sicily.

The next traveler of note to the area was Spartacus. In 75 BCE, the freed gladiator defeated the Roman army with 120,000 of his fellow former slaves. Like Hannibal, Spartacus also chose to take his last stand outside his adopted home of Thurii. Somewhere on the plains of Thurii is the shield upon which Spartacus was slain.[44]

In 871 CE, Paestum was looted, but not dismantled. Natural decay and blowing dust caused the once lovely city to be buried over the next millennium. Then in 1750, a road crew hit upon the yellow limestone pillars. The city

---

[44] Bullitt, p. 156.

was rediscovered. On December 2, 1998, Paestum was made part of an historical and cultural landscape of the World Heritage List by the United Nations Educational, Scientific and Cultural Organization (UNESCO). The UNESCO selection committee noted the importance of Paestum as a link between Magna Graecia and the Etruscan northeast of Italy.

In the 1960s, an Italian, Signor Lerici, invented ground-penetrating radar. He used it successfully to locate ancient archaeological sites in Tuscany.[45] By 1968, Elizabeth K. Ralph, while an Associate Director of the Applied Science Center for Archaeology at the University of Pennsylvania, used a refined form of the device to locate Sybaris. Excavation is continuing.

Today there is still little on the surface of the former Sybaris to tempt an entire cruise ship to include the Gulf of Taranto in its itinerary. The small port of Taranto holds many archaeological riches and work on the gulf is continuing, so new itineraries may be forthcoming. For the adventurous traveler, the toe, arch, and heel of Italy hold many delightful stories of which Sybaris is one. For now, the best means to connect with this story may be on a stop in Paestum, while visiting the Amalfi Coast or Naples.

---

[45] Bullitt, p. 28.

AJACCIO, CORSICA

Napoleon's Mother

When a great man changes control of a continent in a short space of time, it is only natural to ask about the mother that raised him. Napoleon Bonaparte was often ignored as a boy, revered as a man, exiled, and revered again. At age thirty he controlled most of Europe and was headed toward Russia. He was Emperor for Life of France, then exiled to Elba, from which he escaped, and later died on the desolate rock of an island, at St. Helena. Love him or not, Napoleon was the catalyst for France to move from monarchy to republic. At each stage of his career, Napoleon demonstrated devotion to his mother. Their devotion was reciprocal.

During periods of Napoleon's exile and imprisonment, French royals lived in fear that his mother was capable of creating yet another emperor. They held her in check by denying her a passport and by passing laws against Bonaparte family get-togethers. Government spies were assigned to watch the aging family matriarch, as she went from home to church each day. Her moral strength, grace under pressure and devotion to her children were legendary.

Letizia Bonaparte raised her family in Ajaccio, Corsica, until she was widowed with eight young children at age thirty-four. She lived in poverty, washing the family laundry in a stream, until she became Madame Mere, the mother of the emperor in Paris, at age forty-five. At age sixty-two, she left France ahead of the jailors, to settle in Rome. Wherever she went, Letizia Bonaparte kept track of her eight children. Even as each child became a king, princess, or queen, she was always ready to provide a mother's support to whichever child was in need.

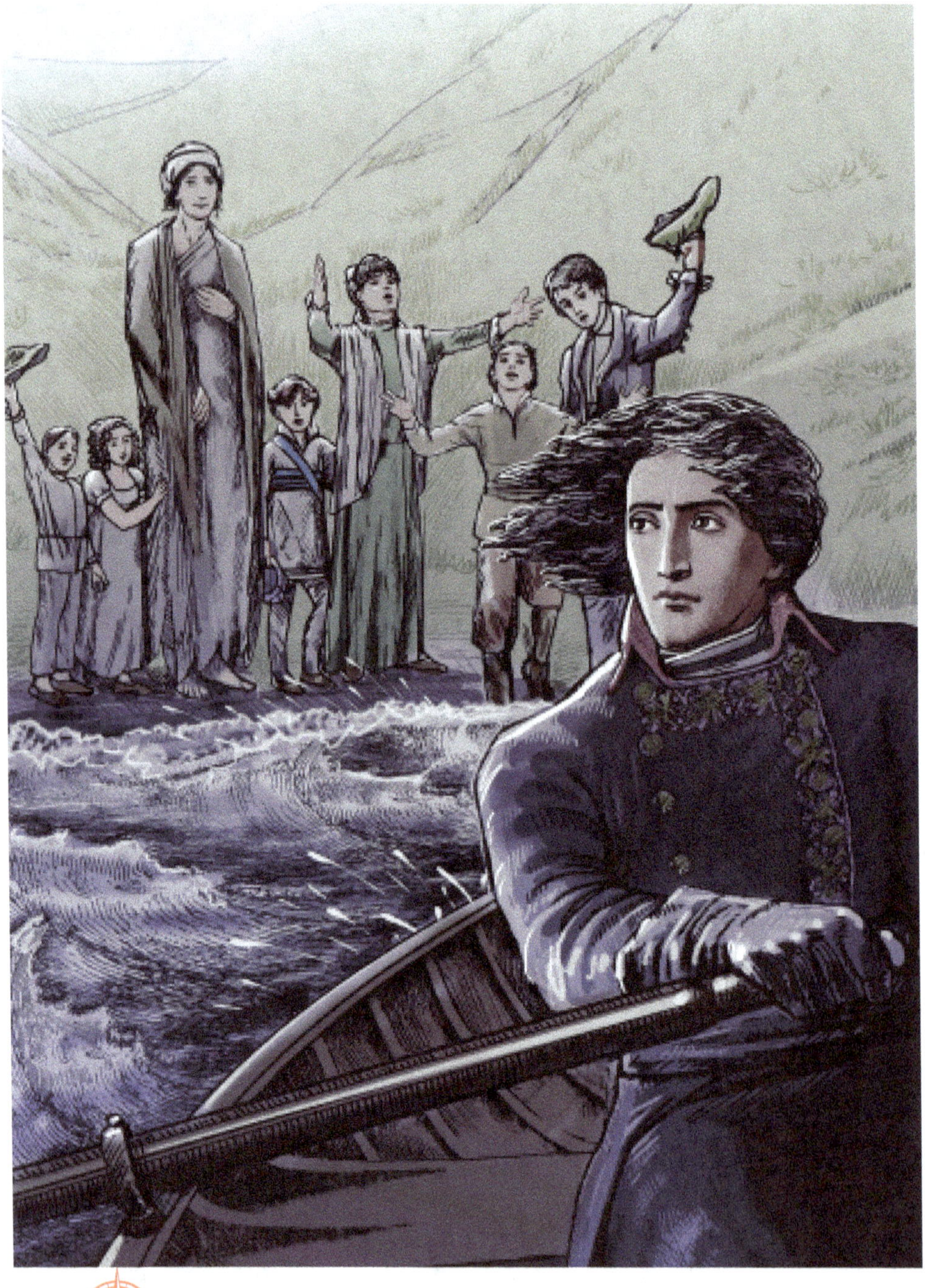

Cruise Through History

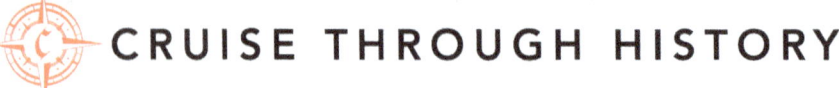

This is the rarely told story of the mother behind the conquering emperor. It is the story of the Bonaparte family of Ajaccio, Corsica, the mother who nurtured their aspirations, and the woman who held the Bonaparte legacy together against all diversity. It is due to the efforts of Letizia Bonaparte that there are numerous Bonaparte museums, which can be visited today. The travel destinations of Ajaccio, Paris, and Rome feature prominently in the story of Napoleon's mother.

Letizia Buonaparte in Ajaccio

Letizia Ramolina was born in 1750, to the Italian captain of the army garrison at Ajaccio, Corsica, and a young woman of a large and long-standing family in Corsica. Their family language was Italian. At the time, Corsica was controlled by Genoa and the residents identified with a special branch of Italian culture.

Corsica of the mid-eighteenth century was an island of several primitive villages. The rule of law was vendetta. The families were not usually violent, except when a family member was injured by a person from another family. Then the offended family would come together to avenge the harm. If the individual offender could not be found, vengeance would be taken on any of the offender's family. In this very Catholic land, the absent offender would be shrouded in a "pillar of shame." Killing for vengeance was accepted. Napoleon once said of his grandmother that she could quickly summon an army of 200 to 300 mountaineers of Corsica if the need arose.

In 1750, Italy was not a unified country. The regions of what is known today as Italy were controlled in the northwest by powerful cities, such as Genoa, Pisa, or Florence; in the northeast by Austria; in the center by the Vatican; and the south and Sicily were at times French, Spanish, or Prussian-German. The Corsicans favored home rule and much of their energy was spent in throwing off the control of Genoa.

Eventually, the Genoese determined that the cost of retaining Corsica was too high and they sold their interest to France. The Corsicans then sought British aid to remove the French. Letizia grew up in Ajaccio in controversial times.

Letizia's father died when she was twelve. Her mother married a Swiss sea captain in the Genoese fleet. They married only after the captain became Catholic. Shortly thereafter, Letizia gained a half-brother, known by his family name of Fesch. He would become a priest, a cardinal, and her life-long confidant. As Letizia aged, Fesch would be her closest companion.

Letizia was not quite fourteen when she married Carlo Buonaparte. He was a handsome young man of eighteen from a noble family. His father died when Carlo was fourteen and he was sent to the university. When he was not giving parties, Carlo was a perennial law student in Pisa.

In contrast to Carlo, Letizia was a serious young woman. She was certainly beautiful, with her large black eyes, light brown hair, tall, slim figure, and lovely smile. She rarely smiled and was not one for frivolous conversation. They were a handsome couple, but an odd social combination.

Fifty male cousins escorted Letizia to her wedding. Part of her dowry was her personal army. Before she left Corsica, that army would be put to good use.

The young couple moved into Casa Buonaparte in Ajaccio. In the three-story home, Carlo's mother and her brother, who was the Archdeacon of the church, occupied the first floor. The newlyweds had the second floor. A cousin and her husband occupied the top floor. When the cousins argued, Carlo's cousin from the upper floor would douse Carlo with wastewater as he leaned out of the window. Since he was a budding lawyer, Carlo sued his cousin.[46]

Eventually, Letizia and Carlo controlled the entire Casa Buonaparte. This was fortunate as Letizia was pregnant twelve times in the twenty-year marriage. Carlo continued to spend time in Pisa, dressing lavishly and giving parties. Letizia kept the household going by being frugal. She never disapproved of Carlo's expenditures. Letizia knew that if her young family were to attain status they would need to dress for the part.[47]

---

[46] Lawsuits for irritations between and within families were common in eighteenth century Corsica.

[47] Letizia sent Napoleon to a nursery school for girls at age five. Historians have drawn comparisons to Hercules, whose mother did the same. Hercules was dressed as a girl at age five and sent to a girl's school for his protection.

While Letizia went to mass every day, Carlo became embroiled in Corsican politics. The great Corsican nationalist, Pasquale Paoli, was leading the charge to seek British aid in ridding Corsica of control by Genoa. As the handsome orator, Carlo gave speeches on behalf of the less flamboyant Paoli. Dressed as French royalty, Carlo went to Rome on a mission to the pope on behalf of Paoli.

In 1768, Genoa sold Corsica to France. Fighting broke out between the new owner, France, and the fiercely independent local Corsican population. Letizia was six months pregnant with Napoleon, when she took the year-old Giuseppe into the Corsican hills to the Paoli military camp. There they hid from the French troops fighting Corsican nationalists in Ajaccio. She lived in a cold, wet cave; unable to light a fire for fear it would disclose the position of the camp. By the time Napoleon was born in 1769, he was the first Buonaparte to be a citizen of France.

In 1770, Louis XV married Marie-Antoinette. As the king's gift to the children of Corsica of noble birth, without the means to attend a royal school, Louis XV offered scholarships with stipends for uniforms and books. Carlo put on his best royal appearance to seek places for his oldest children, Giuseppe and Napoleone.[48] Ten-year-old Giuseppe did not like school. Nine-year-old Napoleone flourished. Napoleon dropped the Italian "e" from his name and the "u" from Bonaparte, learned French, and tried to fit in at school despite his Corsican accent.

Carlo spoke French and performed well as a peace ambassador to the French palace on behalf of Corsica. He had completed his law studies without securing an income-producing position, so in an audience with the king, Carlo asked for a stipend to grow mulberry trees in Corsica. The project was approved, although funding would not come for many years, and only upon the intervention of Napoleon. Carlo and Letizia looked elegant in the French royal court, but rather overdressed, when they stopped by to visit Napoleon at military school outside of Paris.

---

[48] The Buonaparte family all had Italian names. This would change to French-appropriate names when Napoleon attained stature in the military.

When Letizia was thirty-four and Carlo was thirty-eight, he died of stomach cancer. Of the twelve births, Letizia was left with eight children. The oldest, Giuseppe, was sixteen, Napoleon was fifteen, and the youngest was a newborn baby. Carlo spent his family inheritance, and most of Letizia's dowry funds, by the time he died. He left Letizia to handle the housework herself and to care for six children under the age of ten, not in boarding school or the military. Letizia's savior was her half-brother, Fesch, in his early twenties, who had become the Archdeacon of Ajaccio. Thanks to Fesch, the family maintained at least a minimal existence, had sufficient housing, and some education.

When the French Revolution erupted in 1789, more than twenty years had passed since Letizia was forced to hide in the hills. Corsica and the Bonapartes were thrust again into the center of controversy. Paoli returned to Corsica to resurrect his leadership. Letizia's third son, Lucciano, decided at age fourteen to leave school in France, return to Corsica, and go into politics. Lucciano gave an inflammatory speech that accused Paoli of being a British agent. Corsica split into Paoli and Bonaparte factions. Paolists sacked Casa Bonaparte in

Ajaccio, as Letizia ran into the Corsican hills with her four youngest children. Her army of cousins aided her in her escape.[49]

Letizia lived in poverty in the countryside, accepting food from generous villagers, and washing the family laundry in a stream, as she waited to be rescued by Napoleon. Giuseppe and Lucciano were in hiding. The oldest daughter, Elisa, was in France, in a royal school, and thus in danger of being detained by one political faction or another.

Paolists roamed the island looking for Bonapartes. The old family friend, Paoli, issued a decree banishing Bonapartes from Corsica. Letizia was in a desperate situation. Her first concern was for her children, particularly those whose status was unknown to her.

As if in an unbelievable dream, Letizia looked over Corsican cliffs to the sea and saw a three-mast ship sailing up the coast to her location. She prayed that it might be Napoleon. She grabbed the children and ran down to the beach. There she saw a longboat, being rowed to shore by a single occupant. No sooner did the boat hit the beach than Napoleon jumped out and ran to Letizia. There, on the beach, the mother and son had just a few moments for a rare display of tears. The last of the Bonapartes of Corsica jumped into the boat as Napoleon rowed back out to sea.

At age forty-two Letizia left Corsica. Although she would later have the opportunity to refurbish Casa Bonaparte in Ajaccio, she would never live there again. Napoleon left his mother and siblings in Toulon, France, and returned to his military post. A passport given to Letizia at the time listed her as age fifty-six.[50] No doubt, her circumstances had taken their toll on her beauty.

---

[49] The eight Bonaparte children to survive infancy and to live as adults, with their Italian and adopted French names, were: Giuseppe/Joseph (1768-1844); Napoleone/Napoleon (1769-1821); Lucciano/Lucien (1775-1840); Maria-Anna/Elisa (1777-1820); Luigi/Louis (1778-1846); Marie-Paola/Pauline (1780-1825); Maria-Annunziata/Caroline (1782-1839); and Girolamo/Jerome (1784-1860).

[50] Monica Sterling, Madame Letizia, Harper & Brothers, New York, 1961, p. 81

Madame Mere in Paris

Letizia spent the next twenty years living in France, with brief trips to Ajaccio and Rome. Her fate during this time, and that of her children, was dependent upon the rise and fall of the fortunes of Napoleon. Leitizia was at all times a strong woman, who possessed an internal definition of self. She did not acknowledge defeat as she begged for bread in the streets of Toulon to feed her family, nor was she infatuated with living in a palace as the mother of the emperor, Madame Mere.

Never opposed to looking the part of the emperor's mother, Letizia was careful to use the good times to save for the unknown future, even as her children raised their living standards to the extent of their income. The Bonaparte children lived in France as though the present was permanent. Their mother knew better.

When Letizia first landed in Toulon, the place was in anarchy. Violence was all around her. She kept moving the children to avoid harm. Their access to school was intermittent. Food was scarce. Letizia joined other mothers in the streets, begging for bread.

When Napoleon received military pay, he sent it to his mother. She preferred to retain the funds, live as modestly as possible, and return to washing clothes in a stream. The oldest son, now called Joseph instead of Giuseppe, was able to secure a position as a war commissioner for the French republic. His status enabled the family to receive a two-room flat in Marseille. There was no furniture, no heat, and no fresh water.

All of France was in upheaval. The British aided the royalists, represented in Corsica by Paoli. Napoleon was a soldier in the army of the French constitutional government, a government that was so mired in its corruption that it could hardly function. The French National Guard threatened to revolt. Roving bands of revolutionaries sought to execute the nobility.

It was in the midst of turmoil that the military genius of Napoleon was recognized. With a small force of government troops he gained victories over forces several times larger. When the French leadership formed a Directory, to replace the constitutional convention, Napoleon was made commander of the Army of the Interior. He was only twenty-six.

Josephine de Beauharnais was a thirty-three-year-old, divorced mother of a thirteen-year-old daughter and a son, when she charmed the twenty-six-year-old Napoleon. They married without Letizia's permission. Napoleon had evidently forgotten his outrage when his brother Lucian secretly married an innkeeper's daughter. Letizia's disappointment over the marriages of Lucian and Napoleon was moderated by the marriage of Joseph to the daughter of a wealthy former French royal. The in-laws hoped to keep their heads by mixing with working people.

The change in Bonaparte family fortunes dates to May 15, 1796, when Napoleon led 38,000 hungry French troops in a victory over more than 80,000 Austrian forces. Napoleon was hailed as the liberator of Italy. Letizia arrived in Genoa to celebrate the victory and was hailed as a Madonna. She modestly replied that she was at that moment the happiest mother in the world.

Over the next six years the remainder of the Bonaparte children married. Pauline married twice. Her first marriage to a dashing captain ended with his death in battle. Her second marriage, to Prince Camillo Borghese of Rome, established her royal title and domicile in Rome. Louis, the fourth of the five Bonaparte sons, married Josephine's daughter. Letizia did not appreciate that choice at first, although she and her young daughter-in-law eventually became close.

As Napoleon rose in power in France, eventually becoming the Emperor for Life at age thirty, he was able to provide substantial dowries for his sisters and high military positions for their husbands. The whole family became royalty. The youngest Bonaparte daughter became a queen when Napoleon appointed her husband king of Naples. The youngest child, Jerome, had his first marriage annulled and then he married into German royalty. Napoleon gave his older brother, Joseph, governance of lands in Spain that made him a prince. The oldest daughter, Elisa, became a princess when Napoleon made a similar arrangement for her husband. In addition to royal titles, each of the Bonaparte children became wealthy through various land and business dealings. Letizia realized that she was the mother of more royalty then any single mother before her. She was the leading mother figure of her age, having diapered and disciplined the leaders of Europe.

Only Lucien evaded the largesse of his brother, Napoleon. Lucien made a fortune in business in Spain. Secretly, he married for love the daughter of a tradesman. Lucien would not annul his marriage in favor of a royal marriage arranged by Napoleon, to benefit the politics of France. Their brotherly feud saddened Letizia. Eventually, the pope became involved. He took Lucien's side. Publicly the pope spoke of the sanctity of marriage and the sin of divorce. The pope's decision may have been influenced by Napoleon's previous seizure of papal lands.

Napoleon endowed Letizia with the title of Protectress of the Hospital Sisters and Sisters of Charity. She enjoyed her ability to oversee the benevolent side of the government. The position also came with one million francs a year for household expenses.

Letizia enjoyed seeing her children revered as royals, although she refused to live in the palace. Napoleon purchased a house for her in Paris and a country home southeast of the city. As her children spent lavishly on their new lifestyles, Letizia quietly made financial investments in Corsica, Italy, Spain, and London.[51] Her private portfolio grew.

Letizia was also given substantial sums by Napoleon to refurbish Casa Bonaparte in Ajaccio. After the Paolists had trashed it, it became home to British officials. When the British left, they removed the remaining furnishings. Letizia was able to restore and redecorate, but never had the opportunity to reside there. The last time that the home was utilized by a Bonaparte was in 1799, when Napoleon held a lavish dinner there during a military campaign.

Letizia filled her time as the mother of the emperor by playing cards in her country estate, enjoying her grandchildren, and with visits to Rome. In Rome, each member of the Sacred College of cardinals welcomed her as a celebrity. She toured many of the holy sites in Italy. When Letizia was presented to the pope, they had a long discussion.

After nineteen years in France, Letizia saw the fortunes of her family begin to falter. She was pleased when Napoleon divorced Josephine to marry the great-niece of Marie-Antoinette, the eighteen-year-old Austrian princess,

---

[51] Sterling, p. 154.

Marie-Louise. Their son, born in 1811, and Napoleon's only legitimate child, was given the title of the King of Rome. He would never see Rome. Even though the divorce was for the purpose of securing an heir to the throne, the pope excommunicated Napoleon. Napoleon and Josephine remained close to the day she died.

Napoleon's actions to secure an heir to the throne caused his enemies to unite. Palace intrigue increased among ungrateful nobles, the same nobles who were elevated to their stature only a few years earlier by Napoleon. Anti-Bonaparte rumors flared while Napoleon was absent from Paris fighting wars to maintain far-flung territory. He then had a string of military defeats: Spain and Russia in 1812; Germany in 1813; and Waterloo in France in 1814.

When the French Senate repudiated Napoleon, the entire Bonaparte family fell apart. The Bourbon French King Louis XVIII took the throne. Napoleon was exiled to the Italian island of Elba,[52] where he was mockingly given the title of "Sovereign for Life." His wife left for Austria with Napoleon II.

The father and son would never reunite. Napoleon II died at age twenty-one, a prisoner of the Austrian court. Josephine died about the same time, at age fifty-one, the age that would claim Napoleon, seven years later.

The Bonaparte children were allowed to keep their titles, although they were meaningless, as the government harassed the siblings. Caroline and her husband were driven from Naples. Joseph was forced from Spain. Elisa, Louis, and Jerome dispersed. Only Lucien fared well as he installed a swimming pool in his home in Rome. Pauline remained secure in Rome, where her in-laws afforded her protection from the politics of the time. She visited Napoleon in Elba to try to cheer him.

Letizia was sixty-four and her hair was grey. She packed up her homes in Paris and the country and left for Rome. Always the frugal businesswoman, Letizia did not depart Paris until she had bargained hard with the new minister of war, who purchased her city home for 800,000 francs.[53]

---

[52] Elba became French in 1891. The Mulini Palace built by Napoleon on Elba is now a museum.
[53] At this time the value of a franc was about equal to a U.S dollar.

Madame Letizia in Rome

Letizia went to Rome, where she began residence in Lucian's home. Soon she and Pauline called upon the Italian navy to escort her to Elba. There Pauline staged parties, Letizia played cards, and Napoleon rebuilt the Elba water and sewage systems as he had in Paris.[54]

Letizia was satisfied with life on Elba, as for once, in a long time, she knew where her children were. They were out of harm's way. Napoleon was not satisfied. He heard the rumblings from France as the reinstated Bourbon king seized property and reversed the civic advances Napoleon had made. One night, guards on Elba came into Letizia's room looking for Napoleon. She claimed no knowledge of his location. After all, she was only the mother.

Napoleon left Elba with his loyal troops and quickly stormed Paris. There the brothers Napoleon, Joseph, Lucian and Jerome were reunited.[55] Letizia was pleased to see the boys together again. At age sixty-five, Letizia entered the palace hall, once again as a noble.

Napoleon's resurgence was short-lived. By June 22, 1815, he met his Waterloo for the last time. He tried to escape to America, but was apprehended by the British and incarcerated at St. Helena. St. Helena, the desolate rock, off the African coast of Angola, was then, as now, a British possession, so far from the rest of the world as to discourage contact. Letizia was not allowed to visit Napoleon. She prayed with Fesch for a sign that Napoleon had escaped and was living anywhere else.[56]

Letizia's longtime financial and real estate investments, spread across several countries, served her well. She was able to assist her children in need as fallen nobles, and to purchase a fitting home in Rome. The three-story, seventeenth-century palace on Palazzo Venezia became the center of her world. It was there

---

[54] Napoleon also built the Louvre, which he stocked with variously acquired treasures. See this itinerary, The Traveling Horses of Saint Marks, for another side of the story.
[55] Louis remained in Florence, ill with syphilis.
[56] Napoleon died May 5, 1821, of stomach cancer, like his father. He was buried on St. Helena, and then reburied in Paris in 1840, in the Invalides, with full honors. See Correlli Barnett, Bonaparte, Hill and Wang, New York, 1978.

that Madame Letizia entertained foreign dignitaries and Vatican officials. She used the spacious home to collect Bonaparte memorabilia, such as busts of the children and Napoleon's deathbed. Letizia occupied the first floor, kept the second floor for visiting family, and housed her household servants on the third floor.

For a woman so invested in her children throughout her life, to have children and even grandchildren predecease her was painful. Elisa became ill and died in Trieste, in 1820, just prior to Napoleon's death. Pauline, the princess Borghese, separated from her husband, and having had her only child die young, passed away in Rome of cancer, at age forty-five, in 1825. Several grandchildren passed away from illness and accidents.[57] Napoleon II, heir to the Bonaparte dynasty, died at age twenty-one.

Letizia spent her time in Rome taking walks through the Roman Forum and Coliseum. She became a familiar sight when walking through the ancient

---

[57] The last American Bonaparte, Jerome Napoleon, died, childless, in 1945, when he tripped over his dog's leash during a walk in Central Park.

monuments, an elegant form herself in her long, black, merino wool, empire-style dresses and shawl. People no longer greeted her as "your highness." Instead, they referred to her with affection as, simply, "Madame Letizia."

Just before her eightieth birthday, Letizia broke her hip. She was housebound. French, British, and Austrian authorities restricted Bonaparte children living outside of Rome from visiting their mother. It seems they still feared a resurgence of the Bonapartes. This would occur, despite their efforts, in 1852, when the youngest son of Louis would reign as Napoleon III, from 1852 to 1870.

In 1835, Letizia, almost blind, made a list of female children to receive her jewels. She executed a will, leaving her three-million-franc estate to her four sons, with some minor bequeaths to the children of Caroline and Elise. She left an art collection to Fesch and forgave all debts owed to her.

In January 1836, Letizia suffered a protracted illness. A screen was placed in her bedroom so that her admirers could file through as she lay dying. Letizia Bonaparte, the widow of Corsica, the mother of the emperor of France, and the exile in Italy, died in her bed on February 2, 1836. It was unfortunate that she did not live long enough to see the Arc de Triomphe completed and dedicated to Napoleon later that year.

Visiting the Homes of Napoleon's Mother

Due to the proficient collecting efforts of Letizia, there are three well-stocked Bonaparte museums open today. One is the Mulini Palace on Elba, where Letizia sent many of the Bonaparte furnishings from Paris at the time of the exile. The others are in Rome and Ajaccio.

The museum in Rome began at the home of Madame Letizia, where she collected paintings and busts of the children. She also collected memorabilia having the Bonaparte bee emblem of the emperor. There are works of the famous sculptor Canova, depicting Letizia and Napoleon. The elegant building, facing the Italian Parliament and having a more direct view of Italian politicians than the adjacent former home of Mussolini, still dominates the

square. The Bonaparte name is prominent across the top floor. It now houses a private corporation and a Madame Letizia snack shop. The museum is open to the public in the former home of a Bonaparte cousin, on the banks of the Tiber, at Ponte Cavour.

The third museum is Casa Bonaparte in Ajaccio, Corsica, Napoleon's birthplace and museum. It sits on Place Letizia, so constructed and named by Napoleon. A more extensive museum collection of the times is in the Ajaccio Town Hall. Also in Ajaccio is the Fesch Museum, where there are several important works of art by Bellini, Botticelli, and Titian.

Letizia was first interred at the Sisters of Passion Church in Tarquinii, near the cruise ship port of Civitavecchia. In 1851, Napoleon III moved Letizia from Italy to her home in Ajaccio. A century later, in 1951, Prince Napoleon, a descendant of Jerome, and royalty of Belgium, Italy, and Germany, moved Carlo's body to rest next to Letizia.[58]

---

[58] In 1840, Napoleon's body was brought to rest in Les Invalides, near the Military Museum in Paris. One million people lined the route of his coffin. In 1940, the body of Napoleon II was taken from the Hapsburg family vault and brought from Vienna to rest next to his father.

OLBIA, SARDINIA

At Home with Garibaldi on Caprera

As a freedom fighter, Garibaldi fought hard and traveled light. He evidenced no concept of domesticity. Still, his relationships with woman became as legendary as his success in battles to create independent nations. In part, the women in his life contributed to his success by healing his wounds, raising funds for his troops, and writing about his successes in order to exploit the Garibaldi legend. In his way, Garibaldi appreciated all of their efforts.

Each time Garibaldi was a weary soldier in need of restoring his enthusiasm for battle, he would retreat to a little desolate island off the coast of Sardinia. Caprera was home and refuge to Garibaldi during the latter part of his life. It was there that he established a homestead for his final wife, his lovers, and his remaining children.

This is the story of the domestic side of the life of Garibaldi, such as it was. Garibaldi did not have a soft side to his nature. He was consistently a soldier. Still, the story of the warrior in his female relationships and at home is as colorful as his military encounters. The Garibaldi home of twenty-five years in Caprera is now a museum that provides additional insight to the man, whenever it is opened to visitors.

The Warrior and His Women

The women in Garibaldi's life added to his legend by their joint exploits and in their prolific writings. Some historians attribute to the anarchist, Mazzini, the beginnings of the Garibaldi legend, through his elaborations of Garibaldi's

South American exploits for London audiences. Others credit the attention of the then famous author Alexandre Dumas, who enjoyed following Garibaldi, with giving Garibaldi notoriety. However, Dumas did not focus great works of fiction upon this amazing non-fiction character. Garibaldi's own writings, including "The Thousand" and "The Rule of the Monk," about nuns committing torture, were produced after 1870, while in retirement in Caprera, long after the warrior mystique was well established. Credit must be given to the women in Garibaldi's life for providing favorable publicity at all the right times to create the public attention that Garibaldi craved.

In contrast to the rambling Garibaldi diary, written from his distant memory, and the embellishments of Dumas and Mazzini, the writings of Garibaldi's daughter Anita, his nurse Jesse White, his British patron Madame Schwartz, and a would-be lover and wealthy daughter of a Hamburg banker, Marie Esperance, who wrote under the *nom de plume* of Elpis Melena, had the indicia of reliability from first-hand knowledge, even if they were greatly influenced by devotion. Although Mazzini and Dumas wrote of Garibaldi's heroic deeds in battles, it was Garibaldi's women who created the Garibaldi mystique. It was this Garibaldi mystique that translated into volunteers for armies and donations of funds to feed, clothe, and arm them. Garibaldi's women were integral to enabling his goal of the unification of Italy.

As big a part as the women played in the future of Italy and the accomplishment of his self-styled purpose in life, Garibaldi was off-handed in his approach to women. His courtship, whether for an evening or for marriage, was a simple two-sentence approach. He would identify some woman who interested him and court her by saying: "I want you. Will you have me?"

Garibaldi was proud of the fact that as a soldier and conqueror, he never forced himself on a woman. He was honest about never desiring to take on responsibility for the support of a wife or family and offered no illusions of a family home. All of his women had in common their independence, either financial, intellectual, or both. Late in life, when all the guns were silent, Garibaldi was an outspoken supporter of women's rights.

Garibaldi was married three times and had eight known children, four from the first and three from the last of his wives. An eighth child, daughter Anita, was born during a fling with one woman, while he was engaged to another. Garibaldi was not handsome or of distinguished physical stature, although he was described by a man as having the voice of an Othello.[59]

Garibaldi looked splendid playing the part of the South American hombre in Europe, wearing his red shirt and white poncho, while sitting on his white horse. He was not known to have table manners, using his campfire habits even as he enjoyed sumptuous dining. Women of elegance sought his company, such as British Lady Byron and the Dowager Duchess of Sutherland. The duchess allowed Garibaldi to smoke in her boudoir. His fiancée, the wealthy widow Emma Roberts, was a Garibaldi consort for two years. In the end, Garibaldi chose as lasting companions those women who were closer to the earth.

Garibaldi would say that the love of his life was his first wife, Anita Ribeiro da Silva, whom he married in 1842, in Montevideo. His tributes to her in death may have been a glimmer of remorse that he was not more attentive to her needs in life. It was not in Garibaldi's nature to admit wrongdoing or ask forgiveness.

Garibaldi spotted Anita in South America at a time when he was ready for companionship. At the time she was married to a fisherman. She eagerly accepted his two lines of introduction-courtship-proposal, and they were off on an adventure. They were married upon the eventual death of her husband. Legend has it that on their wedding night there was an attack on Garibaldi's troops and Anita picked up a gun and shot three of the enemy. It was a good match.

---

[59] Georg Brandes, Creative Spirits of the 19th Century, Books for Libraries Press, Freeport, New York, 1967, p. 436.

In his memoirs Garibaldi would describe Anita as having given birth to their children practically on horseback. The first child, Menotti, was born in Uruguay, during a battle on September 6, 1840. Garibaldi describes riding off to find linen for the child, when his troops were attacked. He and Anita went with the soldiers into hiding, holding the infant close for warmth as they forded rivers. A statue of Anita in Rome depicts Anita on horseback with a baby on one arm and a rifle in her hand.

Garibaldi's two oldest children with Anita were sons who eventually fought with their father. Of the two daughters, the youngest died while locked in a room with her nurse for their safety. Unable to be released during a fire, the two perished. For the remainder of his life Garibaldi would not allow locks on doors of his home.

Anita became seriously ill during the Rome campaign of 1849. Garibaldi and his 3,000 volunteers were forced to march to San Marino, where they had a safe haven. Horses were scarce so Garibaldi gave his to Anita. After the troops were allowed to disperse for their safety, Garibaldi and Anita sailed to Venice. They were forced to land and hide in marshes to avoid enemy troops. Locals who may have wanted to assist them were timid to do so for fear of repercussions from the Austrians or the French. Legend has it that a farmer gave a bedroom to Anita, where she died. She took her last breath while soldiers came in the front door just as Garibaldi went out the back. The children were safely away in Nice at the time with Garibaldi's mother.

During the northern Italian unification campaigns of the 1850s, Garibaldi was a recognized hero. Women were delighted to meet him as he traveled to England in search of donors to his volunteer army. For two years he was engaged to Emma Roberts and a frequent guest in her London home, while recuperating from battles. Emma's friend Jesse White was barely twenty years old when she accompanied Garibaldi to battle and nursed him and his troops. White idolized Garibaldi and Mazzini. She wrote for the English and Italian press of their conquests and achieved some celebrity on speaking tours. White was imprisoned in Genoa because of her exploits with Mazzini and Garibaldi. Upon her release in 1859, she and her husband went to Sicily to aide Garibaldi in the campaign for Palermo.

Oddly, Garibaldi does not mention White in his three-volume memoirs. Italy has remembered White. There is a plaque in Florence where she died in 1906, commemorating her accomplishments. Her home in Lendinara, south of Venice, is a shrine to her and her work in the unification of Italy. Jesse White's book, "The Birth of Modern Italy," was published in 1909.[60]

Garibaldi found life with Emma Roberts to be "undisciplined."[61] He complained that she did not keep the regular bedtime hours of a good soldier. No doubt frequent baths and changes of clothes were not his cup of tea either. While Jesse was in prison and Emma was in London, Garibaldi made a trip to Caprera to enjoy the company of Battistina Ravello, the daughter of a seaman. Garibaldi and Ravello had a daughter, named Anita, in honor of his first wife. Anita would grow up to write tributes to her father.

Two other women figure prominently in Garibaldi's life at this time. Madame Schwartz was a British friend and patron. She seemed to know all the women in his life at the time, but kept out of the emotional fray. She delivered military messages for Garibaldi. Once in Sicily she was arrested and put into a dungeon to die. According to her account of the trauma, her jailor recognized her from her youth at a time when she had done a good deed. He released her. When Schwartz next saw Garibaldi and told him of her narrow escape, he made a casual remark that it was good to have her when he next needed her.

The other woman was Elpis Melena.[62] Melena, by her accounts, had an exciting life. She was born in 1818, as Marie Espérance von Brandt, a German born in England, who spoke eight languages and married at fifteen. Her husband

---

[60] Jesse White desired to become a doctor, but was denied admission to medical school in England as a woman. She found great opportunities to study public health and medicine while on campaigns with Garibaldi. Once Italy was unified in 1870, White turned her full attention to public health. She did research on problems of mental health and physical symptoms, such diarrhea in the street people of Naples. She found that lack of protein rich food and lack of vitamin B were culprits. She also wrote that having two glasses of red wine a day contributed to good health. White went on to study the ill effects on children in Sicily of their labor in the sulphur mines.

[61] Peter dePolnay, Garibaldi, Hutchinson of London, 1957, p. 37.

[62] Elpis Melena, Garibaldi's Memoirs, Vol. 1, International Institute of Garibaldi Studies, Sarasota, Fl., 1981.

committed suicide by the time she was twenty, which freed her to travel to Rome, Greece, Turkey and Egypt. After she was shipwrecked near Tunis, von Brandt took the name Elpis Melena, which means "black hope." She wrote colorful memoirs of Garibaldi, proclaiming to be his mistress, much of which is disputed by the Garibaldi children as fiction. Garibaldi does not mention her in his memoirs.

Garibaldi's second marriage played out like a Shakespearean comedy. On January 24, 1860, Garibaldi married eighteen-year-old Giuseppina Raimond in a church. She was the daughter of a prosperous merchant. The wedding may have been his only concession to the church in a lifetime of declaring the church to be the enslaver of the masses.

The bride was in love with one of Garibaldi's men and was carrying the young soldier's child. The soldier, out of respect for Garibaldi, decamped for Portugal and was never seen again. He wrote to Garibaldi prior to leaving, but there is no evidence that the letter was received prior to the wedding. Immediately after the wedding, on the wedding night, the bride's brother gave Garibaldi one or more of the love letters of his sister to the father of her child. Garibaldi was enraged and promptly returned the bride to her father, saying, "She is not my wife."[63] Garibaldi always maintained that this marriage was never consummated. Still, he waited twenty years to have it annulled.

Garibaldi sought the annulment of his marriage to Giuseppina on January 14, 1880, so[64] that he could marry the mother of his three children, the third of whom was born in 1873. Garibaldi may have been seen with many women in the last two decades of his life, but it was Francesca Armosino who accompanied him to Caprera in his several attempts to quietly retire. Francesca was eighteen when she was brought to the island as a housekeeper. She stayed on the island while Garibaldi was entertained in England by royal women, such as the Duchess of Sutherland. The Englishwoman Caroline Gifford Philipson came to Caprera to write poems to him, but in the end Garibaldi was most comfortable with daughters of sailors and wives of fishermen.

---

[63] DePolnay, p. 119.
[64] The three children with Francesca were Clelia in 1867, Rosa in 1869, and Manlio in 1873.

The Garibaldi story, which began in Nice where he was born, and came to a crescendo in Sicily at the turning point in his battle to unite Italy, ended on a quiet island off the coast of Sardinia, inhabited by more goats than people. Garibaldi died on Caprera in June 1882, and is buried there, despite his request to be cremated. He was 75, an old age for a man who constantly put himself in the field of battle. He lived to see the unification of Italy, including Rome and Venice, of which he was deprived of having a part. As rarely happens with heroes, Garibaldi lived to be lauded as the unifier of Italy.

A Visit to Caprera

Garibaldi purchased most of the land on the sparsely populated island of Caprera in 1855, prior to the unification of Italy, with funds supplied by his brother. With members of his family, he constructed a self-sustaining compound with a home, stables, livestock pens and gardens. Garibaldi moved to the island in 1856. It was here that he was buried in 1882. His small granite-clad mausoleum and home can be visited, by appointment.

A tour of the homestead moves through the small rooms, with a long pause in the bedroom in which the warrior died. The room is revered as a shrine. The clocks are stopped at the moment of his death, 6:20, on June 2, 1882. His glasses, ponchos, weapons and miscellaneous memorabilia are lovingly displayed. The red shirt is there.

There is a library in which most of the books are inscribed gifts. Two of the paintings in the home are of note. One is a painting of the young Garibaldi son, Manlio, who died at twenty-seven of illness. The other is a painting of Garibaldi by his daughter-in-law, Constance.

Outside the home are the gardens. Garibaldi was an avid gardener. He planted the few trees on the island. Near the gardens and small buildings associated with the farm, is a cemetery. The children of Garibaldi who predeceased him are buried there, as are two daughters from prior relationships, and his third wife, Francesca.[65]

Garibaldi's first child with Francesca, Clelia, born in 1867, lived on the property until her death in 1959. She is credited with preserving the home as an historic site to commemorate her warrior-father. The compound became a museum in 1978.[66]

---

[65] Buried on Caprera near Garibaldi are his children Rosa (1869-1871), Anita (1859-1875), Manlio (1873-1900), Teresita (1845-1903), and Clelia (1867-1959). His third wife was Francesca Armosino (1848-1923).

[66] At the Garibaldi Museum there is a modest charge to visit the house and another smaller fee to roam the grounds. The museum hours are 9am to 6:30 pm. Reservations are suggested, as tour sizes are limited. All tours are in Italian. Tele. And Fax: 0789.727162.

SARDINIA
LAND OF THE GIANTS

The island of Sardinia, off the west coast of Italy, has been home to ancient Greeks and historic Romans. Prior to being the residence of easily recognized and familiar people, there was a large population of indigenous Sardinians. These people are not known to have come from some other place. They lived on Sardinia for more than 2,500 years, before they faded from view in the fifth century of the current era.

The language of the ancient island dwellers is unknown. They left nothing in writing. These indigenous people of Sardinia are known as the Nuraghe, a name assigned to their unique architectural monuments. Such structures are found only in Sardinia and in small sites in a very few other places.[67]

From about 1700 BCE, to about 1860 CE, when remnants of Nuraghe people were dismantled, there were 6,500 Nuraghe towers throughout Sardinia. The distinctive conical and flat-topped towers were one to three stories, built entirely of fitted stone without mortar. The towers were the highpoint at the center of some, but not all, Nuraghe villages. Thus there were many more Nuraghe habitation and ceremonial sites dotting the Sardinia landscape, which indicate that at its height there was a large Nuraghe nation.

The other distinctive remnants of Nuraghe culture are their burial chambers. These aboveground, corridor-shaped, flat-topped stone vaults were faced with large flat and imposing stone walls. The height of the center stone, over the

---

[67] One such place of similar architecture was recently uncovered on a beach, after a severe storm washed away several feet of soil, on a northern island of Scotland. The site is just a few hundred yards from the boyhood home of Robert Lewis Stevenson, but that is another story, in another itinerary.

doorway to the corridor, inspired latecomers to the island to call the early people "giants." Thus the burial sites are known as "tombs of the giants."

This is the story of the Nuraghe nation and their distinctive architectural style unique to Sardinia. There will be no present-day Nuraghe descendants to greet visitors to their homes, sanctuaries, and burial sites. The stones that were not reused to nineteenth century purposes are all that remain to tell the story of the land of the giants.

The Nuraghe Nation

Three thousand years before the birth of Christ ushered in the current era, people roamed across the island of Sardinia. They were herders of native sheep and cattle. They harvested wheat, which they began to plant. As people organized their families into farms, the population grew stable in places inland around the island.

Among the early people there were explorers who ventured west on small ships. There is evidence of contact with the Etruscan people of northwest Italy and with sailors from Cyprus. From travelers, the early Sardinians learned the art of lost wax casting of bronze.[68] They also learned that they were vulnerable to outsiders. A need to build protective structures was realized.

The Bronze Age in Sardinia was from 1700 to 900 BCE. During this time the social structure of the Nuraghe people developed from isolated family farms to a complex social network. Extended families living on farms protected themselves from the weather and encroaching families by building walled settlements with round stone living areas grouped around courtyards within the walls.

---

[68] In lost wax casting, a wax figure is easily formed and covered in clay. There is a hole at the top and bottom of the clay mold. Melted bronze is poured in the top of the mold, and the melted wax escapes through the bottom. The cast item can then be filed down to remove rough edges. Bronze was useful for household implements, jewelry, and for studs on clothing or warriors' shields. Bronze was not strong, but could be melted easily on an open fire.

The most important feature of the family compound was the spring or well. Water, like motherhood, was revered as critical to sustained life. The wells used 3,000 years ago can still be seen with their carefully fitted stone surrounds.

Natural springs were highly regarded by the Nuraghe. There were special places of reverence at the place of springs, denoted by high walls over the spring, stairs leading down to the water, and benches built into the walls for those who came to participate in ceremony. The ceremonies must have included dousing with water, as the floors included drains to capture the spilled water and take it back to the spring. Water was not wasted. Archaeologists have surmised that the springs were places of religious rites. The places could easily have functioned as an early form of bathhouse.

There are small settlements that archaeologists have identified as sanctuaries. These sites are not associated with farms or production of any kind. They are comprised of just a few small living quarters grouped around a courtyard. The dominant structure is a large room with a bench around the wall. These would have served as meeting places, places of reverence, and places of religious practice.

Although the Nuraghe have left nothing in writing to tell of their activities, much can be learned from their art. Many small bronze figures were found of animals and mother figures. If there were deities in Nuraghe culture, they were found in water, women, and animals. Later figurines depict soldiers and boats. One of the most prized bronze artworks of the Nuraghe, now in a museum, is the figure of a wounded or dying soldier attended to by a mother figure.

If the art of the Nuraghe represented their social life, women were well dressed. They wore ankle length tunics of linen. They had bracelets and other adornments, many of which were decorated in a herringbone pattern. Men wore similar tunics at a knee length.

Many boat-shaped bronzes decorated with rams horns and a ram head at the bow have been found all around Sardinia. Nuraghe were not great sailors. The boats are believed to be decorative oil lamps made to suspend from the ceiling.

Not all contact with people from other islands and lands was productive. By the 1300s BCE, the Nuraghe joined with Achaeans, early Greeks, to ward off intrusions from Egyptians. The Nuraghe had begun to build towers of stone in the 1700s BCE, but the need for stronger defenses caused them to build compounds of higher towers, surrounded by walls in which there were similar shorter towers. Inside these compounds soldiers and high-ranking officials resided. Some of the compounds of chieftains included an outer wall, within which crops and/or animals could be maintained.

The Bronze Age coincided with the high point of the Nuraghe nation. The Iron Age, from 900 to 238 BCE, brought the ability to create stronger tools and stronger armaments. Bridles have been found made of iron, indicating that horses were introduced to the island during this time. Nuraghe were able to travel by horse and wagon, instead of riding cattle. However, the Iron Age also brought the Phoenicians from northern Africa and the east. They coveted the Nuraghe homeland. The Nuraghe were mostly farmers, builders, and artisans. The Phoenician sailors were able soldiers. They devastated the Nuraghe.

Pottery from the Iron Age period show signs of Middle Eastern influence, amid the straight lines and dots of earlier Nuraghe pottery. The Nuraghe still baked their bread in large pans. They embellished the loaves with imprinted designs. The indigenous culture was still evident, just not independent of foreign influence and later dominance.

When the Carthaginians came north across the Mediterranean in 650 BCE to conquer Sardinia, they fought the Phoenicians. The Nuraghe culture no longer had control of their island homeland. The Greeks controlled Sardinia from 510 to 238 BCE. At this time the Nuraghe culture went into decline.

The Romans dominated Sardinia from 238 BCE to 476 CE. They arrived to find the remnants of the Nuraghe people. The once protective compounds of Nuraghe leaders held groups of the ancient people struggling to exist. Ceremonial areas were used as modest dwellings. There had not been new structures or new technology for hundreds of years in Nuraghe villages by the time of the Romans. Family farms of a diminished population continued to function independent of Roman control, but the Nuraghe nation had ceased to exist.

Stone Technology

The building epoch in Nuraghe culture was from 1700 to 1300 BCE. Structures were made to last. Wood was scarce and tools to work the wood were primitive. The dominant available material was stone, so stone was used for all but the roofs of dwellings.

Nuraghe is the name given by archaeologists to the stone towers. When they are present they are at the center of a compound. The towers can be one to three stories high. Some have window openings in the upper levels crafted by simply creating a space between otherwise perfectly fitted stones. The towers either have a flat roof terrace, or a conical shape that comes to a perfectly formed peak with an opening, capped by a single stone.

The Nuraghe towers all start with large stones at the base, arranged in a circle. The circle and the stones become smaller as the tower builds to the top. There is no mortar used in construction. There is no evidence of a tumulus of soil or earthwork to support the towers. The towers stand tall and strong due to the skill of the rock masons to place the stones in snug arrangements.

Inside the towers there are often internal stairs, running in a spiral to the top. In the base there are niches inside. Some of the Nuraghe are double-walled with passageways running between niches. In many Nuraghe there are vaults in the floor for water or food storage. Large jars with lips placed just above the ground could be covered with a lid. Since the Nuraghe were skilled brewmasters, the jars could contain beer and fermented beverages.

The openings to the towers are arched at ground level. There may have been doors across the openings although none have been found. If the doors were made of wood or hide, they have long since vanished.

The towers typically open to an internal courtyard with a high, thick wall. Within the courtyard there are openings to other courtyards of residences grouped around smaller courtyards. These are believed to be the homes of the rulers. One opening from a main internal courtyard leads to a storage vault and another to a meeting room.

The meeting rooms were larger than a dwelling place, with a bench around the outer wall. In the center was often found a stone basin for water. Thousands of years before Christian baptism, Nuraghe practiced a water purification ceremony for their people. Water was venerated as the basic element of all life.

In some of the internal courtyards the walls have repeated narrow openings. These enabled airflow, views to the outside, and perhaps played a role in defense. As Nuraghe towers developed, the tall center tower had such openings at the top, ringing the terrace. Smaller towers at intervals in the outer wall repeated the design. Viewed from a distance, the Nuraghe towers appear like turrets in medieval castles. Small stone models of Nuraghe tower groupings exist, which were either artist renderings or instructional models for builders at the time.

The internal courtyard of the Nuraghe tower is accessed through a stone tunnel, high enough to walk through, single file. Outside the tunnel there are groupings of dwellings, all round and all made of fitted stone. The dwellings do not come to a conical top, but remain evenly round from bottom to top. The flat roofs were made of wood.

The dwelling groups are of the same design even when they are found without a Nuraghe tower at the center. These are the farm settlements. All the dwellings have benches around the lower and inner wall for beds and seating. There are niches in the walls and floors for storage. Some archaeologists believe there were fire pits in the center, while others believe the bread was baked outside in courtyard ovens.

Giants' Tombs

Ancient cultures are best known by how they lived and how they died. The Nuraghe buried their dead in vaults above ground, in corridor-shaped stone structures. The corridors had flat tops of fitted stone, so well fitted that they could be walked upon or support a soil overlay. Along the shaft in the center corridor are often found small niches that could hold offerings to the dead.

The front of the corridor is responsible for the name "giants' tombs." Planks of stone form a semicircular wall arrangement across the front. The tallest plank is at the center. The stone slabs become shorter as they fan out to the ends. The planks are supported by the grave corridor at the center and then by walls of stone behind the planks at the outer edges.

The center stone plank has also been called a "stele," the universal name for tall, carved stone in ancient cultures. The center plank has a small curved door opening in the base. Sometimes the stone is carved to have a plain edging. Characteristically, the center stone has a curved top, while the remaining stones of the face have a straight, squared top. In many cases the center stone is fitted in two pieces. The lower half has the door and the upper half has the arched top.[69]

In front of the tomb is an open flat space. Archaeologists believe that this space was used for the ritual burial ceremony. The body was prepared for burial by cleansing the bones. The bones went into the tomb. Of the rest, nothing is known.

Although these are known as giants' tombs, there is nothing to suggest that the Nuraghe were large people. Each tomb could hold hundreds of burials over the time of use. They were more like clan crypts.

Another striking feature of the Nuraghe burial sites are the female deities guarding them. When found intact, they always come in sets of three, as though the Nuraghe believed in a three-part female deity. The deity stones are large, vertical cones with breasts.

As the Nuraghe culture declined, they ceased building new giants' tombs and instead looked for natural caves or depressions in the side of rock formations. The cave openings were faced with just the center stone with the curved top. With whatever resources were available, the Nuraghe uniformly revered their dead.

---

[69] Depictions of giants' tombs have been used as the logo for Sardinian wine. They have become a national icon.

Land of the Giants

Today Sardinia is dotted with Nuraghe sites. Of the more than 6,500 towers that existed by the end of the first millennium CE, only dozens remain. There are still enough structures to delight the visitor with stone buildings that have withstood time. Wooden roofs, benches, clothing and other plant-based accoutrements of the Nuraghe people have decomposed into the soil. The stone structures, benches, tools and art remain.

Up until the middle of the nineteenth century of the current era, most of the Nuraghe towers remained as their builders left them. In the 1800s the island began to accommodate the burgeoning new population of farmers. Enclosure laws were passed that required farmers to enclose their fields to control their flocks and to establish land boundaries. All across the island there were piles of rocks, carefully fitted together by the Nuraghe. The stones were a ready source of wall material, repurposed for nineteenth-century needs. Roads built at the time made use of the smaller stones for base material. Peaceful farmers and road builders dismantled towers that had stood unscathed in battle for more than three millennia.

Of the giants' tombs, those that were easily discovered were long ago picked clean of grave goods and offerings to the dead. Some remained covered by dirt and were discovered recently by archaeologists, who were able to give a detailed account of the finds. Imagine the delight of a researcher who thought he or she was standing on an exquisite patio of interlocked stones, only to discover that they were standing on the roof of an intact Nuraghe tomb.

Today there are Nuraghe sites all around Sardinia to fascinate visitors. They are easily accessible from any cruise port. Whether the cruise ship docks in the south at Cagliari, or in the north at Olbia, near the opulent Emerald Coast, the ability to walk the land of the giants awaits.

PALERMO, SICILY

THE ORIGINAL SICILIAN VESPERS

The thought of Sicilian Vespers may conjure up visions of mob activity in Sicily in recent times. However, the original Sicilian Vespers had nothing to do with the Mafia. It was a populist uprising against the French in 1282. The violence began with an impolite act by a French soldier, perpetrated on a Sicilian lady in front of her husband, and it ended weeks later with the death of thousands of French, their clergy and cohorts, throughout Sicily.

As often happens, the basis of the frustration that led to the full-scale riot was years in development. It began with the unapologetic ambition of Charles of Anjou, the youngest brother of King Louis IX of France. The ambition of Charles was fueled by the pope, who preferred to make a deal with the devil rather than see Sicily and most of Italy controlled by those not under papal control.

The riot that began just outside of Palermo on a lovely Easter Monday rapidly became a war. By the time the war ended, 20 years later, the ambitions of Charles and his popes were compromised. Several popes, kings, and exploiters of Sicilian resources were dead. The war ended in a stalemate, as there was no one left standing who was interested in the reason for the war. All that is left today to commemorate the event for visitors to Sicily is a story and the church of the Holy Spirit of Palermo, where it all began.

Prelude to a Riot and War: The Ambitions of Charles of Anjou

Charles was born in 1227, in the royal family of French kings. He was too far down the ladder of succession to be anything more than another family member needing a purpose in life. He was given a good education, but not much affection. He was also given the French lands of Anjou and Maine and an attractive marriage to Beatrice of Provence. Thus began his lifelong hobby of collecting land.

In the thirteenth century there were three ways to obtain land. Charles easily exploited the means of acquisition by family gift. Land could also be obtained by purchase from the pope or by conquest in a crusade, sanctioned by the pope.

Pope Urban IV desired to see the House of Hohenstaufen, of Germany, removed from control of northern Italy, southern Italy, and Sicily. The pope was uncomfortable being surrounded by Germans, who were not beholden to the papal state. Pope Urban tried excommunicating various heads of the Hohenstaufen family. They were unfazed.

The pope tried to sell Sicily to the English. The English found the price too high and the benefit not compelling. Charles of France was willing to pay the price to gain land with no particular assets, so he became the prime candidate.

Charles had a barrier to his control of Sicily as sanctioned by the pope. Sicily already had a king, King Frederick II, of the German house of Hohenstaufen, who was also the formidable Holy Roman Emperor. Frederick was no fan of the pope. In 1250, Frederick died. His son Conrad IV became king of Sicily, despite excommunication by the pope. Pope Innocent IV called for a crusade against Conrad. During the fighting Conrad died of malaria.

Conrad's son, Conradin, was a juvenile and too young to take the throne of Sicily. Frederick's illegitimate son, Manfred, spread a rumor that Conradin was dead. Manfred was then crowned king of Sicily in 1258.

Meanwhile, Charles was a busy man. He fought throughout Italy to remove German control of lands that surrounded the papal lands in the middle of Italy. He was also involved in making certain that that French Cardinals were in line for pope. By 1265, Charles had conquered northern Italy. In 1266, he defeated Manfred in battle, killing him. Charles took control of Sicily by 1267.

The Sicilian subjects of Charles were not a compliant group. Conradin, far from dead, became a soldier and leader of a revolt in Sicily. Charles was the superior soldier. He easily defeated Conradin and captured him. Charles then beheaded Conradin in a vicious display of control, making it hard for even the French pope to cheer for Charles.

Dealing with Conradin was troublesome for Charles as it distracted him from his main goal, invasion of the Byzantine Empire, the center of which was Constantinople. Charles wanted to control all of Christendom. By 1270, Charles had regrouped and refinanced his troops from the proceeds of onerous taxes on his subjects throughout Italy and Sicily. He sold fiefdoms in Sicily to French lords to fund his planned military exploits.

Just as Charles was ready to sail for Byzantium, his King Louis IX launched a crusade against Tunis. Turning to the south of Sicily, on the north coast of Africa, Charles consoled himself by capturing Tunis. He then went further to capture Albania and Corfu. In 1277, Charles bought the title of King of Jerusalem. Holding a majority of Christian real estate did not satisfy Charles. He wanted Constantinople within his portfolio.

Although Pope John XXI brokered the purchase of the Kingdom of Jerusalem for Charles in 1277, Charles ran out of patience for popes who did not share his vision of control of Constantinople and all Christendom. When John XXI died and was replaced by an unsympathetic Nicolas III, it was the last straw. When Pope Nicholas died in 1280, Charles imprisoned several cardinals, leaving only sympathetic French contenders for the papacy.

Charles was rewarded for his treachery, when in 1281 Frenchman Simon de Brie became Pope Martin IV. Pope Martin IV excommunicated the sitting Byzantine Emperor at the request of Charles. At long last Charles had the sanction of the church to march on Constantinople, which coincidently was at the time the richest city in the Western World.

There were just two more problems lurking in the shadows to hinder the ambitions of Charles. Peter III of Aragon presented a distraction for the ambitious Charles. Aragon was part of Catholic Spain. Peter was married to Constance of Hohenstaufen, the daughter of Manfred. Peter felt he inherited the right to be king of Sicily by marriage. While Charles prepared to invade Byzantium, Peter prepared to invade Tunis, a geographically well-situated place from which to sail to Sicily. The second problem for Charles was his disregard for the population of Sicily and their mounting dislike of him.

Sicilian Vespers

Charles of Anjou had no interest in Sicily beyond exploiting its resources to fund his campaign for Byzantium. He never spent time there, preferring a castle in Naples as the seat of his Sicilian kingdom. The Sicilian kingdom of the time included southern Italy and the island of Sicily. Naples was the usual seat of the king, although it gave the ruler a non-resident landlord aura on the island.

The French generally regarded the Sicilians as incompetent and hopelessly corrupt. Frenchmen were appointed to the best civic positions in Sicily. The regime of Charles was efficient only in collecting taxes from Sicilians. The king was not magnanimous in returning some of the resources back to communities in improved infrastructure and services provided to the people.

The Sicilians despised their French occupiers. They referred to the French who spoke Italian with a French accent as "tartaglione" the stammerers. There was a clear cultural divide between the polished French and the earthy Sicilian farmers and fishermen. Some historians suggest that Byzantine Emperor Michael Palaeologus fueled the antipathy between the French and the Sicilians. The reigning monarch in Constantinople desired to see further distractions to the ambitions of Charles and Spanish king Peter III.[70] Peter had his own plans to acquire Sicily and march on Byzantium.

---

[70] Peter became King of Aragon and Count of Barcelona, ruler of Valencia, in 1276. One of his first acts was to renounce all feudal obligations to the papacy.

Easter Sunday, March 29, 1282, was an occasion for farmers and fishermen to come in from their work and join their families in church. Easter Monday, March 30, was a day of festive activities and community camaraderie. Stories differ slightly on what occurred to alter the celebration of what began as a delightful night of Easter vespers.

The most likely spark to what became a riot was ignited when a group of French soldiers encountered a group of Sicilians just before church. The French invited themselves to join the Sicilians in drinking. In the midst of the festivities, a French sergeant pulled a young Sicilian woman from a group of her friends to encourage her to flirt and dance with him. The French soldiers were careful to check the Sicilian men for weapons. When the sergeant decided to check the woman for weapons and felt within the bodice of her dress, the woman's husband determined the sergeant had become far too amorous. The husband attacked the sergeant with a knife and by the time they were separated the Frenchman was dead.

French soldiers were armed and ready to avenge their comrade. Thus began the brawl that would engulf the island. Villagers joined in to attack the soldiers with rocks and whatever else was in reach. By the time the bells of the church of Santo Spirito rang out for vespers, the French soldiers were all dead in the street.

As news of the incident spread throughout Sicily, villagers rose to attack anyone French, or associated by marriage or family to the French. French monks and town officials were held by citizen mobs and forced to pronounce "cicero," chickpea. The word is almost impossible to say with a French accent. If the captive failed the test, they were executed on the spot.

Six weeks later all of Sicily was under control of Sicilian rebels. Four thousand French and French associates were dead.[71] The only French bastion in Sicily was in the stronghold of a fort in Messina. The Sicilians appealed to the French pope to recognize their independence. Pope Martin stayed true to Charles of Anjou. He excommunicated the rebels.

---

[71] The Catholic Encyclopedia puts the number of French fatalities at 8,000. http://www.newadvent.org/athen/15384a.htm. Last visited 1/25/2012.

Charles had no choice but to divert his ships from sailing to Byzantium. The French fleet left Naples and sailed instead to Messina. Once the French arrived in the Sicilian port, rebels rowed out in a motley assortment of fishing boats and set fire to the French fleet. Any dreams that Charles had of conquering Byzantium went up in flames with his fleet.

As riots targeting the French spread across Sicily, Spanish king Peter III sailed from North Africa to Trapani on the northwest coast of Sicily. Despite excommunication by Pope Martin, Peter became king of Sicily. The Sicilian town folk cheered for Peter as he traveled through Sicily.[72] By October 1282, efforts of the Spanish and Sicilians caused Charles to remove the remaining French from Sicily.

The war to oust the French from Italy continued on the Italian mainland, north and south of the papal state that runs coast to coast through the middle of Italy, north of Naples. As long as he was excommunicating anyone who did not agree with and assist Charles, the pope excommunicated the Ghibellines of northern Italy.[73] King Peter's long-time family friend, Roger of Lauria kept his naval fleet along the southern Italian coast to harass the last bastion of Charles in Italy. Meanwhile, Charles prepared to take his remaining fleet to the east coast of Spain, the homeland of Peter. Charles knew that attacking Catalonia would be a last-ditch desperate act. His options to maintain turf were limited.

Dueling Kings

By February of 1283, Peter controlled the southern Italian coast, as well as Sicily. Charles broke with his traditional style and made a magnanimous offer

---

[72] 600 years later, Garibaldi would travel across Sicily to similar cheers of the townsfolk, as he fought to unite Italy.

[73] The action of the pope set the stage for another well-known story: Romeo and Juliet, amid the factions of the Guelphs and the Ghibellines. The scholar of Italian history will find many of the popes and other characters in this story memorialized in Dante's "Inferno." Dante pictured Peter III favorably, not so the several French popes of the time.

to settle the war with a duel between the two kings: Charles of France and Peter of Spain. Peter accepted.

The duel was set to occur on June 1, at the city of Bordeaux, France, where Charles would have the hometown advantage. The event rapidly became the social specter of the season. A planning committee was made up of six knights chosen by each king. One hundred knights would accompany each king into battle. The event committee even invited a celebrity judge: Edward I of England. However, the pope stepped in to caution Edward, as no pope-fearing king should give credence to a contest between a pope-sanctioned king and an excommunicated ruler. Edward declined to take part.

When Peter left for Bordeaux, he put John of Procida in charge of Sicily. John had been the physician for Peter's father-in-law, Frederick II. John also served as Chancellor of Sicily under Manfred and Chancellor of Aragon under Peter. John is a likely suspect for conspiring with the king of Byzantium to stir things up in Sicily, before the night of the Sicilian Vespers. Peter also replaced his incompetent son, James Perez, with Roger of Lauria (Italy) as head of the Aragon fleet. To complete the picture of the Spanish royal family in Sicily, Queen Constance arrived with the two crown princes.

Charles also made plans to lead Sicily in the future. He was in his fifties and even if he survived the duel, he might not make it back to Italy. Charles appointed his son, Charles of Salerno, as king of Sicily.

When the time for the duel was near, Charles arrived in Bordeaux with a large retinue. In attendance was his brother, the king of France. They no doubt celebrated late into the evening and slept late the next morning.

Peter traveled from Sicily to the Aragon region of southwest France, landing outside Bordeaux. He entered Bordeaux in disguise, fearing a trap. On the morning of the duel, Peter entered the city early with only a modest entourage. He rode to the grounds of the duel, vacant in the early morning, and drove his lance into the arena grounds. Peter declared to the few officials present that he had fulfilled his obligation to be present in person. Peter then rode quickly from the city, crossing back into his territory at Fuenterrabía (Hondarribia).[74]

Nothing was accomplished by the duel at Bordeaux. Nothing was accomplished by the War of the Sicilian Vespers either. The war ended in a stalemate in 1302, with the Treaty of Caltabellotta.[75] Pope Boniface VIII brokered the treaty, after four prior popes either failed to end the war or exacerbated the hostilities by their financially motivated devotion to Charles.

The war ended as those still alive could not remember what motivated instigation of the war. Charles of Anjou died of illness in January 1285, while preparing to invade Catalonia. Upon the death of Charles, Pope Martin IV was driven out of Rome. He died that year, to be replaced by Honorius IV. Three French popes would be seated, as the legacy of Charles, before installation of Pope Boniface VIII returned control of the papacy to Italians.

Toward the end of 1285, Peter also died, while preparing for battle. His queen Constance became a nun. She sold her jewels to finance ships for Roger of Lauria. The pope counseled Constance in 1291, to use her influence with Roger to release a Florentine ship headed to the Holy Land. She died in Barcelona in 1302, at age fifty-four. John of Procida preceded her in death in 1299.

Only Roger of Lauria lived past the treaty that ended the War of Sicilian Vespers. He commanded fleets on both sides of the conflict, before he died of natural causes at Valencia in 1305. Had he lived, he would have revived the dream of Charles to raid the Byzantine Empire.

Sicilian Vespers Enters Popular Culture

Today the church of the Holy Spirit remains standing in Palermo. It sits within the small Sant'orsola Cemetery, almost as if forgotten. The impact of

---

[74] See: Itinerary I – London to Rome – Hondarribia, and the story of the castle at the border built by Peter's son, Alfonso. It was carefully restored in the 20th century as a hotel.
[75] Caltabellotta is a hill town in the south of Sicily, north and west of Agrigento.

that evening of vespers in 1282 has never been forgotten. The phrase, "making it to Sicily in time for vespers" has become synonymous with peasant revolt.

Giuseppe Verdi based his opera, *Vespri Siciliani,* upon the events of 1282. The "Night of the Sicilian Vespers" was given as a title by the press to a series of Mafia murders in New York City in 1931. Even the Italian national anthem has a reference to the "vespri."

PALERMO/ MARSALA, SICILY

Garibaldi and the Thousand Take Sicily

Giuseppe Garibaldi, the Italian patriot, was born in Nice, in 1807. At the time, Nice was part of Sardinia, a state of Italy. Italy was carved into sections, ruled by various foreign powers and the Vatican. Garibaldi grew to adulthood dedicated to ousting foreign rule and focused upon national unification. Garibaldi gave his life to the unification of Italy, achieving success in 1860, and earning his place as an Italian national hero.

Travelers may see statues and monuments to Garibaldi in various places: at the United States Capital, just outside the old Supreme Court chambers, which are inside the new north wing; in the Museo National of Uruguay, in Montevideo; pointing to the Vatican, in Rome; on Staten Island, New York; in Taganrog, Russia; and in Buenos Aires, Argentina. The name Garibaldi is familiar to many, but not many know why, other than historians and passionate sons and daughters of Italy.

Garibaldi was a simple person, who retained his straightforward persona even as he became a legend. He was a controversial personality, who wanted to be always at the center of a battle. The famous writer Alexandre Dumas found Garibaldi to be a good subject, traveled with him, and became his biographer. So much has since been written about Garibaldi, including his lengthy autobiography, that it is a challenge to describe his life in a short story.[76]

---

[76] As of 1983, Garibaldi was the subject of 200 works in the Library of Congress in Washington, DC. Clara M. Lovett, Giuseppe Garibaldi, 1807-1882, Library of Congress, Washington, 1983.

It would seem a sacrilege for a world traveler to reach a Sicilian port without knowing Garibaldi, the liberator and unifier of Italy, since his successful campaign began in the Sicilian port of Marsala. Up to that time, Garibaldi was better known around the world and more appreciated as a freedom fighter in foreign venues than he was at home. When Garibaldi reached Marsala, with his ragged and motley force of about 1,000 troops, the fate of Italy and his own stardom took an abrupt upward turn. This is the story of Garibaldi and the Thousand as they took control of Sicily and turned Italy toward independent nation status.

Who Was Garibaldi?

Simply put, Garibaldi was a freedom fighter of the mid-nineteenth century. His ultimate passion was the unification of Italy as an independent nation. In twentieth century terminology, Garibaldi was a guerrilla warrior, not a statesman or politician.[77] The battles were fought most often with a volunteer army having much popular support, but no overt national backing. He fought for liberation of Uruguay from Spain, Hungary from Austria, Balkans from Russia, and Australia from England.

When there were no nations to liberate, Garibaldi fought for worker's rights, women's rights, and individual freedoms. Abraham Lincoln once sought out Garibaldi as a general of the north. However, Garibaldi's terms of becoming supreme commander of the army and the guarantee of full abolition of slavery were too steep for the United States President to meet, so no arrangement was made.[78] Garibaldi was no hypocrite. He despised the pope and the Vatican as institutions of slavery. He could not fight for the unification of a country that allowed slavery to continue.

---

[77] Ed Bearrs, former National Historian for the United States, National Park Service, and expert on the history of war, says that generals of one war always start by fighting battles in the manner of the last war. Garibaldi was successful in numerous battles by using his inferior strength to fight from multiple positions in the landscape, while the French and Austrians lined up, shot their single shot rifles while out of range of Garibaldi's men, and then advanced.

[78] Denis Mack Smith, Garibaldi, Hutchinson of London, 1957, p. 121.

Part of the popular appeal of Garibaldi was his simplicity of thought. He had no ulterior motive to his battles. Pope Pius IX once said of Garibaldi that only he and Garibaldi made no money from "Risorgimento," the reorganization of Italy under one king.[79] Garibaldi was like a monk in that he kept few personal possessions, traveled light, and met his needs from the kindness of strangers as he went along.

For the writer Alexandre Dumas, his biographer, Garibaldi was a rich source of fresh material for stories. For the anarchist Giuseppe Mazzini, his friend, Garibaldi was a fool who could be sent into battle wherever and whenever Mazzini could incite a riot and use Garibaldi lore to lure investors to his cause. For Count Camillo Benso di Cavour, the chancellor to Italian king Victor Emanuel, his nemesis, Garibaldi was a pain and the devotion of the king to the self-appointed general was a constant source of frustration.

For women of all ages in Europe, Scandinavia, the Balkans, and the Americas, who adored him and made his red shirt attire a worldwide fashion statement, Garibaldi was a hero. For his troops, his faithful followers, Garibaldi was their commander. Garibaldi was loved, adored, compared to Jesus Christ, hunted, and hated. He was never a neutral persona. For his part, Garibaldi simply loved his mother, his wife Anita, and Italy.

The Making of a Hero

Legend has it that Garibaldi was born at sea during a thunderstorm. Actually, he was born near the sea on July 4, 1807. Garibaldi was never a good student. Out of necessity, he learned horsemanship and shooting in South America.

Garibaldi's first infatuation was at thirteen, although it was the girl's father who left a lasting impression upon him. The father would talk to Garibaldi repeatedly about what it was to love one's country. The girl and her father were in a small boat that was crushed in a storm. Garibaldi swam out to save them. He heard both calling to him and went to the father first. He saved the father, but the girl was lost.

---

[79] Peter dePolnay, Garibaldi: The Legend and the Man, Greenwood Press, Conn., 1960, p. 18.

Most of Garibaldi's life from youth to hero occurred by luck rather than by intent or skill. He met Mazzini, who recruited him in a revolution against the church and politics of Italy. On behalf of the conspirators, Garibaldi joined the Sardinian navy. Tasked with inciting a mutiny of the ship, Garibaldi stole a boat instead and headed for Genoa. Soldiers came looking for him so he dressed as a local and went to Nice to hide. He was arrested in France, but escaped through a rear window as the soldiers entered the front door. When he read in a local paper that he had been condemned to death for leaving the navy, Garibaldi hopped onto a ship bound for South America. The evening that the ship was sailing, while soldiers were present, Garibaldi jumped from the deck to save a boy from downing. His identity went undetected and the rest is history.

Garibaldi traveled at sea and in South America from 1833 to 1846. He supported himself initially by making candles. Then he met some Italian exiles and joined in the Uruguay liberation movement. He was arrested in Argentina, escaped, and was captured. Tortured and left hanging by his wrists for hours, Garibaldi would not reveal his cohorts. When enemies literally tried to smoke him out of tall grasslands in Uruguay by lighting a fire, Garibaldi followed the fleeing animals to safety and then dined on roasted rattlesnake from the fire. He rousted the beer drinkers in a tavern in Montevideo to form a volunteer army and bought cheap red shirts to outfit his troops. By 1848, Garibaldi was a gun-slinging hombre, a good horseman, and an experienced leader of soldiers looking for their next battle.

Meanwhile, Garibaldi was becoming a hero in Europe thanks to the creative writing skills of Mazzini. His death sentence was forgotten as he returned to Italy to fight the Austrians in the north and to diminish the pope in Rome. However, when the French intervened and put Pope Pius IX back on the throne,[80] Garibaldi needed to make a hasty exit.

---

[80] Pio Nono, Pope Pius IX, began his papacy with a desire for true reform and to reconcile with the revolutionaries. However, he came to see that the papal lands were a patrimony of the Vatican, and by the time of his death in 1881, the people reviled him. They threw mud on his coffin during the funeral procession.

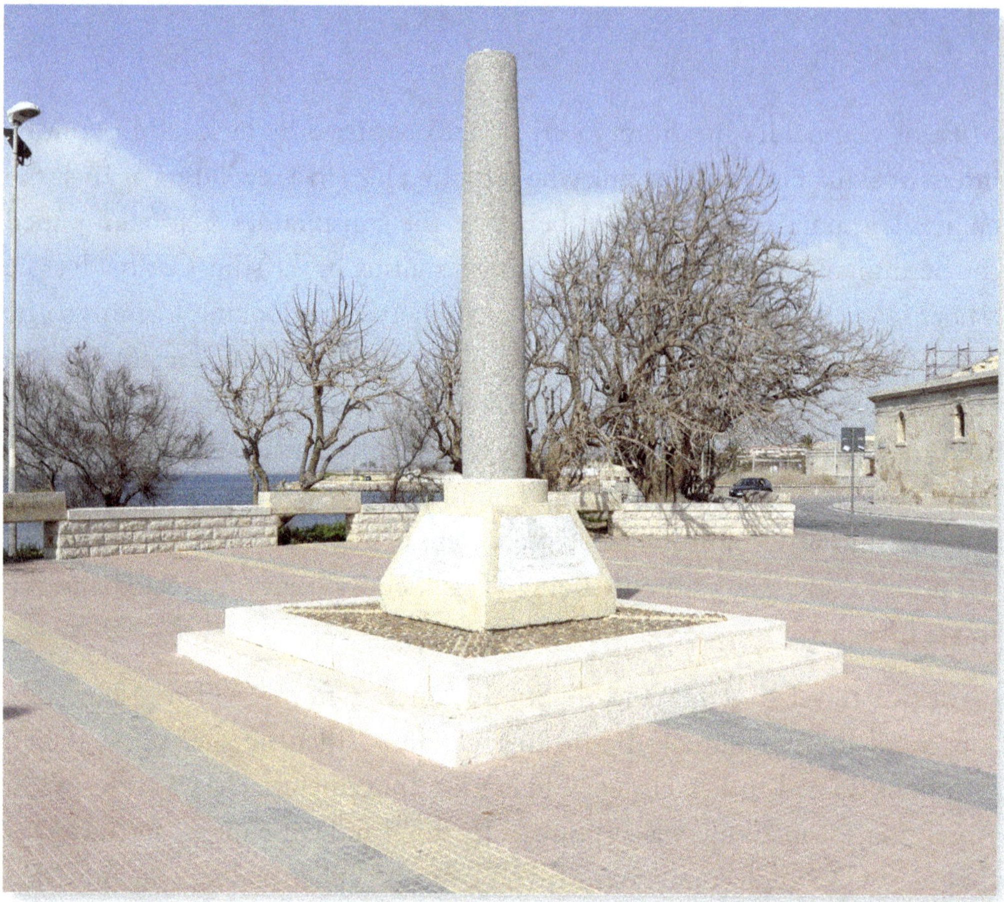

11. V 1860
SBARCO DEI MILLE
DUCE GARIBALDI
PROGETTO STUDIO GIACOMARRO

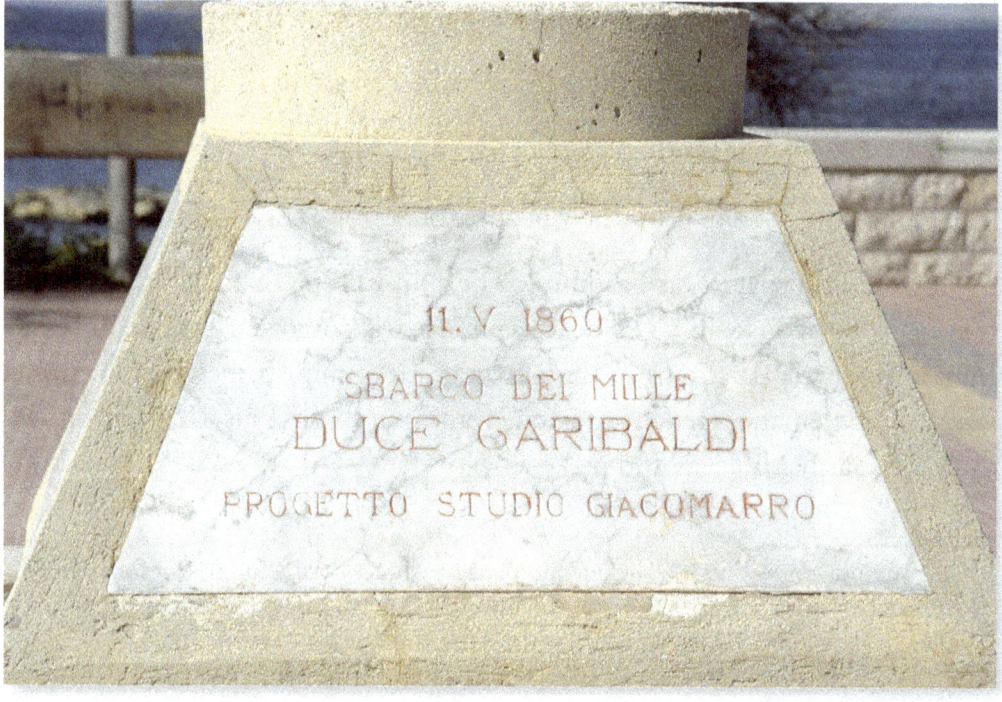

Garibaldi lost his wife in the flight from Rome. He sailed off to New York, where he returned to making candles. From 1852 to 1856 Garibaldi traveled to Australia and back to South America. Ironically, it was Cavour, who detested the popularity of Garibaldi, who gave in to the wishes of Victor Emmanuel and invited Garibaldi back to Italy to fight the Austrians. Thus Garibaldi again became the general of a volunteer army, wearing the uniform of no nation, who would become the midwife and father of modern Italy.

The Thousand and the Unification of Italy as a Modern Nation

To understand the magnitude of Garibaldi's achievement, it must be remembered that before Garibaldi, Italy was divided along lines that had largely existed since the Middle Ages. The city-kingdoms of Italian royalty were easy prey to the powerful neighboring kings of nations. Northern Italy, including Venice and Mantua, were controlled by Austria. A French Bourbon king ruled the lower half of the boot of Italy from Naples down and including Sicily. The Vatican controlled Rome and the papal state comprised much of central Italy. That which was left between the papal state and the Austrian north was under Italian king Victor Emmanuel II. This included Tuscany, Lombardy, Liguria, the Piedmont, and Sardinia.

As a result of Garibaldi's expeditions in 1860, Victor Emmanuel became king of all Italy except Rome and Venice. Cavour negotiated with the French to cede Nice in exchange for help against the Austrians to obtain Venice. Final unification to include the papal state came in 1870, without participation of Garibaldi, but as a direct consequence of his accomplishments.

The Thousand was the affectionate name given to the troops raised by Garibaldi to invade Sicily in 1859. This motley crew of volunteers had neither training nor government sponsorship. The king would accept their successes, but never were the soldiers given official recognition. The Thousand was a unique band. They fought not expecting any spoils of war, but solely out of selfless patriotism. Their conquered territory was liberated, not captured.[81]

---

[81] George Macaulay Trevelyan, Garibaldi and the Making of Italy, Longmans, Green & Company, London, 1911, p. 33.

The Thousand wore red shirts instead of a formal uniform. Garibaldi had begun to wear the shirts as he found them the least expensive clothing. He found more to clothe the Thousand, who became known as the "red shirts."

The Thousand actually numbered 1,089 at their full strength. They were comprised of 150 lawyers, 100 doctors, 50 engineers, 30 sea captains, and 20 chemists. Also included were scientists, artists, teachers, and merchants in varying numbers. There was one woman, Rosalia Montmasson. There were a few Hungarians among the Italians. There were no peasants. The lack of peasants was due to the absence of guaranteed financial support, or even basic supplies. Instead, peasants stayed on the farms and fought with farm tools and anything of iron when the enemy came near.

The Battle for Sicily and Naples Is Launched at Marsala

> Within a few years, and perhaps within a few months, who will remember these little woes which now occupy us so much? Only one thing will always be remembered; it will always be remembered that within these two years Italy was made!   Alessandro Manzoni, Milan, 1860[82]

On May 11, 1860, two ships carrying the Thousand slipped into the Sicilian harbor at Marsala. They were behind schedule as one boat had a hole and would not have left the mainland had Garibaldi not employed an old trick of straw, mixed with cow dung, taken below the waterline by some strong and dedicated swimmers. The intake of water to the hull of the ship sucked in the mixture and made the hull watertight. Garibaldi then boarded this ship as a sign of confidence that it would make the journey down the west coast of Italy to Sicily. The other ship sailed well, but ran aground as it entered the Marsala harbor.

---

[82] The two years were 1859 and 1860. George Martin, The Red Shirt and the Cross of Savoy, New York, 1969, p. 626. In the introduction to the 1971 translation of the Giuseppe Garibaldi Autobiography, by Howard Fertig, translated by A. Werner and introduction by A.W. Salomone, note 73.

Being late was fortuitous as the two ships passed a Bourbon man-of-war heading out to sea. Left in the harbor were British shippers of Marsala wine, who turned a blind eye to the lightly veiled, but still obvious, Italian troop ships. There were a few Bourbon troops in the garrison. Quickly, the Thousand went ashore to begin the assault on Sicily.

Garibaldi eluded attacks on his small fleet as he sailed past Naples, by sending out prior intelligence that he would be landing in Rome to attack the pope. Once on the dock in Marsala, Garibaldi had the opportunity to use a little needed skill he had with telegraph transmission. The telegraph operator in the port realized that the mysterious ships were not friendly when he saw hundreds of red shirts jumping onto the docks. He sent out an alarm message to Naples. Garibaldi quickly commandeered the telegraph to send a message that the prior transmission was a false alarm. He received a return message lambasting the telegraph operator for incompetence. The Marsala garrison quickly surrendered the harbor to the Thousand.

The Thousand fought their way from Marsala across the short distance northeastward to Palermo. Although they were outnumbered ten to one, the Thousand fought out of patriotic spirit and with some tactical savvy. The French Neapolitans would line up, fire, and then charge. The Thousand would lie down as though shot, wait for the Neapolitans to charge, crawl forward, and then rise and charge fully loaded to shoot. The Neapolitans sustained heavy casualties at every encounter.

The Neapolitans had made no friends in Sicily during their time in charge and it cost them the island. As the Bourbon troops were retreating toward Palermo, they murdered locals and pillaged their farms. As the Thousand went into pursuit, the locals grabbed poles with nails at the end, and any metal implements they could find, and poked at the trained Bourbon troops, throwing them into disorder.

On May 24, 1860, under cover of dense fog, Garibaldi's Thousand waited and watched the Bourbons march out of Palermo. Outnumbered three to one, the Thousand fought in small groups. Within the city of Palermo, the citizens helped the Thousand by erecting barricades to impede Bourbon troop movements and then attacked them in dead ends with knives and hatchets.

When Garibaldi captured Palermo he met with the Neapolitan generals on a British ship. The Neapolitans were keenly aware that Cavour had not given Garibaldi official title, so they refused to acknowledge him as the victorious general. The British forced the issue. Cavour relented and the king made Garibaldi a general. Garibaldi then gave the Neapolitans three days to clear the dead and wounded and retreat into several citadels. Meanwhile Garibaldi received reinforcements, including a visit from Dumas.

The Neapolitans gathered their strength at Milazzo, which is east of Palermo, along the northern coast of Sicily, and the last city before Messina at the narrow Messina channel, gateway to the Neapolitan mainland. Milazzo sits on a narrow isthmus of vineyards. There the battle was hand-to-hand combat, vineyard to vineyard. Dumas came to watch from the safety of his personal yacht. Later, after the battle which saw the Neapolitans run for the sea, Dumas would report that crowds shouted: "Viva Italia; Viva Garibaldi; Viva liberty; Viva Dumas; Viva Victor Emmanuel!"

Once Garibaldi secured Sicily, the Thousand crossed the Straits of Messina and headed to Naples. Neapolitan general Bosco had deployed three battalions at Milazzo and his force was spent. Garibaldi secured Naples by September 1860. He declared all victories in the name of Victor Emmanuel.

Proudly, the newly acknowledged general waited for his king to review the Thousand at attention in Naples. The king and Cavour arrived in Naples and arranged for Garibaldi to ride with the king in the royal carriage. The king waved to the cheering crowds aware that the tribute was for Garibaldi, but that he could benefit by association. The king left the Thousand standing and never attended their tribute. Garibaldi felt used. There was nothing more he could do. Garibaldi left for Caprera, his home in Sardinia, with a sack of fresh vegetables and some dried codfish.

Two years later Garibaldi returned from Caprera to fight for the king in a battle for Rome. Cavour gave some inconsistent commands on when the Thousand could fire. As a result Garibaldi was unprepared. Garibaldi was accidentally shot in the foot by an Italian officer sent by Cavour to take the lead over the red-shirt volunteers. At this time Garibaldi was fifty-five. He was suffering from the long-term effects of a life in the field and did not resist standing down from command.

It was logical for an aging fighter to become a statesman. Garibaldi's talents were not as a statesman. He had been elected to represent Nice in the parliament and the next year Cavour gave Nice to France. As a dictator of Sicily for only a brief period, Garibaldi had shown that he had no talent for civic management. Factions were beginning to stake their turf in a battle to control the lands of Italy that Garibaldi had unified. Unification was threatened. Garibaldi needed to make a choice between democracy and unification of Italy. He chose the nation. Garibaldi announced that all his victories were in the name of King Victor Emmanuel. Freedom could wait.[83] At least Italians would govern Italy.

Today there are no visible vestiges of the campaign for Sicily that began in Marsala, except for the obelisk marking the landing of the Thousand near the harbor. Although the chief contribution to the Italian economy from the area is Marsala wine, patriotism is still strong 150 years after the event. Garibaldi inspired Sicilians to proudly become part of Italy.

---

[83] This caused an irrevocable split with Mazzini, who died in 1872, in Pisa.

PALERMO/ TRAPANI

Slave Revolts of Segesta

Thirty years before the famous slave revolts of Spartacus horrified Rome, two slaves made the quiet farming town of Segesta infamous. They led an army of slaves through Sicily for four years. The ruling center of the slave kings, Salvius and Athenion, was in northwest Sicily.

Segesta is a lovely setting for the story of a slave revolt in Sicily. While this was the second major slave revolt in Sicily, it was the first for this prosperous farming area. Prior to the revolt, Segesta was a thriving port city, a leading center of trade in its time. After the revolt of 104 BCE, which lasted until 100 BCE, Segesta went into decline. By the seventh century of the current era the city was abandoned.

Segesta is a short drive from the ports of Palermo, to the northeast, and Trapani, to the west. The temple of Segesta is a landmark visitor destination, as are the theater and archaeological sites of its early habitation. The temple was begun by the city leaders of Segesta as a monument to their success. That the temple was never finished is part of the story of life in Segesta. It is a lasting visible impact of slave revolts in the history of the area.

Life in Segesta 500-100 BCE

The original inhabitants of Segesta were the Elymi people. They may have come from Turkey around the time of Troy, in 1200 BCE. One theory for their appearance in Sicily is that they were refuges from Troy, blown off course[84]. They interacted well with the Greeks. They used Greek writing, but they were a distinct people.

The area of Segesta provided a quiet harbor, fresh water rivers running down to the bay, and hot springs, so enjoyed through the ages for healthful bathing. The steep hill just above the bay, the site of the city of Segesta, was easily protected. The slopes and fertile plains were farmed. The area quickly became a source of wheat. The grassy slopes were home to shepherds. Life was good in Segesta. By 400 BCE the residents enjoyed substantial prosperity.

There was an area outside of the city used for cult worship of the Elymi. Using their wealth and their contacts with Greece, the Segesta city leaders employed Greek temple builders to build a great temple in Segesta. The temple looks like an unfinished Greek temple. It was never dedicated to a Greek god. The place remained a point of pride for the city and its unique cultural traditions.

In 416 BCE and 409 BCE, the people of Segesta were at war with the city of Selinus. Selinus, a Greek trading post, sat due south of Segesta on the coast of Sicily. Selinus marked the border of the indigenous territory of the Elymi people to the west and Greek domains to the east.[85] Most of the time everyone was amiable, even when the Selinuntans and Segestians competed for trade with the Carthaginians. However, when the city leaders of Selinus decided to expand, they threatened Segesta.

The first time Selinus expansion moved toward Segesta, the aggression was easily rebuffed. Upon the second incursion, in 409, Segesta enlisted the aid of Carthage in suppressing Selinus. The result was that Selinus was destroyed. For Segesta, the cost of war was a distraction that ended work on the temple.

Segesta recovered economically from war with Selinus. By 150 BCE, the Romans were making inroads into Sicily. The Romans suppressed the Greeks. Segesta was a Roman-aligned city. Commerce expanded to their mutual

---

[84] Sandra Benjamin, SICILY: Three Thousand Years of Human History, Steerforth Press, Hanover, New Hampshire, 2006, p. 24.
[85] Today both Segesta and Selinus, now known as Selinunte, are archaeological sites in western Sicily.

benefit. This enabled Segesta to engage in building large civic structures, such as the theater. Individual residences of the time were lavishly adorned in mosaics. Stones from houses, unused since the time of the Selinus wars, in addition to stones from the inside of the temple, were repurposed to newer structures.

The basis for wealth of the landed few in Segesta was the export of farm products, including wool. Products came down the mountain to ships headed to distant ports in Italy and northern Africa. Life was good for those who owned land and sheep.

The prosperity of the landowners was dependent upon their ability to manage slave labor. Farming crops and tending sheep were labor intensive. Without slaves the economy of Segesta would collapse. When the slave revolts of 104 BCE began in Segesta, they threatened more than the livelihood of the slave owners. They threatened the existence of the city.

When the slave revolt ended in 100 BCE, Segesta never recovered. By the second half of the first century BCE, the city became a small town. The walls of the town were moved inward. Sometime between the seventh and eighth centuries CE the area was abandoned. In the twelfth century the area became repopulated with Muslim farmers from North Africa.[86] The Christians arrived in the thirteenth century to displace the Muslims. The mosque was destroyed. Within fifty years the latest inhabitants lost interest in the area. For hundreds of years the area was quiet. Traces of farming disappeared. Only the largest of the stone monuments, the unfinished Greek-looking temple, stood out on the quiet hilltop.

Slaves and Slave Revolts in Ancient Sicily

Slavery, as a reprehensible institution, existed for thousands of years prior to Spartacus leading his fellow gladiators from the arena. In early slave revolts in ancient Italy, the slaves typically rose from bondage while the masters were away. They "married" the wives of the household and replaced the masters. The former slaves then became the new slave owners. It never occurred to them that there was a different social order, in which individual human life was of value. Being free in ancient society meant being able to own others.

Slave revolts have been documented in Rome in 501, 460, 419, 259, and 217 BCE. The slave revolt led by Spartacus was from 73-71 BCE. Its fame has risen above others, as it was large in scope and well documented. Spartacus led a group of trained gladiators out of the coliseum arena to terrorize Roman civilization. Rome never recovered. As a consequence of the weakened society of Rome, there was civil war from 49 to 45 BCE. To put this all in context, Julius Caesar was murdered in 44 BCE. Civil war resumed from 43 to 31 BCE.

The first slave revolt of note in Sicily lasted from 141 to 132 BCE. Rome had been sending slaves to Sicily to quarry rock in order to build large civic structures, such as theaters. The slaves were Roman conquests on the fields of battle throughout the Roman domain. Often prisoners of war were sold into slavery rather than killed. Some of the slaves had been born free, or were of aristocratic families.

---

[86] Segesta, La Medusa Editrice, Marsala, 2006, p. 27.

Housing and feeding slaves was a burden passed onto the landowners of Segesta by their Roman benefactors. The further the slaves were from the armed Roman legions, the bolder they could become. Segesta became a farming area, with a small population of landowners, managing a large population of slaves, who were former soldiers. The situation was far from stable.

Landowners unable to fully care for their slaves looked away as their slaves broke into small raiding parties to steal from neighbors or travelers. As long as the slaves did not confront their masters the situation was tolerated. Eventually, several farming areas erupted at the same time. The farmers of Sicily lost control and called upon the Romans to invade with their armies to restore peace.

As a result of the first slave war, large numbers of slaves were slaughtered by armed troops from Rome. The war lagged on for nine years as the Romans sent troops in small batches, enough to kill random strikes by slaves, but not enough to restore order out of the chaos. Rome appealed to nearby kingdoms for troops. The appeals to kingdoms whose people were at times enslaved by Rome were not acknowledged.

The first slave war wound down with the continued reduction of the slave population. Rome then restocked the farmers of Sicily with new conscripts. As the slave population of Segesta began to rebuild, the attrition rate of Roman soldiers increased. So many wars in a far-flung kingdom left Rome ill prepared to protect its domain. A second slave war in Segesta was inevitable.

The Short Violent Reign of King Tryphon

The Second Slave Revolt in Sicily began in Segesta in 104 BCE. It is also known as the Second Servile War. The flash point of rebellion was the initial attempt of the Roman authorities to increase the ranks of Roman battalions by reducing the number of slaves.

The Romans were preparing to wage war far to the west in parts of present-day Germany. They offered freedom to Italian born slaves in Sicily, those imprisoned for such matters as non-payment of taxes. Many non-Italians thought they should also be released. Among them was Athenion, a slave steward in charge of the slaves of a large estate in Segesta.

Athenion was born in Sicily. Historians report that he was a brave man and a capable leader. He began his protest of continued slavery with the 200 slaves who worked under his command. By the end of the week he had recruited slaves from neighboring farms to lead a band of 1,000.[87] Even some of the free poor joined the revolt to share in captured farm goods.

Athenion was a practical man. He knew that freed slaves still needed to eat and that without some workers left to tend the fields, the rebellion would die of hunger. He kept the strongest slaves as part of his army and left the weaker ones to continue to farm. Appealing to their sense of ancient customs, those left behind were told that the gods advised Athenion to provide care for the plants and animals.

The slave revolt spread quickly through Sicily. Slaves ran to find the slave army. So many slaves joined the revolt so quickly that the size of the slave army became a logistical problem. They needed a new ruling order. The leader of the fighting slaves was Salvius. He had proven himself to be a nimble tactician in skirmishes with the Romans. As he led swarms of slaves around Roman encampments, the outnumbered Romans ran from the scene. Salvius armed his troops with that which the Romans abandoned.

Athenion and Salvius joined forces. Salvius became king and Athenion became his general. As king of the slaves, Salvius wanted a new identity, so he crowned himself King Tryphon. At this point the joined forces reached about 30,000 slaves.

The next year was a glorious one for King Tryphon. The slaves were ordered to avoid cities where they would be distracted by luxury and degeneration. Instead, the slave army swarmed Roman troops, gaining food, arms, and horses. Tryhpon personally commanded about 2,000 infantry out of a core army of 20,000 slave-soldiers

---

[87] Theresa Urbainczyk, Slave Revolts in Antiquity, University of California Press, Berkeley, 2008, p. 57.

Defeats were few and victories came easy for the king. One attack began as a disappointment, but in the end added to his ranks. Tryphon chose to attack the central Sicilian town of Morgantina. He expected a quick welcome from the slaves of the city. Instead all was quiet. The slave masters of the town anticipated the arrival of Tryphon. They promised their slaves freedom if they would stay on the farms.

At first the slaves of Morgantina were willing to avoid a fight. They were unhappy but secure in place. Tryphon looked as though he would move on to the next town. The slave owners boasted of their victory too quickly. They recanted offers of freedom as soon as they saw the back of Tryphon. Their slaves realized they had been tricked and ran out of the city after the departing Tryphon.

As a team, Athenion and Salvius were effective. They established a command town near fresh water, which was easily defended. They chose loyal and intelligent advisors. They rebuilt a slave-dependent society into an armed hierarchy. Salvius enjoyed his role as King Tryphon. He wore purple robes and toga when he received official visitors.

The good times for the king did not last long. Happy in his role as king, Salvius was not anxious to seek out Romans to vanquish. Athenion was less patient. He pushed the king to his first defeat. As King Tryphon marched out with his entourage, a large and loyal, but not well-trained battalion, the Romans were waiting under the command of a new general.

Rome was not content to let the second slave war run as long a course as the first. Rome was dependent upon the wheat from Segesta and throughout Sicily. Three years into the rebellion, Rome was suffering a famine. A tested war hero was chosen as counsel to Sicily. The general, Manius Aquillius, was sent to quickly subdue King Tryphon.

In their first clash on that day in 101 BCE, the fighting was intense. These Romans did not run away when outnumbered by slaves. There was hand-to-hand combat. In the end, the Romans withdrew. On the field of battle, King Tryphon lost 20,000 of his rebel army. Athenion was injured, although not a mortal wound.

After the battle King Tryphon became ill. He died of unknown causes. It could have been the aftereffects of battle or a random disease. Athenion was there to don the purple robes. As the new king, Athenion was less gracious in his recruiting style. He ordered the death of any slave owners who would not submit and the death of any slaves who would not join the rebel army.

Although more ruthless than Salvius, Athenion was not as able a tactician in battle. When Athenion led his army against Manius Aquillius the fighting was just as intense. In close combat arms were lost and the battle was again fought hand-to-hand. This time the Romans did not withdraw. Ten thousand rebels lay on the field of battle when Athenion was captured.

Manius Aquillius enjoyed his victory parade in Rome in 100 BCE. Behind him in chains were 1,000 slaves captured in his triumph over the slaves of Sicily. No longer enslaved farmers, they would become gladiators, sent into the coliseum to fight wild animals to entertain Roman citizens.[88]

Segesta Today

All that remains today of the glorious ancient city of Segesta is the temple, the theater, and the abandoned houses, in various stages of archaeological excavation. The green fields surrounding the mountain where Segesta once stood are still lovely. The gentle slopes reach to the water. There are few farms and no large new settlements.

The temple at Segesta stands out against the landscape as an incongruous feature. It is as beautiful today as it was when it was built to boast of the success of the city. Unlike Greek ruins throughout Sicily, the temple at Segesta is, as it was, unfinished.

---

[88] Urbainczyk, p. 59.

AGRIGENTO, SICILY

The Elements of Empedocles: Agrigento to Etna

The Valley of the Temples at Agrigento is as impressive today as it was 2,500 years ago, when it was constructed. The magnificent temples to the Greek gods established Agrigento as a major site in the constellation of Greek outposts of the ancient world. One young boy grew up among the newly built temples believing that as distinguished citizens of Agrigento, his family members were movers and shakers of the world. When he became an adult he believed that he not only lived among the gods, but that he was a god.

This is the story of Empedocles, who was born in 490 BCE. He walked through the temples in his home of Agrigento, the same temples visited by tourists today. He traveled the Greek world collecting adulation, but never stayed away long. In 430 BCE Empedocles jumped into the crater at Mount Etna to prove that he had moved from mortal to god.

Empedocles never made it to god status, despite rock-star recognition during his lifetime. He did leave a legacy of philosophical teaching that is immortal. His 5,000 line poem, bits of which were rediscovered in 1990 and published in 1999, confirm his contribution to material physics, mystic theology, shamanism and magic, physical and spiritual healing, democratic political institutions and the merits of a vegetarian diet. He believed in reincarnation, as each life well lived spiraled a mortal being closer to the world of the gods.

Aristotle generously credited Empedocles with inventing rhetoric. Others considered him a fraud. Empedocles may have "borrowed" philosophy from several contemporaries and melded them into what he thought might be a superior result.

The immortal life of Empedocles provides prospective to the impressive mortal-man-made temples set against the imposing natural feature of Mount Etna. Thus this story begins at the Valley of the Temples in Agrigento, moves through the life and teachings of Empedocles, and ends at Mount Etna.

Valley of the Temples

During the sixth and fifth centuries BCE, the residents of Gela on the southeast coast of Sicily, moved westward to the central coast. They founded the town of Agrigento and immediately began building large temples to the gods. With the North African Carthaginians temporarily at bay off to the western part of Sicily and the Romans not yet a threat, the Greek colonies enjoyed a peaceful time in which they developed large cities with imposing edifices. The style of the time, Doric, comes from an area of the Greek peninsula and is seen most notably in the artistic feature of the column capitals of Agrigento temples.

There are seven temples in the Valley of the Temples dedicated to Greek gods. As a group the Valley of the Temples, which actually sits on a ridge, became a World Heritage Site in 1997.[89] The oldest feature is the Temple of Heracles (Hercules), at the center, begun in the sixth century BCE. The temple is a straight and narrow double row of columns of which one row has been restored. The Temple of Vulcan is barely visible due to erosion and neglect. The Temple of Asclepius is located away from the group on the ridge, near a spring. The medicinal qualities of the water may have given inspiration to the temple's dedication, as Asclepius is the god of medicine.

The Temple of Zeus and the Temple of Castor and Pollux, also known for a time as that of Demeter and Persephone, at the western side of the site, are the least well preserved. They may have been victims of an earthquake and not finished. In 406 BCE, there was another Carthaginian invasion and further construction was evidently abandoned. In its prime, the Temple of Zeus may have been the largest of Doric temples. Items unique to this temple are the giant statutes integrated into the architecture. One of the statutes is realigned on the ground nearby the temple ruin and another is in the museum.

---

[89] http://www.valleyofthetemples.com/valley_of_temples.htm last visited 2/2/2012; The World Heritage Site listing and designation on December 7, 1997, are at http://whc.unesco.org/en/list/831 last visited 2/2/2012

The Temple of Concordia, with 34 standing columns, may be among the best preserved Doric temples in the world. Part of its success is due to its reuse, 800 hundred years after construction, as a church in the fourth century. In its repurposed state, some of the destruction of Greek temples carried out by Christian fanatics in the fourth through sixth centuries bypassed this temple. The Temple of Concordia was given a substantial restoration in 1748. No doubt, eighteenth century popularity of travel to places of classical antiquity helped to instigate the effort.

The majestic temple at the edge of the ridge is that of the Temple of Hera, also called the Temple of Juno. Enough remains to enable imagining its beauty in ancient times. There are residues evident of the fire of 406 BCE that destroyed much of the structure.

The presence of the Valley of the Temples had an impact on non-Greeks. In the Roman times, toward the end of the first century BCE and the beginning of the first century CE, Cicero and then Virgil wrote of the valley. More recent aficionados include Alexander Dumas, Anatole France, E.M. Forster and the playwright buried in Agrigento, Luigi Pirandello.

Growing up among the Valley of the Temples during their time of glory certainly had an impact on Empedocles. In his major treatise on the foundations of life, he refers to four "roots": earth, air, fire and water. These elements are each represented by a Greek god. Temples to three of the four gods can be found in the Valley of the Temples.

Empedocles the Man

Empedocles was born in Agrigento, in its early days, when it was called Acragas. He was born into a wealthy and politically well-connected family. His grandfather, also called Empedocles, was a hero of an Olympiad, having raced a single horse to glory.

Empedocles was well educated. He traveled at least as far as Thurii, on the southern coast of Italy, and to Athens.[90] During his travels he met some of the brightest thinkers of his day. In his poetry he later chronicled the praise paid to him during his visits. He was delighted to know that his fame preceded him. At one point, he tells the reader that he traveled to the land of the Magi. It is not known where he went, or when, or if this excursion was metaphysical rather than actual.

Empedocles enjoyed the studious life. He walked around town with a somber expression as though he was always deep in thought. He emulated some of the well-known scholars, even to their dress. One of his contemporaries wrote that Empedocles affected a certain look with his flowing purple robes, a gold belt and copper sandals. He wore a laurel-wreath around his head, as did the priests who attended the oracles at Delphi.[91]

Empedocles was known to be charitable. Nothing is written of his building a palace for himself. He did, however, provide a dowry for young girls of Agrigento, who were not necessarily of his family. He was praised for his generosity. He was followed about town by a flock of young boys, for whom he may have provided an education.

Empedocles enjoyed being an orator and a poet. His teachings were accumulated in a lengthy poem. He also believed in democratic principles. He, like his father, is credited with ousting a tyrant and for keeping Agrigento democratic. Historians recorded that at one point Empedocles was offered the position of king, which he declined. Declination of an authoritarian position heightened his popularity. It is not known who offered the position or where the kingdom was to be. As wonderful stories of Empedocles spread throughout the Greek world, fashion, fable and fact all merged.

---

[90] Thurii plays a role in the story of Sybaris in this Itinerary.
[91] Gordon Campbell, "Empedocles (c. 492 – 432BCE)," Internet Encyclopedia of Philosophy, p. 2, http://www.iep.utm.edu/empedocl/ last visited 2/2/2012

Empedocles the God

The concept for which Empedocles is most well known is his identification of the basic four elements, or "roots" as he called them, of all existence. The roots of all life are earth, air, water and fire. The roots are the product of the gods: Hera is the earth, Zeus is fire, Persephone is water and Aidoneus is air. Of these, only Aidoneus is not represented at the Valley of the Temples.

The roots in varied proportions are found in all life: plants, animals, and humans. As the roots swirl through the sphere of life they combine and recombine to make all forms of living things. Hurling of the roots through the sphere of existence is caused by Love and Strife. Love brings things together and Strife breaks them apart. In an existence totally controlled by Love, all is peaceful and together. When Strife is dominant there is chaos of separated roots. In the beginning all spirits lived in the bliss of Love. Strife broke them apart.

Empedocles relied on his "roots" to create a cosmology that can be regarded as resembling a theory of evolution. Plants evolve into animals and animals evolve into humans. In the development of humans, Love brought together parts that at first did not work. A body might have had too many arms and no head, or a torso with a head and no limbs. Such aberrations did not last. Strife broke apart the ineffective products of Love, until successful combinations of roots resulted in functional humans.

The concept of reincarnation was central to the Empedocles cosmology. Once an animal was created, it could, in subsequent lives, become a higher and higher order of an animal, until it became human. For this reason, eating meat was forbidden. The animal sacrificed at an altar in the Valley of the Temples, or consumed at an evening meal, could be the future progeny of the city. To avoid such cannibalism, only a vegetarian diet could be consumed.

The hierarchy of evolution did not end with becoming human. Empedocles wrote and preached that humans should aspire to lead a moral life to bring them closer to the world of the gods. By being a pacifist and a vegetarian, a mortal could find a path to immortal life as a god. If a person ate meat or killed in battle, they would be reincarnated as another mortal to be given another opportunity to lead a better life. Empedocles felt that he was at the top of his journey. By becoming a vegetarian he was certain that immortality would be his fate.

Empedocles also had novel ideas about perception, vision, and the movement of light. Some of his ideas have inspired later thinkers, such as Euclid, whose theories on light and optics inform modern knowledge. Empedocles felt that vision was the result of particles from an object reaching the eye. For him there was a physical transference that was absorbed in sight.

Part of the fame that Empedocles enjoyed, which gave him superstar notoriety during his travels, came from stories that he healed the sick and raised the dead. There was some factual basis to the story of his healing hundreds of people suffering from an early plague. The illness that beset a community came from drinking foul water. Empedocles was able to lead an effort to divert a fresh water stream into the source of drinking water and the community began to recover. His ability to raise the dead was derived from some theatrics. Empedocles preserved a dead woman for thirty days and then displayed her as fresh. The purpose of the feat was to indicate that she had not previously died, but awakened to die again later.

Once the stories of healing and raising the dead spread, other stories of the god-like ability of Empedocles appeared. He was thought to have the ability to control the wind and the rain. People believed that he could control the effects of aging. Although Aristotle wrote that Empedocles lived to age 60, others wrote that he lived to be 109.

As Empedocles compiled his opus effort in the poems of "Purification" and "On Nature,"[92] he combined his observance of the empirical with his view of the spiritual. It becomes hard to distinguish where the physical science ends and the mystical begins. Was the woman who was dead for thirty days actually alive in the spiritual sense? As the poem grew to 5,000 lines, the boundaries of real and supernatural blurred. Clearly the practice of ritual sacrifice had to be abolished. Multi-god worship and bloodletting were a hindrance to Greek society achieving the prior glory of the world of Love.

---

[92] Scholars now believe there was one long poem, not two and that the fragments were all part of a single lengthy opus. Divining the etiology of scholarship does not impact this story. What was known of Empedocles was known through the surviving writings of later historians and philosophers. In 1990, an ancient papyrus was discovered within the Egyptian collection of the University of Strasbourg and believed to be the fragments of the Empedocles poem. The findings were published in 1999, giving rebirth to the study of Empedocles in minute pedagogical detail.

Immortality at Mount Etna

Empedocles was delighted to be revered as a god when he traveled to the coasts of Italy and Greece. He wrote of his enthusiastic receptions in his poem. He was certain that his life well lived brought him to the highest order of mortal. For him the next step was to join the gods.

The four states of human existence through which a mortal would become a god were: prophet, minstrel or poet, physician and leader.[93] In his judgment, Empedocles achieved all four during his lifetime. He was ready to join the immortals and pass his wisdom to those on earth through the ages. His poem tells the reader that Empedocles reached the highest state of purification. He was a god.[94]

---

[93] Campbell, p. 5.
[94] Richard Parry, "Empedocles," Stanford Encyclopedia of Philosophy, 2005, p. 7. http://plato.stanford.edu/entries/empedocles last visited 2/2/2012

As the story goes, Empedocles went out from Agrigento to a garden. He spent the night there with some of his students and followers. In the morning they awoke and he was gone. He had hiked up to the top of Mount Etna and tossed himself into the fire of Zeus. One of his students recounted that Empedocles said that he was a god and that his next step was to combine his roots in the fire and become immortal.

There are some differing accounts as to how Empedocles ended his life. A legend holds that as he threw himself into the fire of Mount Etna, he yelled to his followers that he was a god and as proof of his godliness there would be nothing left of his mortal self. However, the volcano tossed back one of his copper sandals, rendering proof of his common mortality.

Another story is that Empedocles lived to the age of seventy-seven. On the way to Messina his chariot overturned and he broke his leg. He died as a result of the injuries. This version could have been confused with the death of the grandfather of Empedocles, who was a charioteer.

In an act of unintended irony, the port at Agrigento, Port Empedocles, was built in part with stone quarried from the stones of fallen temples in the Valley of the Temples. As Empedocles is still considered one of the distinguished residents of Agrigento, perhaps this port may be the Temple of Empedocles that he would have so appreciated.

Some Fragments of Empedocles Poetry[95]

45. Fools! they have no far-reaching studious thoughts who think that what was not before comes into being or that anything dies and perishes utterly.

344. It is not possible to draw near to god even with the eyes, or to take hold of him with our hands ... but he is sacred and ineffable mind alone, darting through the whole world with swift thoughts.

383. For before this I was born once a boy, and a maiden, and a plant, and a bird, and a darting fish in the sea.

390. From what honour and how great a degree of blessedness have I fallen here on earth to consort with mortal beings!

---

[95] The quoted fragments come from: K. Paul, Trench, Trubner, The First Philosophers of Greece, ed. & translated by Arthur Fairbanks, 1898. http://history.hanover.edu/texts/presoc/emp.html last visited 2/2/2012

TAORMINA
THE FLEEING WOMEN OF SICILY

There is a long history in Sicily of independently minded women running from their amorous pursuers. They are known as Donnafugata, meaning "the fleeing woman." Their stories can be seen in some beautiful Sicilian places, real and imagined.

The oldest story is that of the early fifteenth century Queen Regent of Navarre, Blanche I. She ran across northern Sicily in 1410, ending up back at home in Taormina, where her castle can be admired today. The fictional town of Donnafugata, not far from Palermo, appeared as a character in Giuseppe Tomasi di Lampedusa's novel of nineteenth-century Sicily, "The Leopard." A real stone-and-iron seventeenth-century castle of Donnafugata was expanded upon in the nineteenth century, after an earthquake. This castle can be visited outside of Ragusa in southeastern Sicily. More recently, the nineteenth century Queen Maria Carolina fled from Naples to seek refuge in a western Sicilian valley. That valley is now home to twenty-first-century vintners, who salute her memory in Donnafugata wines.

Chasing Donnafugata around Sicily covers a millennium of Sicilian history and the circumference of the island. No visit to Sicily would be complete without a visit to at least one Donnafugata. These are the stories of the fleeing women of Sicily.

The Legend of the Fleeing Woman

Blanche I of Navarre was reputed to be the most beautiful woman of her time. She was a descendant of beautiful women named Blanche. Her progeny included at least two lovely Blanches. Her family stature and her gene pool were the source of her wealth, ability to travel, and her woes.

The Blanche of this story was born on July 6, 1387, in Pamplona, Spain. She was the second child and heir to King Charles III of Navarre.[96] Blanche was married by proxy to Martin I, the younger, king of Sicily, when she was about eleven and he was twenty-eight. Imagine the groom's delight when he finally married Blanche in person in 1402. She would have been a very lovely fifteen years old.[97]

The marriage did not last long. Martin died in 1409, after a military victory he led in Sardinia. The only child born in the marriage died in infancy. At twenty-two, Blanche had dominion over Sicily and a part of north-central Spain, Navarre. She was still a beautiful woman. That was her problem.

Rights to the crown of Sicily did not automatically pass to Blanche. The men of Spain and Sicily adored their women. That did not mean they would accept a woman as a ruler. Blanche had to negotiate and fight for the right to govern in her name. She became locked in a contest with the father of Martin I of Sicily, who was Martin I of Aragon. The larger Aragon territory of eastern Spain had always looked down upon tiny Navarre, wedged as it was between Aragon and the rest of Spain, known as Castile.[98] Then Martin I of Aragon died.

On the death of King Martin I of Aragon there was a six-way contest to take control of a large part of Spain. History does not record the widow Blanche as one of the six. Control of Sicily was not of apparent interest to the contenders. Control of Sicily became divided between Blanche, who was known in Spain as the widow Queen Blanca, and an advisor to King Martin of Aragon, Bernardo de Cabrera.

---

[96] The Kingdom of Navarre was the Basque area on both sides of the Pyrenees, extending to the Atlantic Ocean.

[97] Actually, Martin was slated to marry Joan, Blanche's older sister. Joan died before the wedding, so Blanche stepped up to the marriage. Martin's first wife died in 1401, thus the marriage to Blanche in 1402.

[98] Castile and Aragon would be combined by the marriage of Ferdinand II, King of Aragon, and Isabel, Queen of Castile. That would not occur for another seventy years, in 1479. This was just in time to support the first voyage of Columbus.

Fortunately for Blanche she was as intelligent as she was beautiful. She quickly occupied the Corvaja Palace in Taormina and convened a Sicilian Parliament there in 1410. Her parliament was made up of local land barons, military leaders from Martin's era, and the church. With all the locals under her control, Blanche was able to distance herself and Sicily from her former father-in-law and his would-be successor, who were an ocean away in Spain.

The Corvaja Palace was a strategic choice for a headquarters. Located on a main square of Taormina, next to the church, it was recognized for five hundred years as the seat of power. The Arabs built it after they conquered Taormina in 902.[99]

Blanche had astutely included a local nobleman, Bernardo Cabrera, in the Sicilian Parliament. He proposed to marry Blanche as a means to end succession controversy and garner a beautiful wife. He offered to give her male credibility with which to govern Sicily. Blanche was not easily swayed. Bernardo was sixty years old in 1410. Blanche had been previously offered in marriage for political expediency. If she were to remarry, it would be on her terms.

Bernardo was accustomed to dealing with troublesome, ungrateful royalty and persevering to his ends. His father had been a war hero for a prior king of Spain, but was beheaded due to a false charge of treason. When Bernardo was twenty, the injustice was acknowledged, his family lands and fortune reinstated, and he found himself in service to Martin I of Aragon. Bernardo was part of the King of Aragon's forces that conquered Sicily. He would have been responsible for putting the son, Martin I of Sicily, on the throne. Bernardo was richly rewarded for his efforts. He was heir to his father's fortune and he

---

[99] Of course Blanche added some lovely refinements, such as the Norman style addition for meeting rooms for Parliament, a balcony, and the moral sayings inlaid around the building. Today the Corvaja Palace houses the tourist information office and an art gallery. The site was originally part of the Roman agora in Taormina, remnants of which can be seen in the floor of the adjacent church of Saint Catherine of Alexandria. The site proves the adage, once a good piece of real estate, always a good piece of real estate. The name Corvaja comes from the aristocratic family that owned the building from 1538 to 1945. http://www.virtualtourist.com/travel/Europe/Italy/Taormina-141901/Things_To_Do-Taormina-TG-C-1.html last visited 4/8/2012

had connections to the royal Aragon family.[100] He had money and power. He desperately desired Blanche.

Bernardo would not take no for an answer. He pursued Blanche. He threatened to lock her in a tower until she relented. Blanche left Taormina and hid in the countryside. Every time Bernardo discovered her location, Blanche would slip away to a new hiding spot.

The legend goes that Blanche went from location to location as she fled around Sicily. She ran for about two years. Then one day Bernardo moved quickly. Blanche was apprehended. Bernardo finally held his love's interest in his tower.

In fifteenth century Sicily a man could require a woman to marry him if he could prove himself a worthy husband. Blanche needed an heir, possibly a son, to succeed her in power. Unfortunately, Bernardo could not perform when the time came. The legend goes that Bernardo tried three times to perform as a husband to Blanche and thus force the marriage. After two months in captivity, Bernardo had to concede to Blanche's desire for freedom. Although frustrated by his loss of a young bride, Bernardo would live another ten years.

Blanche returned to Taormina. She reconvened her parliament and continued to govern as Queen of Sicily. She no longer had to contend with the kings of Aragon. She no longer had Bernardo as a competitor. She reigned for ten years as a single woman.

In 1420, Blanche married again, by choice. She married her former father-in-law's successor to the throne of Aragon, John II of Aragon.[101] Blanche and John had four children. Their son, Charles IV, would become their heir and rule as king of Aragon and Sicily from 1458 until 1461. A daughter,

---

[100] The elder Cabrera, or his father, was connected to Martin I of Aragon through marriage to his sister. It is difficult to know as all three generations are known as Bernardo Cabrera. All three were distinguished in military service to the kings of Aragon.

[101] For those who enjoy royal tableware, the dishes of Queen Blanche and King John II, which bear their coat of arms, can be seen at the Metropolitan Museum of Art in New York, gallery 018. http://www.,etmuseum.org/Collections/search-the-collections/70012352. Last visited 4/10/2012.

Joan, died young like her namesake deceased aunt. A proxy to Henry IV of Castile, the largest region of Spain, married beautiful Blanche II of Navarre. After thirteen years of an unconsummated marriage, Blanche II was sent home, where her family imprisoned and poisoned her for failing to satisfy her husband. Daughter Eleanor was Queen of Navarre until her death in 1479.

Blanche I, Queen of Sicily, Navarre, and Aragon, died at the age of 53, in 1441. She was buried in Spain. Much of the details of her political accomplishments and flight from Bernardo were lost in time. They have been reconstructed from recent finds of Bernardo's letters and woven into the legend of the first Donnafugata, the fleeing woman of Sicily.

"The Leopard"

The town of Donnafugata is a fictional place in the touching novel, "The Leopard," by the real-life last prince of Sicily, Giuseppe Tomasi di Lampedusa.[102] Lampedusa's work chronicles the end of the royal era through the fictional last prince of Sicily, Don Fabrizio Corbera, prince of Salina. "The Leopard," the mark of the fictional royal house, is an affectionate title of the prince.[103]

Lampedusa's prince is a tribute to his grandfather, who, like the character in the novel, was a mathematician and astronomer.[104] The elder Lampedusa discovered two asteroids, referred to in the novel as planets, named after favorite hunting dogs. Donnafugata is modeled after the town of Santa Margherita Belice, outside of Palermo, where Lampedusa spent happy times in his childhood. So many places in the novel can be identified as places from

---

[102] Giuseppe Tomasi di Lampedusa, The Leopard, Alfred A. Knopf, Inc., New York, 1991 edition. (Pantheon edition 1960). Lampedusa was born in 1896, died in 1957.

[103] Some literary critics note that Lampedusa is an island off of Sicily, never inhabited by the real-life royal family. The island is home to Gattopardo, a small animal seen in the Tomasi family coat of arms. The original title of "The Leopard" original title was "Il Gattopardo."

[104] Don Giulio Maria Fabrizio received a prize at the Sorbonne for his scientific achievements. He died in Florence, of typhus in 1885.

the life of Lampedusa, that there are Donnafugata tours to take visitors on the trail of "The Leopard."[105]

It is not surprising that after reading "The Leopard" so many people have wanted to visit its setting. However, the novel was almost relegated to the family attic. Lampedusa, a World War I veteran, went into depression as he saw the bombs of World War II eviscerate family landmarks. He wrote as therapy suggested by his wife, who was a well-regarded analyst.[106] He finished the volume in 1957. It was refused publication by the two leading Italian publishing houses, because the publishers thought it was too royalist and anti-liberal. Lampedusa died later that year.[107]

Fortunately, there were well-regarded intellectuals who actually read "The Leopard." Acclaimed communist, E.M. Forester read the work and proclaimed it to be the best novel to have ever come out of Italy.[108] Published in 1958, "The Leopard" has certainly become one of the most successful Italian novels. In its first two years there were prizes and 57 editions. In 1963, Burt Lancaster played the aging Leopard in the movie version.[109]

"The Leopard" begins in 1860. The prince laments that he is fifty. He sees the mismanaged estates of nobility being bought for a fraction of their value by a rising commercial class of unpolished cheats. His family is steeped in history

---

[105] http://www.sicilytourguides.net/Donnafugata_Belice_tour.htm. Last visited 4/10/2012.

[106] The princess, the Marchese Tomasi della Torretta, met the thirty-four year old Lampedusa in London, while she was hostess in residence for her stepfather, the Italian ambassador to England. He was a former military officer in World War I. She became a Freudian analyst, president of the Italian Psychoanalyst's Association.

[107] He died of cancer in a little room in Rome, much like the prince in "The Leopard."

[108] Forester must have received some criticism for his praise of "The Leopard." The Communist Party of Italy was angered by the non-Marist portrayal of the Sicilian working class. Conservatives decried the decadent royals and the Left was angered by a seemingly critical depiction of Italian unification. Nobility and the clergy did not like their mirror in the book. Ironically, Lampedusa was a self-described antifascist. He was somewhat apolitical. He was a sincere, truthful romantic.

[109] Luchino Visconti directed the film, which received an award at the Cannes Film Festival. 20th Century Fox released a short version of the film in 1963. Twenty years later the original film, with English subtitles was re-released.

and religion. The prince escapes his duties as head of the family and the shifting political alliances of his king and neighbors, by leaving his sedated wife for his mistress, or by leaving dinner parties to create mathematical models.

The prince feels stabilized by the art and architecture of his inherited surroundings. He tolerates the priest who seems to live in his house. His joy is in his nephew, the son of his deceased sister. The nephew's father is dead. He died after squandering the family assets. The prince supports his nephew so that the youth can enjoy a lifestyle commensurate with his noble title.

In the summer the family leaves Palermo and resides in the summer palace at Donnafugata. It is there that the lovely daughter of a newly rich land baron and mayor of Donnafugata becomes enthralled with the prince's nephew. As the lovers explore the seemingly endless rooms at the family palace, the nephew repeats a phrase from the prince, "no house where all the rooms are known is worth living in." Their marriage joins money and title.

Upon the unification of Italy, the prince is offered a senate seat. He is asked to collaborate so that he may help his people in Sicily. The prince is annoyed. He is not vain enough to think the position could enhance his power. He also does not believe the people of Sicily want help, because they do not see themselves as lacking. The people are poor and angry, but they see each new overlord as a new set of obligations, taxes, and deprivations.

The prince dies in 1883. He suffers a stroke on the train back from the mainland Italy, where he sought treatment. Unable to make it to the palace, he dies in a small room, as did his real life equivalent and his author. There is no fear of death. Death is a beautiful woman who flirts with him on the train and seeks him out in his bedroom. He is desirable to her. His last thought is her kiss.

Tribute to Donnafugata

Running through "The Leopard" are memories the prince has of a friend of his grandparents, who came to stay for a while at Donnafugata. These are the real-life memories of Lampedusa. The woman is Maria Carolina of Austria, queen to Ferdinand IV of Naples, and sister of Marie Antoinette. She was the woman with long red hair. She was the inspiration for the nineteenth-century Donnafugata of "The Leopard."

Growing up at Schönbrunn Palace in Vienna, Maria Carolina learned how to run a country at the knee of her father, Holy Roman Emperor Francis I. Although Maria Carolina's husband was often away from Naples, hunting or visiting his mistress, Ferdinand and Maria Carolina had eighteen children. She made certain that each of the seven survivors had advantageous marriages.

Since Ferdinand showed no aptitude for governance, Maria Carolina stepped up as chief administrator. She managed to oust Ferdinand puppets in government and enact reforms.[110] As history would record, most of her accomplishments are attributed to Ferdinand. His foibles are attributed to her.

---

[110] Maria Carolina was a patron of the arts. She established a philanthropic community that supported itself by weaving silk. She negotiated from strength with the pope.

Then the 1789 French Revolution disrupted all the rules and security of nobility. When France declared war on Britain, Maria Carolina put Naples in consort with Britain and its allies. It was an emotional decision, triggered by the execution of her sister in France, and not one of political merit. Napoleon conquered Naples for a while in 1806, causing the royal family to flee.

In 1813, in the midst of Ferdinand's abdication of the throne in Naples, Maria Carolina fled to Sicily. She hid in the palace at Santa Margherita, in Belice, the family home of the Cutò clan, the family of Lampedusa's mother. To Maria Carolina the palace was part refuge and part prison. A year later she returned to her home in Vienna. Shortly thereafter, in 1814, Maria Carolina had a stroke and died. She lived to see her enemy, Napoleon, defeated.

Today the Belice Valley is home to the Donnafugata winery. The owners of the wine estate trace their vineyards back 150 years to the time of Maria Carolina.[111] The label of Donnafugata wine holds the picture of a woman with long flowing red hair. It is a tribute to the nineteenth-century fleeing woman.

Donnafugata as the Fountain of Health

There is one Donnafugata in Sicily not associated with a woman. The Arabic term for enclosed fountain, or fountain of health, became "Ronnafuata" in Sicilian. Eventually, a tenth-century fountain enjoyed by the Arabs in southeast Sicily, outside of Ragusa, became the site of a seventeenth-century castle known as Donnafugata.

The seventeenth-century castle was expanded upon in the mid-nineteenth century. Then fifty years later a Venetian Gothic arcade was added to the Neoclassical and Neo-Gothic structure.[112] The result is an elegant, if quirky, palace arising from lush gardens. Visitors are allowed to inspect the first floor, where they will be treated to a gilded, trompe-l'oeil Baroque interior. The castle would make a wonderful destination for a present-day Donnafugata.

Her era was considered enlightened absolutism.

[111] http://www.wine.com/v6/Donnafugata/learnabout.aspx?winery=17689 Last visited 4/10/2012.

[112] The expansion of Castle Donnafugata was the work of Baron Corrado Arezzo de Spuches (1824-95).

SYRACUSE

Archimedes' Eureka Moment

One of the most memorable of Syracuse residents in its 2,500-year history is Archimedes, the last of the great Greek mathematicians. He was born in Syracuse in 287 BCE and died there in 212 BCE. Other than a brief time in Alexandria for school, Archimedes lived his entire life in Syracuse.

Not much is known of the personal life of the great thinker. He is known to be the son of the astronomer, Phidias. He may have been related to King Hiero, whom he served with his inventions. Given what is known about his life and the penchant of Archimedes to forget to eat and dress when he was engrossed in the proof of a theorem, it is unlikely that he needed to be concerned with being gainfully employed. At an early age, people of distinction recognized his talents, supported them, and wrote of his accomplishments.

Archimedes used simple instruments to decipher complex problems. He often performed his calculations with a stick and a palate of sand. Once he had his proof, it seemed so simple and replicable that he would write an essay of his experiment and send it in a letter to his friends from school. Sometimes he would confound their ability to take credit for his work by sending them the formula, but not the underlying proof. It is the compellation of these letters and a mysterious text discovered in 1998, which give us a glimpse of how the great man's mind worked.

Inventor by Necessity

Archimedes did not focus on the invention of things. Problems needing solutions came to him from his friend and king of Syracuse, Hiero II. Since

Archimedes by his self-description thought things through mechanically and in three dimensions before he calculated a theorem, working with objects was a natural extension of his immersion in mathematics.

During the lifetime of Archimedes, Syracuse was a great port city, often under attack from Rome. King Hiero came to Archimedes and asked him to devise a means to protect the harbor. One such tool developed by Archimedes to address the problem was the claw, or "ship shaker." This devise was used for enemy ships at close range, before their warriors could be deployed to enter the city. The claw was actually a large hook attached to a pole, suspended by another pole over the wall of the city. If the ship was close enough to be caught by the hook, the pole could be used to raise the ship, shake it, and sink it tail end first.

The claw was a simple mechanical devise that depended upon geometrical calculations of scale and weight. Archimedes calculated that a long pole could be tilted and thus lift a heavy ship from the water without extraordinary effort. The claw would allow the ship to dangle, heavy weight down, leaving it in a vertical position for shaking or sinking. Imagine Archimedes as a child in his bath, playing with toys and beginning to understand the properties of objects that would later solve problems for a king.

From a further refinement of the ship shaker, Archimedes devised block and tackle systems for sailors to lift heavy cargo. These simple mechanical objects invented by Archimedes are in use today. The system exemplifies the Archimedes reasoning process of using physical objects as models to approach a problem, in this case sticks, rocks or bricks, and rope, followed by a mathematical theorem to work through the relative mathematical proportions of weight and counterweight, that would allow a sailor to lift much more weight with the block and tackle than a man could lift unassisted.

Another invention, the "death ray," may have been more concept than real. The idea of the death ray was based on mirrors placed on the shore at strategic locations and at angles that would reflect the sun to a single point on an approaching ship. The ray of heat generated by reflected sunlight could then start a fire on the approaching wooden vessel.

In recent years reconstruction of the death ray device to prove its likelihood of success was undertaken by self-proclaimed "myth busters," a team from MIT and a United States sponsored science decathlon during the first term of President Obama. The myth busters found that under ideal conditions of sunlight and with a stationary object, not far from shore, such a fire could be made to occur on a target. Historians believe that it is more likely that the bright ray reflected from the shore scared the attackers and they retreated to the sea. Either way, the device would have been an effective protection tool.

The utility of another device invented by Archimedes is in wide application, even today. This is the "water screw." The invention came about as a practical solution to the problem created by the desire of King Hiero to have a large ship built to carry as many as 600 passengers. The hull of such a ship would have been so large as to take on bilge water faster than it could be bailed away. Archimedes solved the problem with a device that amounted to a simple cylinder with a large screw-styled flange within. When turned by hand from the top, water at the lower level could be raised to the top and discharged. The simple, but elegant and effective device, the Archimedes Screw, is in use today in such applications as grain elevators and ships.

Physics Takes a Bath to Solve a Problem

King Hiero may have been Archimedes' biggest patron, given that the king was so often reported as having brought problems to him for a solution. The most famous of the assigned riddles for resolution involved the gold crown. The king commissioned a crown, for which he furnished the gold. When it was completed, the king was certain that the crown had the correct weight, but he was suspicious that the sculptor had replaced some of the gold with silver. By simply considering the weight of the crown, no difference could be detected.

Archimedes had this problem on his mind when he took his famous bath. As he watched his body displace water in the tub, he realized that mass has a relationship to displacement of water. He jumped from the tub, sans towel, and went running through the streets exclaiming, "Eureka, Eureka." Translated from the Greek, he was yelling, "I have found it." No doubt the citizens of Syracuse who were startled by his appearance were not surprised when they saw that the happy fellow was Archimedes. He often lost himself in thought when working on a problem. He could be excused the loss of a towel or toga.

To the surprise of the crown's sculptor and the satisfaction of the king, Archimedes was able to show that in fact the crown had a quantity of silver mixed with gold in its construction. The weight of the crown and its likeness in a solid gold bar differed when weighed while suspended in water. Once he performed the physical test, Archimedes then worked through the equation, now known in physics as hydrostatics.

Archimedes did not invent the lever, but he came to understand the ratio of weight to be lifted and length of the lever that made it work. Like so many of his theorems, he first worked through the physical relationship. Then he reduced the problem to an equation. He is attributed with the saying, "Give me a place to stand on, and I will move the earth."

Another Archimedes invention is the odometer. He evidently liked to play with gears. In one simple apparatus, a ball will drop into a container each time the gears have revolved as the wheels of a cart to which they are attached have gone a mile. In another device, the moon and sun revolve with the earth in separate orbits by means of sophisticated connected gears to which each solar system object is attached. Archimedes also used gears to improve the catapult and pulley systems. Part of the genius of Archimedes was to think conceptually as well as in practical application.

Mathematician by Personal Preference

When not presented with tasks from his king, Archimedes preferred to fill his days contemplating mathematical questions, such as the value of pi. When mathematicians refer to "exhaustion," they are making a reference to methods of reduction to the smallest infinitesimal value. The value of pi, π, has been the question of the ages for mathematicians everywhere. Archimedes came about as close as anyone with the determination of between 3.1429 and 3.1408. While a difference of .0021 is not likely to haunt the typical traveler, most have ambled though beginning geometry reciting the Archimedes formula for the area of a circle as equal to pi multiplied by the square root of the radius of the circle, πr^2. This is an important formula if you are building columned temples, which are to last more than a millennium.

Archimedes went on to calculate the square root of 3 as between 1.7320261 and 1.7320512. The actual value has been determined to be 1.7320508, so Archimedes came close using only sand and a stick as a calculator. He then went on to calculate the internal area of a parabola.

Archimedes really hit his stride when he was challenged to determine the number of grains of sand in the world. King Gelo, son of Hiero, said it could not be done. To do so, Archimedes needed to first invent a numbering system that could accommodate myriads, that is quantities in units of 100 million. The truly curious will be pleased to know that the number of grains of sand that fill the universe is eight vigintillion. The Archimedes formula is 8×10^{63}.[113]

---

[113] The treatise is known as the "Sand Reckoner."

Archimedes' personal favorite among his spatial mathematical and geometric calculations was the relationship between the sphere and the cylinder. When a sphere is fit into the smallest possible cylinder, the sphere has a volume and an area of two-thirds that of the cylinder. Archimedes desired that his tombstone include a sphere and a cylinder.

Death and Discovery

Somewhere unknown there is a tombstone of Archimedes with the sphere and the cylinder. It is known that Archimedes died in Syracuse in 212 BCE. The death ray may have scared away Roman ships, or may have set one on fire, but the tenacious Romans came back to Syracuse under a cloud shadow or during the night. A Roman soldier came across Archimedes while the mathematician was deep in thought. Thinking that the older man was being impudent or hesitant to heed a command, the impatient Roman ran his sword through Archimedes. He died on the spot.

The Romans were not pleased with themselves at being responsible for the death of Archimedes. They revered him. The great Roman orator, Cicero, came to Syracuse around 75BCE, to look for his tomb.[114] The story is that Cicero hunted for the tomb based on ancient lore and eventually found it in untended condition. The tomb was identified by the sculpture of the sphere in the cylinder on the top of a memorial stone. Cicero credits himself with restoring the burial area. Today there is a large tomb in Syracuse within an ancient burial ground regarded as the tomb of Archimedes.[115] Honest guides will tell you that the definitive site of the burial is still unknown.

Other than writing letters to his friends and with the exception of the essay of the "Sand Reckoner," Archimedes left much of his work in the sand. In 500 CE, his letters were collected and reprinted into comprehensive texts. Much knowledge of Archimedes today comes from those texts.

---

[114] Cicero was born in Rome 106 BCE and executed there as a matter of political expediency in 43 BCE.

[115] The tomb regarded as that of Archimedes is within the Necropolis Grotticelli, not far from the visitor information center, across the stone quarries from the Greek Theater, the Roman Amphitheatre, and the altar site of Archimedes friend and patron, King Hiero II. The stone quarry is the site of the Ear of Dionysius, which is another story.

Plutarch, the Greek essayist and biographer of the first century CE, said of Archimedes:

> "It is not possible to find in all geometry more difficult and intricate questions, or more simple and lucid explanations. Some ascribe this to his natural genius; while others think that incredible effort and toil produced these, to all appearances, easy and unlabored results. No amount of investigation of yours would succeed in attaining the proof, and yet, once seen, you immediately believe you would have discovered it; by so smooth and so rapid a path he leads you to the conclusion required."[116]

The letters of Archimedes remained the sole font of knowledge of the mathematician/inventor until 1906, when there was the discovery of a surprise text hidden for centuries. The twentieth-century discovery of the Archimedes Palimpsest is a tale worthy of a movie mystery. Any discovery of a palimpsest can be an exciting event.

Palimpsests are layers of texts created by ink on vellum. Vellum was manufactured from goatskin, which was expensive a thousand years ago when first used, and is even more valuable today to collectors. Vellum can remain preserved for long periods of time, even after the ink used to write on the vellum has faded.

In the middle ages, vellum was regarded as more valuable than the words inscribed there. Often the ink was scraped away and the vellum reused. With modern technologies of ultraviolet lights and x-rays, layers of texts can be discerned on vellum, even when the vellum has been reused several times. Deciphering the layers of writing in a palimpsest can result in finding texts thought lost for centuries.

The modern tale of the Archimedes Palimpsest began in 1906, when a Danish academic, Johan Ludwig Heiberg, made a trip to Constantinople to view a thirteenth-century parchment. He thought he would be examining a text of prayers. He was, no doubt, ecstatic to learn that he was viewing palimpsest. The assembled scholars were able to determine that lying under

---

[116] J.J. O'Connor & E.F. Robertson, "Archimedes of Syracuse," MacTutor History of Mathematics, 1999, p. 4. http://www-history.mcs.st-and.ac.uk/Printonly/Archimedes.html. Last visited 1/25/2012

the thirteenth-century prayers was a tenth-century edition of treatises of Archimedes. The excitement mounted when they realized that these treatises were previously unknown.

The parchment, now identified as the Archimedes Palimpsest, had spent centuries in the monastery library in Constantinople, before being identified by Heiberg in 1906. In the 1920s it was sold to a private collector. Then in 1998, the Archimedes Palimpsest sold at a Christie's Auction for $2 million. It is now at home at the Walters Art Museum in Baltimore, Maryland.

Among the treatises of Archimedes discovered on the palimpsest is the only known copy of "On Floating Bodies," in the original Greek. Also on the text is a dissection puzzle, such as Archimedes used to render three-dimensional objects into two dimensions as he worked out in the sand a means to calculate their size in a theorem. The document holds the solution to the riddle of the relationship of the sphere and the cylinder, which Archimedes thought to be his greatest achievement.

The location of the tomb of Archimedes, under his sphere in a cylinder epitaph, has yet to be found. The recent discovery, in the twentieth century, of the recording of his mathematical solution to the sphere and cylinder puzzle leaves travelers to recognize that history is never complete. Part of the joy of travel and discovery is the knowledge that there is always more to come.

SYRACUSE
THE DIONYSIUS EAR

Dionysius I, also known as Dionysius the elder, grew to power in Syracuse in fourth century BCE, by making paranoia into an art form. As a Greek ruler of an ancient Greek outpost in eastern Sicily, he would have been expected to promote democracy. Democracy made him feel insecure.

Dionysius was born in 430 BCE and died in 367 BCE. He left some lasting impressions in Sicily. Of political importance is his check on the spread of the power of Carthage on the island, making it safe for Greek commerce. For visitors to Sicily today, there are two vestiges of the Dionysius era. One is the wall built to protect his city and the other is a natural rock feature, which is a monument to his paranoia, the Dionysius Ear.

Capitalizing on Paranoia

Dionysius had modest beginnings as a clerk in a public office. In his younger days, he was a champion of the poorer classes, who, like himself, sought opportunities. Ironically, the man who achieved and maintained power as a tyrant obtained his first real civic advancement through the democratic process, so synonymous with ancient Greece.

When Dionysius was thirty, he was elected a general in a democratic process. Greece had been at war with Carthage for control of Sicily from the time Dionysius was twenty-one. In four years, he was able to distinguish himself in battle. Thereafter Dionysius rose in rank and power incrementally based on merit. When he stood for election he was experienced in military and civic service. He was honored to utilize the democratic process to become the supreme military commander in Sicily. He then promptly forgot his roots.

Dionysius was known to play his peers against each other. He may have built his popularity, and possible success, on his ability to be more political than able as a military leader. Such a circumstance would be consistent with his insecurity, protectionism, and paranoia, for which he became increasingly well known.

Dionysius perfected the early use of the mercenary troops for personal political and strategic gain. He is believed to have faked an attack on his life, early in his military career. That near brush with death justified his obtaining six hundred mercenaries as his personal guard. Over time he increased their number to one thousand, without arousing the suspicion of any detractors, until it was too late.

Well positioned and well armed, Dionysius was able to set aside democracy in Syracuse and take control as the supreme tyrant. Oddly enough, he was able to maintain good relationships with Sparta, even though the city was suspicious of tyrants and had unseated a few. Dionysius had what the Greek peninsula wanted, and that was a clear ability to trade with Sicily. As long as Dionysius was at war with the Carthaginians and kept them in check, mainland Greece was his supporter.

Keeping up an army of mercenaries and the cost of continual war with Carthage was expensive. To fund the needs of Dionysius, the people of Sicily were heavily taxed. Dionysius also removed gold from the statues in temples, justifying his actions with silly excuses. No one was going to argue with the tyrant when he said that Zeus would be better off in the temple in the winter with a woolen cloak instead of a golden one, or that removing the golden beard from gods was more suitable to their familial hierarchy.[117]

Over time, Dionysius dominated the citizens of Syracuse by capitalizing on their fear of Carthaginians. He then went on to plunder areas of the Adriatic, including an assault on Delphi. For him, the Adriatic was the Sea of Dionysius, all part of his domain. Dionysius instilled suspicion, fear, and self-doubt among those who reported to him, as he felt insecure and suspicious of everyone. These traits served Dionysius well as he rose from town clerk to supreme tyrant of one of the wealthiest and most powerful cities of the ancient Greek world.[118]

Sword of Damocles

Being at the top of the world order of Syracuse did not give Dionysius any peace. His paranoia was so extreme that he slept in a chain mail vest. His bed was positioned in the center of a moat and accessed by boards, which he pulled in at night. He had spies and eavesdroppers everywhere. Guests were quartered so that he could overhear their conversations through the walls or floorboards of their rooms.

One carefree and solicitous courtier was the young and unsuspecting Damocles. Damocles thought he was being complimentary when he told Dionysius that as supreme tyrant Dionysius had everything going for him. Dionysius offered to trade places with Damocles. Foolishly, the young man accepted.

---

[117] http://www.in2greece.com/english/historymyth/history/ancient/dionysius_elder.htm. Last visited 1/25/2012.

[118] Dionysius is credited with the invention of the catapult in 399 BCE. It was later perfected by the addition of wheels by the Romans.

When he next came into a banquet, Damocles was directed to sit on the throne of Dionysius. He was surrounded by every luxury. Then Damocles happened to look above him. There, hanging by a hair tied to the hilt, was a sword pointing down at his head. Dionysius made his point that the great man with everything lives in constant fear of losing it all.

Whether the story of Damocles and Dionysius is myth or fable, it is a story that has lasted over the millennium as a tale of caution. It was certainly an act consistent with the personality and gamesmanship of the tyrant.

The Universal Man

Dionysius began his life as a clerk, so it is known he was literate and not solely an armed soldier. As he secured his position as a military and civic leader, Dionysius wanted to be known as a great writer and poet as well. He surrounded himself with poets and philosophers, such as Plato. Although he may have made great effort to hide his admiration for Plato, the great philosopher may have been the only guest to feel secure around Dionysius. Dionysius is not known to have challenged or held him against his will. Plato, who was known to offer riddles to contemporaries, was likely intelligent enough to be solicitous to Dionysius.

Since Dionysius was the center of his own universe, his treatment of others, who may have also contributed to the arts, was not always respectful. He was known to imprison poets who failed to compliment his work, only to pull them from the jail so that they could perform at dinner. One such poet, who was jailed and reclaimed, was then asked to listen to Dionysius recite his own poetry. The poet is reputed to have asked to be returned to his cell.

Dionysius was not without recognition as a writer. Whether his efforts were deserving of merit, or were simply given accolades out of political convenience, is not known. He did win a competition at an Athens festival for his play, "The Ransom of Hector." Shortly after learning of the success of his play in 367 BCE, Dionysius was dead.

Of his death, the most popular story is that his physicians at the direction of his son, Dionysius the younger, possibly poisoned Dionysius. His son succeeded him as supreme tyrant of Syracuse. It is also possible that he partied so long and hard upon learning of his success in the theater that he over did it and drank himself to death. Another possibility is that the man who was so insecure and paranoid actually died a natural death after a night of celebrating another achievement.

The Dionysius Ear

The visitor to Syracuse today is able to see two remnants of the life of Dionysius. One is the wall of Syracuse, built with a great deal of effort, and the other is an interesting natural feature at the opening of a rock quarry.

The wall around Syracuse was built over a five-year period beginning in 402 BCE. It has been identified as one of the many wonders of the ancient world. Some historians estimate that to build the wall, 300 tons of stone would have been installed each day over the five years of construction. Hundreds of slaves and political prisoners labored to cut stone to build the wall. Visible today in the quarry are the marks of ancient stonecutters. The horror of working in the quarry for Dionysius is not felt today, as the visitor walks through what has become a quarry garden.

There were fourteen towers on the wall. Today remnants of the wall exist, bisected by modern roads. No doubt some of the fitted stone from the wall and towers have been incorporated into later-built structures over the two ensuing millennium.

The quarries in Syracuse, from which early Greeks obtained stone for buildings including the nearby Greek theater, are enormous.[119] Within the quarries are caves used by early Greeks for shelter and repurposed by Dionysius as prisons. One such cave has an opening that is elliptical, as an ear, and has perfect acoustics. The cave is known as "Orecchio di Dioniso," The Ear of Dionysius.[120] The legend associated with the cave is that the paranoid Dionysius held his prisoners in this cave, so that he could hear their whispered conversations. With all that is known about Dionysius the legend has credibility.

The visitor to Syracuse today has nothing to fear from Dionysius or his quarry. The area is a lovely place to walk through deep history, test the acoustics of the Ear, and enjoy the climate of eastern Sicily.

---

[119] The Greek theater at Syracuse continues to offer productions in the summer months of the even years. Sicily, Eyewitness Travel, DK, London, 2011, pp. 136-139.

[120] Caravaggio, who is worthy of his own story, named the cave for Dionysius in 1608. The artist visited Sicily to enjoy the light and warmth and left his mark on an entire school of art. His dubbing the cave "Ear of Dionysius" was a commentary on the eavesdropping, paranoid king.

ARGOSTOLI, CEPHALONIA AND ITHACA

Fantasy and Fairies: Cave Nymphs at the End of the Odyssey

At the close of the Trojan War, around 1250 BCE, the surviving kings went home to their families. The last to arrive home was Odysseus, king of Ithaca. His ten-year odyssey home from the war was chronicled in Homer's Odyssey, the companion tale to the story of the Trojan War in the Iliad.[121] Much of the tale of the Odyssey relies upon mythology. That Odysseus lived on Ithaca is a widely accepted fact. The location of his palace remains a mystery.

The gateway island to Ithaca is Cephalonia, part of the Ionian Islands off the west coast of the Greek mainland, in the Ionian Sea, separated from Italy by the Adriatic Ocean. Ithaca and Cephalonia are known for their caves, home to fairies and other local lore. These islands comprised the kingdom of Odysseus.

This is the story of the homecoming of King Odysseus to the magical land that was his kingdom. It is the story of the caves, the occupants of which have existed in fantasy, fact, and on faith. Although ancient manmade landmarks on the islands are few, the beauty of the beaches and landscape are tangible evidence that these islands were worth the effort of a decade-long odyssey to return home. The vistas remain unspoiled for the present-day cruise ship visitor.

---

[121] See Itinerary III. Eastern Mediterranean -Troy Lost, for the tale of the Iliad and the Trojan War.

End of the Odyssey

King Odysseus was known to the Greeks as a god-like hero and to the Romans as a reluctant and deceitful warrior. Thus Odysseus is a great subject for various stories of heroism and cunning.[122] Odysseus resisted leaving home to join the war effort by feigning insanity. His ruse was exposed when the general of the Trojan War, Agamemnon, placed the son of Odysseus in the path of a plow. Odysseus avoided hitting his son.

Odysseus then went forward to recruit Achilles in the battle for return of Agamemnon's sister-in-law, Helen, the wife of Menelaus. Achilles' mother hid him to avoid him joining the battle. She dressed him as a girl and deposited him in a nursery for female children. Achilles was prophesized to be facing glory and death. Odysseus received the prediction that he would have a long journey home.

During the Trojan War, Odysseus proved himself a capable leader and a soldier of valor. He was the first to jump from ship onto Trojan soil, despite prophesy that the first to land would die. When the Trojan prince Hector offered to resolve the controversy with a one-on-one battle, Odysseus was the first to volunteer. He is credited with the idea of sending a large wooden horse, filled with Greek soldiers, to breach the walls of Troy. Odysseus led the soldiers hidden inside the Trojan Horse.

Odysseus began his journey home accompanied by twelve ships. The journey could have been a short one, through a familiar course. However, at his first stop, Odysseus angered the gods. The gods used the winds to give Odysseus a circuitous and repeated course of travel, before he was allowed to reach home in Ithaca.

At the outset of the journey to Ithaca, Odysseus was driven off course by storms. He landed in the home of the Lotus-Eaters, where the Cyclops captured the travelers. Odysseus seduced the Cyclops with a barrel of wine. Once asleep, Odysseus was able to drive a stake into the one eye of the monster.

---

[122] Greek Homer idolized Odysseus, Romans Virgil and Ovid had their own depictions of Odysseus as a cunning womanizer. Modern writer James Joyce used Ulysses for his wanderer of twenty years.

Unfortunately for Odysseus, the Cyclops was a son of Poseidon, the god of the sea. Odysseus and his men safely boarded their ships, only to be blown back to the eastern Aegean Sea, near their starting point, after they had sailed close to home.

Odysseus and his armada were guests of Aeolus, god of the winds. They left with a bag of winds, not to include the much needed western wind. The sailors opened the bag, thinking it contained gold. Foolishly, the sailors allowed the winds to escape, lengthening their journey.

For eleven of the twelve ships the journey home was cut short. The next stop on the journey was the land of the cannibals. Only the ship holding Odysseus made it back out to sea.

Odysseus and his men next visited the goddess Circe. The men feasted on cheese and wine, until Circe turned them into swine. Only Odysseus was spared, as the sole man to enjoy the charms of Circe. The goddess found that she loved the warrior and so she released his men from her spell as a sign of adoration. Odysseus in turn decided to stay on the island with Circe indefinitely; that was, until his men persuaded him to move on toward home.

The homeward journey took the sailors to the end of the world. The spirit of the mother of Odysseus appeared to him there. She told of her grief at passing before he could arrive safely home. She also warned Odysseus of the one hundred suitors courting his wife for the wealth of his kingdom. His wife, Penelope, was portrayed as faithful, refusing to marry until she completed her knitted shroud. Each night Penelope would pull out her stiches, to repeat the knitting the next day as a means to forestall remarriage.

Circe proved an admiring friend. She gave Odysseus a map home that would avoid perils, such as the Sirens, who lured sailors with their song, only to have them crash on the rocks. The ship was able to navigate between the whirlpool, Charybdis, and the six-headed monster Scylla, lurking at the Straits of Messina. The ship came close enough to Scylla for the monster to pick off six of the sailors. Finally, the ship landed on the island of Thrinacia. Hungry for meat, the sailors hunted down and killed the cattle of the sun god, Helios. For this transgression, the ship encountered a storm from which Circe could not save them. All but Odysseus perished at sea.

Odysseus washed up on the shore of the island home of Calypso. It was his fate to remain the lover of the island goddess for seven years. When Odysseus finally tore himself from the charms of Calypso, he ventured out to sea, only to be shipwrecked once again. This time he landed on the beaches of ancient Phaeacia, known today as Corfu.[123]

The king of Corfu was a friend to Odysseus. Told of the warning given to Odysseus by the spirit of his mother, the hosts of the long adrift Odysseus delivered him to Ithaca at night and in disguise. Odysseus arrived at his palace in the clothes of a slave.

Meanwhile, Penelope devised a contest for her suitors. The one who could string the bow of Odysseus and drive an arrow through twelve ax handles could have her hand in marriage. None of the one hundred men could string the bow. The slave stepped forward and easily strung the bow and shot the arrows through the target. Thus revealed to his son and faithful servants, Odysseus turned the suitors into a mass of corpses.

Penelope was not convinced that the man before her, who had no doubt aged over the ten years of the journey and the efforts of the war in Troy, was her husband. She asked that the wedding bed be moved. Odysseus proved his identity when he told her it was impossible to move the bed, as one leg was a live tree. Only her husband would know that fact.

Over the course of the ten years Odysseus traveled along the coast of Turkey to North Africa, then west to the gates of Hercules, the entrance to the Mediterranean. This was the end of the world to the Greeks. Then the ships were blown eastward from southern Spain to the west coast of Sicily, where they traveled up through the Straits of Messina, the waters of whirlpools and exposed rocks. Odysseus went as far north on the coast of Italy to near Naples, before going south to Cyprus. The ships were close to home in Cephalonia, when they were blown back into the Mediterranean.[124]

---

[123] Some scholars identify Phaeacia as Cyprus, not Corfu. Cephalonia may be the ancient Ithaca, rather than just the smaller island.

[124] The course of travels from Marianne Nichols, Man, Myth, and Monument, Morrow, New York, 1975, p. 214.

The Caves of Fairies, Nymphs, and Nazis

Odysseus came ashore in Ithaca at the cave with two entrances, Marmarospilia cave. It was one of many caves in his kingdom to have importance in ancient and modern history. Historians believe that the cave where Odysseus entered Ithaca may have been at Polis Bay. The town of Stavros, inland of Polis Bay, is thought to lie at the base of the hill of the palace of Odysseus. The hill is Pilikáta. The local museum boasts artifacts from the cave and hill that are related to the time of Odysseus.[125]

The Ithaca cave was the source of twelve bronze tripods and caldrons, which date from the ninth to eighth century BCE. Although too late to belong to Odysseus, they support stories related by Homer of twelve gifts to Odysseus as a king. The items are consistent with the history of Odysseus as a king of Ithaca, although his palace has yet to be located. The residents and caretakers of the cave were sea nymphs. They would have been the first to greet Odysseus as he ventured home.

A narrow strip of sea separates Ithaca and Cephalonia. Polis Bay, in Ithaca, is almost directly across from Sami country and the caves of Cephalonia. Habitation of the area goes back to about 50,000 BCE. The areas were clearly Greek in the time of Odysseus. Nymphs lived in the caves, which could be navigated by boat, although ancient seamen had no reason to bother the domains of sub or super humans. Local farmers stayed out of the caves, unless the turf above gave way, exposing internal lakes.

The east coast of Cephalonia is Sámi country. Some historians consider this area to be the home of Odysseus, the place where he came ashore through a cave.[126] There are two caves in the area open to tourists. Each has a long history and its own mythology.

---

[125] Schliemann, who dug at Troy, also dug around Ithaca. He bought items from locals, such as a spear, flute, and coins, that he attributed to Odysseus, but which dated to the first century CE.

[126] A large tomb of the age of Odysseus has been discovered in Poros, on the eastern edge of Cephalonia toward the southern tip of the island. Archaeologists hope to continue looking there for the palace of Odysseus.

Melissáni Cave-Lake was thought to be home to the mythical Pan, often depicted as the half-man and half-goat flute player. Knowledge of the underground grotto and lake slipped away in modern times until a young goatherd fell into the lake when she unexpectedly encountered an area where the ground had collapsed into the lake. Townspeople tried in vain to save the girl from drowning. The cave-lake now bears her name.

Guidebooks tell the story of a nymph named Melissáni, who drowned herself when spurned by Pan. Today oarsmen take tourists into the Melissáni Cave in small boats. The secret home of Pan is a popular attraction on a warm day.

Nearby is another cave, the Drogaráti. Deep in the earth is an opening the size of a concert hall. There is no lake and no river. The moisture drips down through the earth to form large stalactites. During World War II, Nazi soldiers camped in the cave. They shot the ends off of the stalactites for target practice. Recently, there have been concerts in the cave. Today visitors walk down the slick stairs to the opening of the cave and are treated to a cool walk through a long hidden wonder. The cave was opened to tourists in 1963.

Lasting Natural Beauty

In 1953, an earthquake rocked Cephalonia. Since then, small towns have grown slowly, offering lovely accommodations to locals and visitors. The big draws are the beaches. Clean and sparsely populated, the beaches offer spectacular vistas for relaxing. The capital and harbor town of Argostoli is small and seems fresh and new, even though the area dates to ancient times. Dense vegetation reaches down to the beach areas. It is easy to imagine Odysseus reluctant to leave and anxious to return home.

CORFU

Elisabeth and Her Achílleion Palace

The Ionion Greek Island of Corfu, along the west coast of Greece in the Adriatic Sea, has a long history of fashionable residents. Unlike those Greek Islands, filed with rocky fields and modest houses, Corfu Island, and particularly Corfu Town, has enjoyed hosting residents of luxury.

In Corfu Town there is an arcade of restaurants and shops, called the Liston. It is a place where upscale residents can enjoy sitting in sidewalk cafes and looking across the cricket grounds toward the old fortress and the bay. Visitors who mingle with the locals in the Liston are continuing a five-hundred-year-old tradition in Corfu. This is the place to walk up and down the arcade, window-shopping, to see and be seen.

The Italian cities of Venice, Genoa, and Murano, published Golden Books, Libro 'd Oro in Italian, a listing of the local nobility. They were published in the seventeenth through twentieth centuries. The books may have been used as a tax register, or a registry of official noble title. These were particularly important in the early twentieth century, after the demise of Fascism. Fascists had eliminated all titles during their control of Italian politics. Later, former Italian nobles sought to reestablish their birthright using Libro 'd Oro as proof of their heritage.

One of the earliest examples of a Golden Book was that of the Libro d'Oro of Corfu, first published in 1572, long before listing nobility was a social consideration in Italy. Corfu attracted royals to its beauty and climate from so many places that it was evidently necessary to have a proper accounting of who was a noble from where. As people strolled down the Liston, it was important to know with whom they were rubbing shoulders.

Corfu is a Greek island, more influenced by Venice than Athens. The legacy of Greek gods is evident in Corfu, but as an island under the protection of Venice until the Napoleonic wars, the culture is Venetian. Corfu officially became unified with Greece in 1864, under the Treaty of London. The architecture, language, and customs remain heavily Venetian influenced.

The island paradise, with deep blue waters and warm climate, was a popular tourist destination for wealthy Europeans in the late nineteenth and early twentieth centuries. Among the European royals who found Corfu an attractive getaway from the cold climates and palace intrigues, was Empress Elisabeth of Austria. She was affectionately known as "Sissy."

This is the story of Sissy, the beautiful empress, with the tragic family history. Far from Vienna, she built a quirky castle south of Corfu Town, which she dubbed the Achílleion Palace. There she blended Greek tragedy with her own story to create her environment. Sissy died tragically in 1898, and the Achílleion Palace continued on to build its pedigree.

"Sissy"

Elisabeth was born Her Royal Highness Duchess Elisabeth Amalie Eugenie, on December 24, 1837, to royal parents, the Duke Maximilian and Duchess

Ludovika of Bavaria. Upon her marriage to Franz Joseph I of Austria, Sissy became queen of Austria. In 1867, she was also crowned queen of Hungary. At times her royal family conquests also resulted in her titles of queen of Bohemia and Croatia. From the time of her idyllic childhood, she preferred to be known as Sissy.

Sissy's contribution to the history of royals in Europe was less in politics than in convention. She had a disdain for rigid court protocol and the conventions of a proper princess or empress. She had the freedom and financing to go anywhere and express herself, so she did.

Sissy's free nature was in part a product of her childhood. Her father preferred to roam the Bavarian towns looking for circuses for entertainment. Her mother was not a disciplinarian. As the youngest of five children, Sissy had a protected, but glorious childhood.

The carefree life came to an end when she married Franz Joseph I of Austria. Sissy was not yet seventeen at the time of the wedding and the groom was twenty-four. They were first cousins, as their mothers were sisters.

Initially Princess Sophie, the mother of Franz, arranged the marriage between Franz and the oldest of Sissy's siblings, Helene. Helene was a somber young woman. Next to her, Sissy's fair hair and gay mood was more appealing to Franz. When the children of the two families first met, Franz refused to propose marriage to Helene. In defiance of his imposing mother, he demanded to marry Sissy, or not marry at all. Sissy and Franz were married in Vienna, on April 24, 1854. At a very young age, and with little preparation, Sissy became a queen.

Sissy had little time to adjust from her free-roaming childhood to the stiff court life of the Austrian royalty. She was married about one month before she became pregnant. Sissy's mother-in-law Sophie, who was also her aunt, considered Sissy too young and irresponsible to be a mother. Sophie took the infant archduchess, named her Sophie, after herself, and raised the child without consulting Sissy. One year later, Sissy gave birth again. Sophie removed the second infant daughter from Sissy, named the baby Gisela, and continued to keep mother and children separate.

Sissy reacted to the isolation and rigidity of court life in Austria with physical complaints. She excused herself from court functions, lorded over by her mother-in-law; by claiming she had a headache. Pamphlets were spread about the palace regarding Sissy's inability to produce an heir to the throne. The hateful epistles suggested that Sissy be sent home. They were likely the work of her mother-in-law.

While there is no indication that Franz stood up to his mother to demand that his wife be allowed some control in the household, and especially with regard to her children, he was attentive to Sissy. Franz took Sissy with him on his official travels. With his mother left in charge of the palace and his beautiful wife in his company, alone, Franz too could have some sense of domestic peace.

Of the places that the young royal couple traveled, Hungary was Sissy's favorite. Sissy first visited Hungary in 1857. The Hungarians were a people struggling to assert their independence under Austrian control. With these people, Sissy built a cathartic bond. Rather than promote independence from Austria, as Sissy's mother-in-law feared, Sissy's compassion and grace toward the Hungarian people endeared them to the Austrian royal couple, and particularly to Sissy. When Sissy was crowned the Queen of Hungary in 1867, she was almost thirty and no longer a child. She faced coronation with a sense of self-assurance and dignity, built over her years at court.

It was during their travels as a royal family that the oldest child, Sophie, became ill. While mother-in-law Sophie touted the illness as proof that Sissy was not competent to be a mother, the child contracted typhus, a disease for which children are routinely vaccinated today. Little Sophie died at age two.

The death of Sophie was followed within months of news that Sissy was again pregnant. This time she gave birth to an heir, the Crown Prince Rudolf, born in August 1858. With her mother-in-law silenced, an heir to the throne established, and at the mature age of twenty-one, Sissy began to express herself more freely.

Sissy was a beautiful woman. With her mother-in-law constantly making her feel unwelcome in the Austrian court, Sissy would count on her appearance to maintain her status with her husband. Maintaining her beauty became an obsession with Sissy.

Sissy was always tall and slender. At five feet eight inches, she was taller than Franz. At around 110 pounds, Sissy was fearful of ever being heavy. She watched her diet, not eating deserts, a difficult thing to do in Austria. She exercised compulsively. If her weight increased, she would fast for days. There is some indication that when she would eat a heavy meal, she would induce vomiting. Sissy had beauty secrets that her adoring female subjects emulated. As a slim, fit, woman, Sissy was an independent woman. It was an unusual trait for a nineteenth-century royal.

Sissy flaunted her sleek appearance in her clothing and in the lovely appearance of her long hair. The royal hairdresser would spend hours in order to treat and style Sissy's tresses. She had special facial creams concocted to keep her face looking young. Gray hairs were plucked from her scalp. He body was massaged and creamed. Style mattered to her. Women all through Europe copied her style. Sissy was the trendsetter of her time.

European woman of the mid-nineteenth century were moving from large skirts to a more flowing silhouette. Sissy was at the head of the style movement. Whether in ball gowns or daily riding attire, Sissy would use the practice of a tight-laced corset to keep her looking trim to compliment her natural figure. She was a proponent of the eighteen-inch waist. Style mattered even if it made a woman ill. That her mother-in-law abhorred the practice of a too-tight corset, as it was the antithesis of the pregnant look, only made style more important to Sissy.

Sissy's mother-in-law continued to dominate the royal household. Sissy was again denied any input to the education and daily affairs of Rudolf. She was often ill. She would refuse to eat. Her mother-in-law was convinced that the problem was the tight-laced corsets from Paris that caused Sissy to be ill. Doctors suggested a change of climate. So it was that Sissy was introduced to the warmth and beauty of Corfu.

For almost ten years after the birth of Rudolf, Sissy traveled the world and gave primary attention to her appearance and her education in literature and languages. She enjoyed life again as she had in her childhood. She visited her family in Bavaria. She rode horses every day and kept a gymnasium in every residence. She attracted the attention of noble men in distant courts. From Corfu to England, Sissy was a public figure of beauty.

Back in Vienna, Franz was having little flings of his own. He was rumored to have taken a stage actress as a mistress. It was time for Sissy to come home. She had been learning Hungarian and Greek. She was ready to dominate the household and be her husband's partner in world affairs. The coronation in 1867, of the couple as the king and queen of Hungary, was a royal homecoming. While in Hungary, a fourth child was born to Sissy and Franz, Valerie, in 1868. Sissy was thirty-one and at the top of her realm.

For the next twenty years, Sissy lived her life as she chose. She defied her mother-in-law to assert herself in Rudolf's education. He was a sensitive child, who did not warm to the idea of a military education. Sissy indulged her two youngest children, Rudolf and Valerie. Valerie was hers to dominate, free from the meddling of Sissy's mother-in-law.

Mother-in-law Sophie died in 1872. She did not live to see Gisela married in 1873, to a second cousin on Sissy's side of the family, Prince Leopold of Bavaria. Rudolf married in 1881. He married Belgium Princess Stephanie. They had a daughter they named Elisabeth.[127]

Sissy continued to travel and to spend time in Corfu. She and Franz maintained a cordial relationship. Much of their life is known from the correspondence they maintained. Then, in 1889, Sissy's life fell apart.

In 1889, Sissy's mother, father, and a sister died. While in mourning for her family, Sissy received the shock of her life. Crown Prince Rudolf died of a self-inflicted gunshot wound, while in the presence of a lover. The lover was also shot in an apparent murder-suicide. The deaths occurred in the hunting lodge of the crown prince in Mayerling, Austria. The tragedy has become known as the Mayerling Incident, the subject of the press at the time and later fictionalized in books and movies.

Always a public icon, Sissy withdrew from public life, upon the death of her only son, and crown prince, Rudolf. The marriage in 1890, of Valerie to her

---

[127] Sissy's granddaughter Elisabeth was the heir to all her jewels and valuables, which were not state property.

second cousin, the Archduke Franz of Austria and Tuscany, did not pull Sissy from her melancholy. Sissy withdrew to Corfu, where she began to build a retreat from life, the Achílleion Palace.

Empress Sissy was assassinated in 1898, at the age of sixty. The twenty-five-year-old Italian anarchist, Luigi Lucheni, stabbed her on the street in Geneva, Switzerland. He had been stalking Sissy for days. He carefully made a narrow, sharp, metal file, attached to a wooden handle. When he approached Sissy on the street, he seemed to stumble into her and then he ran away. Because the puncture wound was small, and as Sissy was wearing a tight corset that restricted her blood flow, she had no idea that she was mortally wounded as she continued to walk to the pier and board a boat. The wound had punctured her heart. Sissy slowly bled to death as she sat on the ship.

When Franz learned of Sissy's death he was first concerned that she had committed suicide, in the aftermath of Rudolf's death. Appearances were important, as he was a Roman Catholic monarch. When the news of Sissy's death reached Hungary there was an immense outpouring of grief. Geneva went into mourning. Sissy's death evoked more grief in Europe than had the death of the crown prince.

The assailant was apprehended, tried, and convicted. Switzerland did not have the death penalty. He was tried as a common murderer and given a life sentence, thus depriving him of making a political statement. He had wanted to kill a royal, any royal, and Sissy was near at hand. He later hung himself in his cell.

At the time of her death Sissy was the longest-serving royal of Austria. She has been memorialized in literature and movies, not always in a sympathetic light. Her story lives on, as she defined herself, in the palace she built on Corfu.

Palace of the Dying Achilles

Empress Elisabeth began work on her palace south of Corfu Town in 1890, the year following the death of Crown Prince Rudolf. Critical biographers of the empress attribute to her a Thetis complex. Thetis was the mother of the half-human, half-god, Achilles. True, Elisabeth had an often expressed passion for Homer's Iliad, the story of the battle for Troy and the return of Helen to her Spartan Greek husband.[128] In Elisabeth's time, the Iliad was at the core of the curriculum for the well educated. Achilles died at Troy. Elisabeth was a grieving mother. She worked through her grief by filling her time with her new palace.

The palace would be known as the Achílleion Palace. It became a quirky blend of fantasy and elegance. At the focal point of the garden a fountain was built. In the fountain is the statue of a dying Achilles. Achilles is shown in pain, eternally trying to remove the arrow from his heel. It is easy to attribute this monument as one to Rudolf.

The parallel between the tragic death of Rudolf, with his lover, and the death of Achilles is not hard to draw. Paris, son of the king of Troy, ignited the war that brought down his father's kingdom when he became involved in a contest between female gods. The goddesses each promised Paris power, money, or the love of a beautiful woman if he would give the goddess, whose gift he chose, the golden apple. In the judgment of Paris, there was no need for money or power, as he would inherit those assets. Paris chose the most beautiful woman in the world, Helen, as his prize.

Helen was already married to Menelaos of Sparta, a dull, but solid, husband. In the war, Paris saw Achilles end his brother Hector's life. Paris was not a skilled archer, but his errant arrow, aided by the meddling goddesses, found its mark at the only place of vulnerability for Achilles, his heel.

Achilles died at Troy. The Trojan kingdom died. The age of Greek superheroes died as well. It was the end of a lineage and of an era. The death of Rudolf, the only male heir to the throne, ended the lineage and the era of the dynasty. It was that era which defined Elisabeth's life. That Elisabeth would compare herself to Thetis is understandable.

The palace is built in a neo-classical style. There are Greek statues surrounding the building. Inside there are paintings and statues of Achilles and representations of the Trojan War. The palace and gardens sit on a hill overlooking the Ionian Sea. It is a commanding location for a dream house.

---

[128] See Itinerary III. Athens to Alexandria – Troy Lost. This is the story of Paris, Helen, and the death of Hector and Achilles at Troy, in the Iliad.

Inside the mansion, at the great staircase, there is a huge painting of a resplendent Achilles. He is shown in his full regalia, shield and chariot in hand. He is shown at that point in the Iliad when Achilles loses his sense of decorum and parades the lifeless body of Hector, brother of Paris, around the castle, dragged behind his chariot. It is the moment of victory, but not the best hour for Achilles. A loving mother may have wanted to commission a painting of Achilles at a time later in the Iliad, when he invites the father of Hector to retrieve the body, and arranges a pause in the battle to afford Hector a proper burial. Elisabeth was a mother in pain. She was not yet thinking with compassion of the circumstances that led to Rudolf's death.

There remain some important works of art in the palace. Next to the statue of Apollo is the statue of the Graces. It is the work of noted Italian sculptor, Canova.[129]

---
[129] Canova was courted by Napoleon to produce sculpture. Canova detested Napoleon for looting Italian art and removing it to Paris. Canova eventually produced an

Palace of the Victorious Achilles

Upon Sissy's death, the palace in Corfu remained vacant. In 1908, ten years after her death, Kaiser Wilhelm II of Germany purchased the Achílleion Palace. He removed the statue of the Dying Achilles in the garden and replaced it with a statue of Victorious Achilles. Under the statue there is the inscription, "From the Greatest of Greeks to the Greatest of Germans."

Kaiser Wilhelm made some changes to the palace and the grounds. Notably, he built a bridge over the highway, to connect the palace gardens to the beach. Today the bridge no longer spans the roadway. Ironically, the Germans removed the bridge as an obstruction during their occupation of the area in World War II, so that they could move military vehicles freely along the highway.

Kaiser Wilhelm held the palace from 1908 to 1914. After the First World War, the palace was sold to the Greek government. It was converted into a museum.

The palace may look familiar to fans of James Bond films. The Achílleion Palace was the setting for the 1981 Bond film, "For Your Eyes Only." In the film, Bond and one of the Bond girls go underwater to an ancient Greek Temple. They revive themselves and enter the casino, which is the ballroom of the Achílleion Palace.

Today visitors can roam the palace, with or without a tuxedo. They can step into the dream of a sad empress, at the end of an era, Sissy, Elisabeth of Austria, Bavaria, and Hungary.[130]

---

unattractive sculpture of Napoleon. See this itinerary, port of Venice - The Traveling Horses of Saint Marks.

[130] Instead of a James Bond martini, shaken not stirred, the visitor may prefer a kumquat liqueur, the local specialty.

BARI/ BRINDISI

Frederick II and His Castles: Stupor Mundi

Stupor Mundi means "wonders of the world." As seen by travelers to the east coast of southern Italy, stupor mundi are the plethora of castles built by Frederick II, in the early to mid-thirteenth century. Frederick II may not be well known outside of Puglia. Frederick is a common name among European royalty and later kings.[131] It is easy to become confused. This Frederick was a most uncommon character. Visiting his legacy monuments will make him memorable.

Frederick II was the most notable man of his era. His contemporaries called him "stupor mundi," an astonishing wonder of the world, some out of admiration and others out of jealous irony. Frederick earned his several powerful detractors, among them popes. He also earned the loyalty of his allies. Among his allies were the Muslims subject to random pillaging of property and taking of farms during the period of his infancy.[132] They became staunch supporters of Frederick in his various wars against popes. Such was his resilience as an emperor that Frederick's subjects refused to believe that he was dead for twenty-five years after his demise. They thought he was merely sleeping in the mountains and would wake to reclaim his empire.

This is the story of Frederick II's life and accomplishments. They explain the need for prolific castle building between 1220 and 1250, to protect his several kingdoms. The legends of Frederick's life are true. Frederick's castles, visible today, are his most lasting legacy.

---

[131] Frederick II of this story was a grandson to Frederick II, the one-eyed, Duke of Swabia, a German knight.
[132] Henry Barbera, Medieval Sicily: The First Absolute State, Legas, Canada, 2000, at 132.

Born to be King

Every aspect of the life of Frederick II exemplifies his commanding public persona. He was born to be a king and satisfied his parent's ambitions several times over. Frederick's mother was the queen of Sicily, which included southern Italy, and his father was Henry VI, King of Germany, Northern Italy, and the Holy Roman Empire.

The legendary life of Frederick began with the moment of his birth. He was delivered into the world in the middle of the market square, as his mother lifted her skirts on a cold December day, to the surprised crowd. Queen Constance was forty years old at the time. Critics charged that she was faking the pregnancy. They would be forced to witness the majestic event of the birth of her first son. She wanted there to be no question of his birth, his parentage, and his birthright. No doubt, Queen Constance would have preferred the birth to occur the day earlier. As it was, Frederick was born on December 26, 1194.[133]

Frederick immediately got to work on being great. Before he could walk, the infant was crowned the king of Germany upon the death of his father. By the time he was three, he became Frederick I of Sicily. His career was dealt a setback when Queen Constance died of an infection in 1198. Pope Innocent III became young Frederick's guardian.

The pope could offer young Frederick a wonderful education. However, popes and Holy Roman Emperors were in direct competition for the leadership of the western Christian world. Frederick's father was the outgoing HRE and Frederick was heir to that throne.

Frederick's German uncle invaded the kingdom of Sicily and took over guardianship of Frederick when he was six. The pope fought back with the aide of Otto, a Bavarian count. The uncle was assassinated. By this time Frederick was fourteen. He was ready to assert control of his Sicilian crown.

---

[133] Frederick Hohenstaufen was born in Iesi, Italy, just outside of the coastal city of Ancona.

By 1208, Frederick had come of age. Quickly, the pope arranged the marriage of Frederick to Constance, a widow of the king of Hungary. Frederick added another crown to his collection. The royal couple had two sons, Heinrich VII (Henry) and Enzio.

In 1211, Frederick reasserted his German kingship. His former guardian Pope Innocent III assisted him in this endeavor. Finally, in 1220, Frederick became the Holy Roman Emperor. Innocent III had died a few years earlier and was not there to officiate.

Constance died in 1221 and Frederick married again. The second bride was fifteen-year-old Yolanda, daughter of the Regent of Jerusalem. As part of his wife's dowry, Frederick was also made King of Jerusalem. Frederick could afford to give away a title. He endowed his oldest son, Henry, with the title of King of the Romans.

Yolanda died soon after the birth of their only child, Conrad, in 1228. Frederick's third wife was Isabella, sister of Henry III of England. None of their children survived to adulthood. Frederick also had long-standing relationships with mistresses, from which he acknowledged two sons, Manfred and Tancred.

In 1220, Frederick, King of Germany, Sicily, Jerusalem, and the Holy Roman Emperor, was twenty-six. He had spent most of his time as king mending relationships with princes throughout northern Italy, southern France, and Germany. It was time to assert his leadership on the larger world stage. The means to do so in the thirteenth century was to lead a crusade.

The Reluctant Crusader

A crusade was a twelfth century, pope-sanctioned excursion to rid the holy land of the infidel and enrich the pope's coffers as a result. After the First Crusade, each succeeding venture was more about enriching coffers than vanquishing an infidel. Given Frederick's world standing, the pope tagged him to lead the fifth and sixth crusades. Frederick's first preference in dealing with conflict and international tension was diplomacy. He was reluctant to lead gold-seeking knights into battle. Such reluctance angered the pope.

The Fifth Crusade launched in 1217. Frederick was a no-show. As the knights made their way through Egypt to Jerusalem, they lacked his leadership. Sultan al-Kamil was willing to give up Jerusalem in exchange for expelling the pope's knights from Egypt. When the agreement stalled, al-Kamil sent the knights home in defeat. Frederick was blamed.

To save face and restore confidence in his leadership by the church and the populace, Frederick agreed to launch the Sixth Crusade by 1227. He had become the king of Jerusalem in 1225, when he replaced his father-in-law. There was no way to avoid the trip, so Frederick set sail in the fall of 1227. He immediately claimed to have been infected by the then raging plague and returned home within the month. The pope was furious. He excommunicated Frederick. This would be the first of four excommunications.

In an effort to counter everyone's disappointment, Frederick sailed from Brindisi to the Holy Land in 1228. Since an excommunicated knight could not lead an army on behalf of the pope, Frederick was acting outside of the moral authority. The pope denied Frederick the assistance of any knights. Unaided by a bevy of raiding thugs, Frederick resorted to diplomacy. He negotiated a treaty with al-Kamil in early 1229. As a result, Jerusalem, Nazareth, and Bethlehem were returned to his Kingdom of Jerusalem. In return, Frederick agreed not to use Jerusalem as a walled fort. There were to be no attacks on Egypt.

The restoration of Jerusalem from the infidel without war made Frederick very popular at home. The pope was forced to lift the excommunication, even though the papacy had not profited from the deal. Professional knights, such as the Knights Templar, were not happy. The Templars were rumored to have written a letter to al-Kamil, in which they offered to assassinate Frederick if al-Kamil would hire them. Instead, al-Kamil turned over the letter to Frederick. Left with no immediate prospects for profit abroad, the disgruntled knights turned their attention to Frederick's domain in Europe.

Intrigue and Innocent IV

Inspired by self-interest and Pope Innocent III, nobles invaded the lands of Frederick II, while he was on crusade. He returned in 1229, from a bloodless victory abroad, only to fight for his possessions purloined by the rear guard. Pope Innocent III was obligated to lift the excommunication given the good deeds in Jerusalem. Frederick publicly acknowledged that he was on good terms with the pope. He then proceeded to sack the towns of his detractors, until he regained his ground and secured the position of his crowns.

Frederick's several sons, from his three wives and other relationships, did not inherit either his leadership or tactical skills. The oldest son, Henry, caused so many problems while ruling in Germany that the German nobles were in open revolt. Frederick conceded autonomy to them, such that they happily fought among themselves for hundreds of years, while the remainder of Europe formed strong nations. The new pope, Gregory IX, did not see the utility in Frederick's actions. In in 1234, he issued Frederick's second excommunication. Henry continued to cause problems in Germany. In 1235, it became clear that Frederick had no alternative but to imprison Henry.

The early thirteenth century was the time of the great rivalry between the Guelphs, supporters of the papacy, and the Ghibellines, supporters of the Holy Roman Emperor of Germany and Austria. Political intrigue, capture of opposing family lands, and incarceration of opposing nobility played out all through Italy. Nobles of cities often switched sides without warning, depending on who doled out favors. Family rivalries of the time were immortalized in Shakespeare's Romeo and Juliet. The star-crossed young lovers were residents of Verona, in northern Italy, one of a Guelph and the other of a Ghibelline family.

Frederick, the master diplomat, was able to rise above the Guelph-Ghibelline controversy. He used the dissention between cities to his advantage. In Germany the Hohenstaufen and Guelph cities united under Frederick.[134] When the pope incited Guelph nobles to riot in 1238, Frederick brought order among petty disputants within the year. Even though Frederick stopped short of attacking Rome, Pope Gregory handed Frederick his third excommunication in retaliation for his other victories over Guelph cities.

---

[134] Powerful Pisa was a staunch Ghibelline, as was Ferrara, home to the Este family dynasty. See Itinerary I. Florence.

Frederick installed his son, Ezio, as the ruler of northern Italy. In 1242, when Pope Gregory died, Frederick thought his troubles would diminish. Instead, intrigue heightened.

Pope Gregory's successor was Pope Innocent IV, a master negotiator and notorious foe of anything German, which included Frederick Hohenstaufen. Pope Innocent IV secretly sent funds to German nobles to incite rebellion against Frederick. Innocent IV appealed to the French King Louis IX to assassinate Frederick and Enzio. However, the French king liked Frederick. A political marriage by Frederick's son Manfred pleased French King Louis. The French exposed the plot. The infuriated Pope Innocent IV excommunicated Frederick, his fourth expulsion from the church, a church for which Frederick had no use.

In 1248, the sensitive political balance began to tip against Frederick. He had long suffered from illness that began at the start of the 1227 crusade attempt. Although Frederick championed healthy living and cleanliness, his health was fragile. During one of his ill periods, the Guelph and Ghibelline controversy rekindled in Lombardy. In the Battle of Parma that year, there was great loss of men. A large part of the royal treasury of Frederick was captured during the battle.

In 1249, Frederick had several additional setbacks. His closest friend and advisor, the poet Pier delle Vigne, was exposed for embezzlement and treason, having contributed to the loss at Parma. Vigne had been an efficient administrator, who communicated daily with Frederick's vast empire in Latin, Greek, Arabic, Hebrew, French and German. The poet's constant contact had been credited for stability in the kingdoms. Frederick parted company with Vigne and with his departure lost control of the vast empire.

That same year, Enzio, age twenty-three, was captured in a war against Pisa and was imprisoned by the pope. He would spend the remaining twenty-three years of his life in captivity. Frederick's son Richard died in a battle. Most of the lands in northern Italy were lost from Frederick's kingdom. Those lands that remained were given to the oldest son, Henry VII. Henry led a brief revolt against his father and then committed suicide.

In 1250, Frederick retired in the manner of a thirteenth-century gentleman. He gave up his worldly possessions and became a monk. Of his remaining sons, Conrad IV became king of Sicily and Manfred inherited what was left of northern Italy. Jerusalem had been previously awarded to Conrad. On December 13, 1250, Frederick died in southern Italy. The cause of death was intestinal infection and dehydration. As he was raised in Palermo, Frederick was buried there.

The Stupor Mundi

Frederick II has been credited with shaping twentieth-century Europe. He replaced feudalism with a secular constitutional code for Italy, weakened the papacy, leading to the Protestant Reformation, and delayed the unification of Germany and Italy due to his struggles with the succession of popes during his lifetime. Frederick was a man of superior personal strength and intellect. He made the most of his family inheritance and his papal education.

Physically, Frederick was not handsome or imposing. He had thin red hair and a slim body. After 1227, he continually struggled with his health. He was slated to marry Sancha of Aragon. However, when Sancha's older sister became a widow, Constance stepped up to first in line to marry Frederick, even though she was ten years his senior. Still, Frederick mustered the strength to outlive three wives and several concubines.

Frederick was enamored of Arabic customs. This contributed to his practice of keeping a harem and a zoo of wild animals. He was known to travel with both. The clean lines of Arabic geometric design can be seen in his castles.

Frederick could write and speak Latin, German, French, Greek and Arabic. He is credited with forming a popular version of Sicilian, a precursor to modern Italian. He wrote poetry and music. Frederick was a patron of science and the arts. His favorite pastime was to work with falcons. He wrote and illustrated a well-regarded book entitled, "The Art of Hunting with Birds." For these efforts, Frederick is considered the first scientific ornithologist.

Frederick was a secular leader in a time of domination of the Catholic Church. Unfazed by his four excommunications, Frederick did not campaign against the church. He simply had no use for the political exploits of the papacy. Popes interfered with two tenants of Frederick's life, those of religious toleration and science.

To understand Frederick, it must be recognized that he was raised in an Arabic culture in Palermo. He appreciated the arts and sciences, including mathematics and astronomy, in which the Arabs excelled. At his first adult coronation, where he could control the ceremony, Frederick wore an ancient robe, covered with Arabic inscriptions of good wishes, dated to about 528 CE.[135]

Frederick believed in a secular life for the political ruler and in religious toleration. He hired Arabs in his army. This proved a fortunate arrangement, as no Catholic would continue service during Frederick's periods of excommunication. Frederick also employed Jewish scholars to translate Greek, Latin, and Hebrew texts for his library.

In 1224, Frederick founded the University of Naples. It was a bastion of science, mathematics, astronomy, and physics. It was also the center of study for public administration and secular law. Frederick's chief counselor, Vigne, is believed to have been an alumnus. Historians surmise that Frederick wished to mount substantive scientific and legal arguments to the pope. The popes had the University of Bologna from which to draw upon for scholarship. Fredrick too had a think tank of scholars.

Some of Frederick's experiments on humans to disprove the existence of a soul seemed macabre, if they indeed did occur. Church scholars reported that Frederick locked men in barrels to see if a soul could escape, or deprived children of hearing speech to see if they would spontaneously burst forth in Latin, Greek, or Hebrew. Detractors could have exaggerated such reports, but if true, they exemplify Frederick's desire to show the worth of a secular education.

---

[135] The robe is now in the collection of the Kunsthistorisches Museum in Vienna.

One of Frederick's major accomplishments was the drafting of laws. His Liber Augustalis, compiled in 1231, is credited with the establishment of modern civil law in his kingdom. It remained the basis of civil law in Sicily for almost 600 years, until 1819. The code established uniform local governments and trade agreements. There were provisions that limited taxes. Notably, the code provided a representative assembly. Trial by ordeal was eliminated. The logic was that the strong could always prevail, which was not an indication of guilt or innocence. In total, the code is considered to have been a critical basis for stability in Frederick's kingdom. The Liber Augustalis was followed in 1241, with the Edict of Salerno, in which peace was brokered with a similar document, the Constitution of Salerno.

A consistent item in the civil codes was a prohibition that doctors could not also be pharmacists. The logic was that a doctor may prescribe expensive, but unnecessary, potions to enrich the doctor without benefiting the patient. Frederick's bout of illness prior to the crusades may have prompted his life-long opinion of doctors. He also founded medical schools and promoted cleanliness in daily life. Frederick was a patron of the medical school in Salerno. It was there that Frederick sponsored the study of anatomy.

Frederick's kingdom was not a democratic monarchy. The evolution of society from medieval fiefdoms to a unified nation took a short, but strong, step forward under his rule. That was enough for the time. The emperor continued to hold eminent domain over the land. Heirs could only inherit a castle upon Frederick's permission and by payment of a fee. Married women could not inherit from their brothers. Frederick did offer peace within the kingdom. Private wars were outlawed. Only the castles of Frederick could be reinforced with defensive walls.

Castles of Puglia

The enduring visible legacy of Frederick II exists in his dozens of castles, forts, and civic structures. Emblematic of Frederick's secular life, no churches were commissioned by him. There are no chapels in the castles. These are the stupor mundi - the amazing architectural gems in the Puglia landscape.

The castles may have provided secure residences, fortress protection for the artists and academics Frederick sponsored from throughout his world, or simply hunting lodges from which he emerged with his falcons. The number of structures may also be a testament to Frederick's quest to improve upon each new dwelling with his advancing knowledge of geometry.

In Frederick's buildings there are themes evident of simplicity, perfect proportion, and Arabic geometric design. Although the corner towers of his castles appear identical, some were storage towers for food and water, which could be individually secured in a siege. Thus the castles are beautiful and functional. Some notable examples of Frederick's castles within a short drive from the ports of Bari or Brindisi are:

CASTEL DEL MONTE: Built late in Frederick's life, Castel del Monte may be his ultimate accomplishment. The well-preserved castle sits on a hill surrounded by an open landscape. The octagon masterpiece has eight identical towers, on the points of the eight-sided castle, with eight interior rooms on each of two floors. The geometric proportion is perfect. The front gate faces east.

The emperor may have used the castle as a hunting lodge. During French control of Sicily, Caste del Monte was a prison. His sons Henry, Azzo, and Enzo were imprisoned in the castle after capture in 1266, along with Hohenstaufen supporters. Over the next several centuries the castle had intermittent use as a theater, a refuge from the plague in 1656, a hospital, another prison, and a hideout for bandits in the eighteenth century. In 1876, the castle was purchased by the Italian government for restoration. In 1996, Castel del Monte was listed as a World Heritage Site, as a "masterpiece of medieval military architecture, reflecting the humanism of its founder, Frederick II of Hohenstaufen."[136]

TRANI: Trani was a busy port in the thirteenth century. It was a trading and political center of Medieval Europe. Today the castle still sits at the edge of the sea, a testament to Frederick's architectural prowess.

---

[136] http://whc.unesco.org/en/lost/398 last visited 7/30/2012

BARI: Norman King Roger II built on the site of a former Roman fort in 1132. That castle was razed in 1156. Frederick rebuilt the castle between 1233 and 1240. Unusual for Frederick's castles, the Bari castle has a moat, which may have been filled with seawater, as a holdover from the prior design. Today the castle is the anchor of the old town historic district of Bari.

BARLETTA: Barletta sits on the Adriatic coast between the castles of Trani and Manfredonia. This castle began as a Norman fortress. Then Frederick transformed the site into a palace. The architectural features are more elegant than seen in some of the later castles.

There are more of Frederick's efforts to be seen in Puglia, although not all are complete structures. The Brindisi castle, built in 1227, was an important embarkation site for the crusades. Frederick would be pleased to know that the castle is still in use today as a home for the port police. In Lucera there are still two of Frederick's 1233 era towers visible within the structure modified by the French. Near Altamura are the remains of a hunting lodge where Frederick held his falcons. Frederick kept a mistress locked up in a castle at Gioia del Colle, between Taranto and Bari. This castle was a modification of a structure begun in 1100. Several additional castles can be seen in Sicily.

There was more to Frederick II than his castles. However, the intangibles are harder to appreciate on a tour of Puglia. When in the ports of Bari or Brindisi, a tour to the stupor mundi will amaze even the seasoned traveler with their architectural sophistication and endurance.

BARI
Believe In Santa Claus

Santa Claus, or more formally, Saint Nikolaos, was a real person. His name was Nikolaos of Patara, born March 15, 270. He was a Greek priest, in a Greek town, in present-day Turkey.[137] He died on December 6, 343. Almost 750 years later, his bones were taken to the Greek town of Bari in southern Italy.

From the time of his death to the time of his relocation to Italy, Nikolaos evolved from a generous priest to the patron saint of children, sailors, merchants, archers and thieves. His feast day of December 6 is celebrated around the world as the time to give generous gifts. All of this makes perfect sense, once the true story of Saint Nikolaos is told.

The Life of Nikolaos

In the first centuries of the Christian era, the seaport towns of present-day Turkey were largely Greek settlements. Greek seamen were also early residents of the Italian port city of Bari, on the southern Adriatic coast. Even today, fishermen of Bari speak a language that is more Greek than Italian, in this city which has retained its Greek heritage.

Nikolaos was born into a wealthy family of Greek Orthodox Christians, living on the southwestern edge of modern Turkey, on the Mediterranean Sea. This is the Lycia region of Turkish Asia, which borders on the Adriatic, in proximity

---

[137] As Saint Nikolaos was undeniably Greek, the Greek spelling of his name is used in this story.

to the Greek Island of Rhodes. Nikolaos was known to be a good student. He enjoyed religious study.

When Nikolaos was young he lost both parents in a plague. His uncle, also named Nikolaos, became responsible for the youth. The uncle was a bishop. Thus, Nikolaos fell easily into the priesthood.

Early Christian bishops were powerful church leaders. No doubt the uncle was financially established. Young Nikolaos had the means and the desire to be generous with those less fortunate in his community. His generosity became the foundation of his legend and his eventual rise to sainthood.

As the Bishop of Myra, Nikolaos ministered to the poor. He was the protector of poor and hungry children. Those needy beings leaving their shoes outside their doors would wake in the morning to find gold coins had been deposited in them. Such generosity was attributed to Nikolaos. He gave discreetly, so as not to embarrass the beneficiaries.

Rough sailors, from the dregs of the shipping hierarchy, found compassion and assistance came to them from Nikolaos, rather than harsh judgment for their lifestyle. He was the protector of aimless seamen, those marginalized in town society. In the eleventh century, sailors were encouraged to join guilds by the Emperor Frederick II. One of the earliest sailor's guilds is known as the Association of Saint Nicholas of Bari. They are the descendants of those sailors sent to Myra to collect the remains of Saint Nicholas and bring him to Bari.[138]

Nikolaos lived a long life for the times. When he died at seventy-three, he was buried in a church in Myra, a coastal town in southern Turkey.[139] Immediately, Nikolaos was revered in death. His tomb became a shrine to his gift giving and compassion.

---

[138] Doré Ogrizek, Italy, McGraw-Hill Book Company, Inc., New York, 1950, p. 419.

[139] Myra was the town from which St. Paul sailed to Rome and his martyrdom. Herbert J. Muller, The Loom of History, Harper & Brothers, New York, 1958, p. 389.

The Legend of Nikolaos

The bones of the sainted departed are considered sacred relics. Annually, from the time of his death, the relics of Nikolaos were reported to secrete a clear liquid with the fragrance of rose water. The water was considered to be manna or myrrh, a holy liquid. The precious liquid was believed to have special curative powers. Sailors spread the word of this miracle, making Nikolaos an early de facto Christian saint.

Over the years the legends of Saint Nikolaos grew in number, as they spread like goods on the ships through the Christian world. One deed attributed to Nikolaos was providing dowries to the three daughters of a poor man. Girls of poor families without dowries could not expect to be married. Unmarried women had few options in society prior to the establishment of convents and the opportunity to live as a nun. The story has variations, but is consistent in that Nikolaos threw three gold purses into the home of the man, enabling him to provide a dowry for each daughter. One version has Nikolaos providing the purses over the years as each daughter attained the age for marriage. Upon the third event, the man waited up all night to see his benefactor. He reported having the ability to thank Nikolaos as the third purse was delivered.

Another legend tells the gruesome tale of a butcher who lured young children to his home, where they became cured meat. Such tales abounded around the end of the first millennium, particularly during times of famine. In the legend, Saint Nikolaos finds the butcher and saves the children. In some versions Nikolaos arrives after the children are butchered. He brings three children back to life.[140]

Times of famine produced several stories of heroic acts. In one legend, a famine struck Myra while a ship loaded with wheat destined for the Emperor in Constantinople sat in its harbor. Nikolaos convinced the sailors to remove a large quantity of wheat from the ship. There was enough wheat to feed the population for two years. When the shipment reached its destination the cargo was weighed. Miraculously, there was no diminution of weight.

---

[140] Saint Nikolaos is always remembered and pictured saving people in threes. He gave three purses, saved three children, or three travelers, or three seamen.

As Christian practices evolved in medieval times, nuns remembered Saint Nikolaos by delivering food baskets to the hungry each year on December 6, the remembrance day of the Saint. Festivals sprang up across the old and new Christian world featuring food and gifts for sale in the Christmas season. December 6 became a time to buy small gifts for children at the fairs. Sailors remembered the day by purchasing gifts to bring home to their families.

Saint Nikolaos Travels to Italy

In 1087, the relics of Saint Nikolaos traveled to Bari. Basilicas of the first millennium were founded with the relics of a saint. The city leaders of Venice and Bari knew of the fame of Saint Nikolaos as he lay, intact, in the church at Myra. They reasoned that the fall of Greek Christian control of the city to Muslims in 1081 put the relics at risk. They decided to rescue the saint.[141] The relics could be used to found new basilicas to grace their cities.

There was some debate at the time as to whether Saint Nikolaos was at risk in Myra. The competition between Roman Catholic Venice and Greek Orthodox Bari, as to which should be the guardian of the relics, overshadowed the protests of the resident priests of Myra. Forty business leaders of Bari commissioned the ship first to arrive in Myra. They hurriedly collected the remains. By the time the Venetian ship arrived for the same mission, they were left with the few bones left behind in the crypt.

The relics taken to Bari were ensconced in the Basilica di San Nicola. The remains taken to Venice are in the modest church of San Nicolò al Lido. Questions remain today as to whether each church holds the bones of the same man, or whether the Venetians satisfied themselves with the remains of the uncle of Saint Nikolaos, also a priest named Nikolaos.[142]

---

[141] The remains were removed over the objection of the Greek Orthodox in charge of the church at Myra. Historians point to the jealousy of Roman Catholics in Italy, who considered the Greeks heretics, as motivation for removal of the remains to Bari or Venice. Muller, at 390.

[142] There is some speculation that the remains in the two churches are of the same man, but neither is St. Nikolaos. There are also human remains that lie on a Turkish island between Rhodes and Myra, which are attributed to Saint Nikolaos.

Fortunately for the city leaders of Bari, the relics, newly installed in their crypt, continued to exude the miraculous fluid each year on December 6, the feast day of Saint Nikolaos. The monks were able to bottle the fluid for sale in the church shop. They continue to do so. The miracle of the crypt and the water bottling activity is unimpaired by the change in the calendar.

Greek Orthodox calendars use the traditional Julian dating system. The widely used modern Gregorian calendar is off from the Julian calendar by thirteen days. So the new crypt of Saint Nikolaos would have begun producing fluid on December 19, by the Julian calendar, if it now produces on December 6, of the new Gregorian calendar. Saint Nikolaos may be amused, but not confused. The spirit of his giving continues.

Bari and Venice provided stable homes for their relics. Over time, neither city was plundered for its relics. As the popularity of Saint Nikolaos spread, other churches remembered the saint in frescos and icons. Foreign churches considered themselves fortunate to obtain a bottle of the holy liquid from the crypt of Saint Nikolaos.

Saint Nikolaos Today

Today Saint Nikolaos is revered as a patron saint of Greek Orthodox Christians. His feast day of December 6 is widely celebrated. Many churches have been named in his honor, while others hold statues, frescoes, and icons of the saint. Roman Catholics also recognize Saint Nikolaos as one of their own. He is universally regarded as the saint of gift giving. Saint Nikolaos has evolved into Santa Claus.[143] He has gained interdenominational, if not secular, recognition

The Basilica di San Nicola stands today, as a splendid attraction for visitors to Bari. It contains Roman Catholic and Greek Orthodox chapels to Saint Nikolaos. Consecration of the crypt for the remains of the saint, in 1089, inaugurated construction of the Basilica completed in 1197.

Typical of major architectural feats of the day, particularly those in southern Italy, the Basilica resembles a castle. In fact, the building was used as a castle during part of its history. Also typical of the times, the Basilica received gifts from prominent families, making it a museum of art treasures.[144]

In its millennium of continuous use, the Basilica di San Nicola has been restored several times. There were additions, such as the Baroque adornments. Baroque decoration was inconsistent with the original stark lines of the Basilica. More recently, the Baroque additions have been removed. The visitor to Bari today will enjoy the Basilica di San Nicola, much the same as it was in the twelfth century.

Questions and controversy over the remains of Saint Nikolaos continue. The modern city of Demre has developed in Turkey not far from ancient Myra. In the last decade the Turkish government has demanded that Italy return the bones of Saint Nikolaos, on behalf of the city leaders of Demre. Evidently, the Turkish government has taken the position that the remains removed from

---

[143] The Dutch referred to Saint Nikolaos as Sinter Claes. From there the father of gift giving at Christmas time became Father Christmas, Santa Claus. For those who wish to sever the commercial aspects of gift giving from the religious observance of Christmas, gift giving on December 6 would be historically justified.

[144] The tomb of the patriarch of a powerful Renaissance family, Bona Sforza, is located in the Bari Basilica.

Myra, and not the remains discovered on an island off the coast of Myra, within Turkey, are the actual remains of the Saint. Controversy, over control of the relics of Saint Nikolaos, is ongoing.

In 2005, the mayor of Demre replaced a Russian Orthodox era statue of Saint Nikolaos with a plastic blow-up Santa Claus. There were protests from the Russian Orthodox Church. The statue was given a respectful placement in a nearby garden, but the plastic Santa continued to reign on the city square.

The real Saint Nikolaos may have been jolly and bearded, but not likely pudgy. He was in fact the first secret Santa. Whether gifts are given on December 6 or 19, Saint Nikolaos is a reminder of the joy of giving. The Basilica in Bari is a fitting tribute to the Saint.

BARI/ BRINDISI

COUNTING ZIMBALO'S ANGELS IN LECCE

One of the loveliest towns in Italy is tucked away in the heel of the boot. Fortunately this town is accessible from the ports of Bari and Brindisi on the Adriatic Ocean and Taranto inside the heel of the boot of Italy. Lecce was founded in antiquity. The town holds vestiges of its life as part of Magna Graecia, with a long line of Greek descendants, and of the conquest by Rome. The central town square opens to reveal the archaeology of its heritage, including a Roman amphitheater. This historical wealth is not the only reason to compel visitors to Lecce. The beauty of Lecce, that attracts visitors and renders them reluctant to leave, is seen in Lecce's Baroque period buildings.

It is as though life blossomed in Lecce in the late seventeenth and early eighteenth centuries. The height of Lecce's Baroque period came in the second half of the seventeenth century, a period between 1640 and 1700. The task of residents of Lecce since that time has been to preserve their inheritance. They have done well.

Baroque architecture dominates Lecce. A delicate riot of flowers, wreaths, and angels can be seen inside and outside the churches. As such, it has been called the Florence of the south. Three factors were responsible for the beauty of Lecce. One was the signature yellow limestone building and sculpting material, available in abundance close to town. The second was the talent and prolific efforts of Giuseppe Zimbalo. Zimbalo was a resident sculptor in Lecce. The town was the benefactor of his life's work. The architectural sculptors who followed Zimbalo perpetuated his style. The result is an entire town beautifully sculpted. The third factor was the bishop who was a patron of Zimbalo from 1640 to 1670, at the height of his artistic career.

Angels are Zimbalo's trademark. They grace every building that is decorated with his work. The visitor to Lecce today can spend the day strolling through the narrow lanes and open plazas, counting the angels. This is the story of Zimbalo and his angels of Lecce.

The Art and Influence of Zimbalo

There is a clear demarcation of Lecce pre and post Zimbalo. The ruling families of Lecce, of the late fourteenth and early fifteenth centuries, created massive stone structures devoid of decoration. The round, smooth, stark, white stone towers of Maria, countess of Lecce, princess of Taranto, and later queen of Naples,[145] were built at the turn of the fifteenth century. For the next one hundred years not much was built in Lecce. The town suffered plagues and raids, both of which greatly reduced the population.

In 1539, King Charles V of France, ruler of the kingdom of Sicily, which included Naples and southern Italy, made Lecce his regional capital. The king built an imposing fortress castle, which today dominates the approach into Lecce. The austere city walls also date to the time of Charles V. Buildings in Lecce of this period have sparse decoration.

At the beginning of the seventeenth century, Lecce was a town of diverse influences. Long-time Greek residents of Lecce were joined by Genoese and Venetians, all businessmen who brought their wealth to the city. They adorned their homes and chapels with statues and wreaths in the lavish Baroque style. Lecce became a haven for talented artists who were schooled in the art of architectural adornment.

In a few decades, the emerging city was resplendent in the yellow limestone, known as Leccisu, or Lecce Stone. The abundance of limestone in nearby quarries made it a primary source of building material. That the stone is

---

[145] Maria Enghien, (1367-1446), deserves her own story. She established civil and penal order in Lecce, and was adored by her subjects, except in the Jewish community, the members of which she required to wear identification badges. Ironically, it was the Enghien dynasty that opened Lecce as a free port to Venetian merchants and opened the port to Jewish, Greek, Albanian, Florentine and Genoese merchants, who became the drivers of prosperity in Lecce.

characteristically soft when first quarried and hardens over time made it ideal for external decorative use on buildings. Artisans embellished their every commission with Baroque sculpture.

Giuseppe Zimbalo distinguished himself as a master among the elite sculptors of Lecce. He lived a long productive life perfecting his craft and training his son Francesco to sculpt. Born in 1620, he died in 1710. His most productive years coincided with the glory years 1640 through 1700, of the Baroque style of architecture and abundant building commissions in Lecce.

Zimbalo was physically small and was affectionately known as Lo Zingarello, the tiny gypsy. In fact he was a giant in terms of his ability to influence the architecture and style of an entire town. He did not decorate all of the magnificent examples of Baroque architecture in Lecce. Those buildings that he did not touch still bear his influence. Later artists emulated his style in the buildings finished after Zimbalo.[146]

The powerful Bishop of Lecce, Luigi Pappacoda, first brought Zimbalo to prominence. Pappacoda was bishop of Lecce from 1639 to 1670. During his tenure as bishop there were seventeen convents for monks and eight for nuns. Pappacoda supported public display of wealth by the town barons, who responded with support for church building coffers. Pappacoda was able to engage Zimbalo as his personal architect for the grandiose edifices that would communicate the power of the church to the populace.

Bishop Pignatelli succeeded Bishop Pappacoda. Construction on churches continued, but Zimbalo held few of the later commissions. Pignatelli elevated the younger sculptor Giuseppe Cino to chief architect. Cino added the second story to the Convent of the Celestini, begun by Zimbalo.[147]

---

[146] The cadre of artists included Francesco Antonio Zimbalo (Giuseppe Zimbalo's uncle), Mauro Manieri, Gabriele Riccardi, and Giuseppe Cino.

[147] A notable church rebuilt by Cino in 1687, is the Church of Saint Chiara. To look out upon the beautiful Saint Chiara in style the visitor can stay at the memorable four-star Hotel Santa Chiara. www.santachiaralecce.it. CTH rarely includes restaurant recommendations as cruise travelers rarely have time for on-shore dining. However, if at all possible the local cuisine should be enjoyed at Setefi or Trattoria di Nonna Teti, both down the street to the left as the visitor faces the Church of Saint Chiara.

Zimbalo died in 1710, at the age of ninety. No doubt he passed away a contented man. Times were not so fortunate for Cino. Bishop Pignatelli was evicted from Lecce in 1711. It seems that Pignatelli established himself as overlord and head of the law courts, as well as the ecclesiastical leader of Lecce. His dominance was notable for high taxes and questionable finances. Pignatelli's convents milled the town flour, sold at exorbitant rates, not subject to his taxes. Unable to excommunicate his way out of difficulty, he left town for ten years. Tempers cooled and Pignatelli returned and put Cino back to work.[148]

Over the centuries Lecce would see the return of epidemics and political upheaval. Throughout these difficult periods the yellow stone holding the life's work of Zimbalo and his artistic followers remained constant. When Italy became unified in 1860, the residents of Lecce enjoyed stability and prosperity. Wealthy citizens built villas outside of the city walls, thus enabling the late seventeenth and early eighteenth century Lecce to endure.

---

[148] Rosella Barletta, Lecce City of Art, Edizioni del Grifo, Lecce, 2002, p. 21.

Counting Zimbalo's Angels in Lecce

Zimbalo created a number of sculptural motifs used repeatedly in his commissions. Of these, the most frequently seen are his angels. The visitor to Lecce today could spend hours or days wandering through the town counting angels and never count all of them.

The following are places in Lecce to see Zimbalo's angels. Some of these buildings have their own stories.

Saint Oronzo Square, the Column, and the Church of Saint Irene: The main square, with the Roman amphitheater is the central gathering point in Lecce. It is in this square on Saturday evenings that residents of Lecce mingle with visitors, as entire families come to the square to enjoy the town. A work of Zimbalo dominates the square, although it would be difficult to see any angels.

The large column with the statue at the top is one of two columns that marked the end of the Appian Way, the road from Rome to Brindisi. In 1528, one of the columns fell and separated into drums. When the citizens of Brindisi were spared the plague of 1656 that ravaged much of Italy, they gave thanks to Bishop Oronzo, who took credit for the prayer that saved the whole boot of Italy. Brindisi made a gift of the column to Lecce. In 1681, Zimbalo was given the honor of creating the new ornate capital at the top of the column. The statue of Oronzo was added many years later.

When Bishop Oronzo saved Lecce from the plague with his prayer, he became Saint Oronzo, supplanting the prior patron saint of Lecce, Saint Irene. There is still a church dedicated to Saint Irene in Lecce, although it is more modest than most edifices. The church is just off the square to the left hand of Saint Oronzo, sitting atop his Zimbalo perch. The exterior and interior of the church hold works by other sculptors of the Baroque style, including Zimbalo's uncle Francesco.

Lecce Cathedral: The most impressive square in Lecce is the Piazza del Duomo.[149] The original cathedral was built in 1144, rebuilt in 1230. It took Giuseppe Zimbalo eleven years to create the look of the cathedral seen today. Zimbalo also designed the adjoining bell tower.[150] This is an ideal place to begin counting Zimbalo angels.

Church of Saint Teresa, Church of Saint Anna, and the Basilica of Saint Giovanni Battista: Exiting the Piazza del Duomo and turning left takes the visitor down a narrow street, Via Libertini. On this street there are three small churches, each embellished with Zimbalo angels. The church of Saint Teresa was an early commission and the Church of Saint Anna was built forty years later. The Basilica of Saint Giovanni Battista is sometimes called "del Rosario." Built in 1691, it was one of Zimbalo's last efforts. He was buried here in 1710. Directly across from the Basilica is the Hospital dello Spirito Santo. This is the hospital for the poor. Zimbalo is credited with the decorations inside the hospital chapel.

Basilica of Saint Croce (Church of the Holy Cross) and the Celestine's Convent: The most magnificent of Baroque churches in Lecce, and possibly the world, is the Basilica of Saint Croce. It represents the work of almost all the major sculptors in Lecce over the entire seventeenth century. Work begun by Zimbalo's uncle, before Giuseppe was born, continued until the adjoining convent was begun in 1695. Giuseppe Zimbalo is credited with the first floor of the convent. The second floor and finishing touches were the work of Cino.

More Churches, More Angels: As the visitor continues walking away from the main square of Lecce, past the Basilica of Saint Croce, there are still more Zimbalo angels to count. The Church of Saint Maria, also known as the Church of Saint Angelo, is unfinished. There are still Zimbalo touches evident. Possibly Zimbalo's last commission is the Church of Saint Frances of Assisi. The church and bell tower appear to be smaller versions of the Duomo and bell tower.

---

[149] At the entrance to the square there are statues, three on each side. Represented are Saint Oronzo, Saint Irene, and other church leaders.

[150] The weather vane has a little statue of Saint Oronzo.

Whether a visitor spends an evening in Lecce, or enters the town gate for an afternoon stroll through the narrow streets that open to the Roman era square, they will be watched over by Zimbalo's angels. The yellow stone has hardened over time to assure that the angels will be waiting for many more years in the future.

DUBROVNIK

WALK THE WALL OF DUBROVNIK

One of the most popular cruise destinations on the Adriatic Sea is the city of Dubrovnik. Dubrovnik, with its red-tiled roof houses, has been a familiar port of significance to seafarers since the middle ages. The city enjoyed continued prosperity, while maintaining its original charm, for more than a thousand years.

In 1979, Dubrovnik was added to the prestigious list of World Heritage Sites maintained by the United Nations. Although the city was a victim of the breakup of Yugoslavia in 1991, enduring seven months of shelling from Serbian forces, restoration of its original beauty has been completed. Today, as many as eight cruise ships moor outside its small harbor in a day, sending visitors to fill its streets to the level seen in its earliest history.

Walking the streets of Dubrovnik with a tour guide is a fascinating, if not overwhelming, experience. Fortunately, Dubrovnik has one of the best-preserved city walls of any medieval city in the world. A wonderful way to gain a perspective of the entire city is to leisurely walk the wall of Dubrovnik.

A Short History of the Long-Standing City

Dubrovnik began, as did so many settlements along the Adriatic, as an ancient Greek settlement. As Greek control of the seas gave way to the rise of Italian maritime commerce, the city became known by its Latin name of Ragusa. Ragusa was a convenient stopping place for sailors moving cargo to and from Constantinople, in the east, to Ravenna, in the west. Sitting between the two capitals of Byzantium, Ragusa was controlled and protected within the Byzantine Empire for centuries.

Venice rose to dominate eastern Mediterranean Sea trade by the thirteenth century. Ragusa became a Venetian satellite city, increasing its wealth from the cargo traffic. Former Venetian residents moved to Ragusa where they built numerous homes and businesses.

In 1358, Ragusa achieved independence from Venice. For protection as an independent republic, Ragusa looked eastward toward Hungary. For the next 450 years Ragusa remained independent, even though it succumbed for much of that time to control of the Ottoman Empire, to which it paid an annual tribute.

As an independent city, Ragusa could make its own rules. Its sailors roamed the seas as a neutral, that is, they sought only to be involved in trade, not the politics or land acquisition of other cities or nations. Despite trading from the Americas to India, merchants of Ragusa refused to be part of the slave trade as of 1418. The sailing flag with the word "Libertas," freedom, became the official city flag.

Dubrovnik survived a fire in 1296, which engulfed most of the city. It rebuilt its economy after an earthquake decimated its shipping industry in 1667. It outlived the political upheaval of 1806, when the city surrendered to Napoleon and it survived transition into and out of the Austrian-Hungarian Empire later in the nineteenth and early in the twentieth centuries. At the end of the First World War, in 1918, Ragusa left Austria-Hungary and became Dubrovnik again, within the Serbian-Croatian-Slovenian nation of Yugoslavia. It was not until the seven months of shelling in 1991, during the break-up of Yugoslavia that resulted in Serbia and Montenegro fighting to control Dubrovnik, that the city was in danger of losing the cultural vestiges of over two millennia of its heritage.

Abiding by strict principles of historic restoration, Dubrovnik was slowly repaired. Its status as a World Heritage Site was preserved.[151] As a result,

---

[151] http://whc.unesco.org/en/list/95. Last visited 11/16/2012. World Heritage Sites can lose the designation if the features of the site that contributed to the listing are substantially impaired. Listed sites will become endangered, subject to periodic review, until there is a suitable remedy, or the site is removed from the World Heritage list. For example, the Adriatic coastal city of Budva, in Montenegro, a contemporary of Dubrovnik, smaller, but just as charming, was threatened with delisting by the WHC as the city was to be engulfed by the construction of a new resort.

Dubrovnik endures as a prime cruise port city. For many years to come, Dubrovnik will beckon travelers to walk the wall.

Walk the Wall

The old city of Dubrovnik is completely enclosed by a defensive wall. One trip around the wall is 1.24 miles. Just inside the secondary city gate, near the Dominican Monastery, there is a broad stairway to the wall. The climb is brief and the rewards are great.

A walk along the wall provides a vantage point 80 feet above the city streets. There is plenty of room to move about, even when there are tour groups passing by. On the landward side the wall has floor space of almost 20 feet and on the seaward side about half as much. Occasionally, small round guardhouses are built into the wall.

The wall was originally built in the tenth century, but it has been strengthened several times in the last thousand years. Modifications were made in the thirteenth century and more modern improvements, using the best advancements in architectural technology of the time, were added in the late fifteenth to the mid-sixteenth century. Any damage caused by the earthquake in the seventeenth century or the twentieth century war have long been repaired.

The walk around the wall of Dubrovnik starts above the Dominican Monastery and moves eastward toward the fort and the old port. The first panoramic look at the city provides a sense of how densely packed was the population of about 20,000 people. Most buildings housed multiple families. The preferred apartments were those up the stairs, where there was light and better ventilation. The clay tile roofs vary in age and color from brown to red. It easy to see how the fire of 1296 could move quickly through the town of wooden houses. The broad pattern of streets of stone and brick structures dates from that time.

The Dominican Monastery was built in 1315. It is one of the larger buildings in the city. The monastery is a multistory, four-sided building, with an inner courtyard. The monastery was built to run along the inside of the wall, but due to the size of the complex, and the desire to keep the courtyard of the cloister square, the outer wall of the city needed to be adjusted to take an outward jog. The monastery now houses a museum that includes multiple works by Titian.

Moving eastward along the wall, the next point of note is at the Ploče Gate. This gate led to the Revelin Fort and the storage houses. The fort is the most recent and strongest of the city fortifications. Built in 1538, it provided safe haven for art treasures during turbulent times. It was in some of the houses near the port that visitors were kept in quarantine for a month as a precaution, to keep plague-stricken arrivals apart from the city population. If the visitors survived their illness, or any illness they contracted while in quarantine, they could be admitted to the city.

The wall curves along the contours of the port and, looking inside the city, along the walls of the monastery. The wall then runs parallel to the dock and over an archway that opens from the city to the pier. Inside the city, the building closest to the wall is the Sponza Palace. The building was begun in the fourteenth century to house the mint. Enlarged in the early sixteenth century, the palace served as the customs house. It now contains the archives.

The wall continues at a right angle toward the sea and then runs along the outside of the largest complex in the city. This is the governing Rector's Palace. Onofrio della Cava, who is responsible for several notable city landmarks, designed it in 1435. The Dubrovnik government offices have been replaced by the Cultural Historical Museum. Just beyond the palace is the seventeenth century Baroque style Church of Saint Blaise, the patron saint of the city.

As the wall continues straight across the harbor to the Fort of Saint John, there is a panoramic view of the inner harbor. This fort now houses the Maritime Museum. Below the wall is a small outcropping of rocks from which people still come to fish and to swim.

The lovely little island with dense vegetation, seen just across the water from the city wall, is Lokrum. It is now a nature preserve of exotic plants. The Benedictine monks first built an abbey on the island in 1023. The earthquake of 1667 left the abbey in ruins. The present-day natural history museum is housed in the former palace built by Austrian Archduke Maximilian in 1859.

The wall is narrower as it runs along the seaward side of the city. Looking inward there is an old section of town with many churches and random streets, unlike the near perfectly parallel streets running across the north side of the

city. There are places along the wall where the walkway opens to a plaza. These are good places for a group photo.

At the eastern most point of the city is the Bokar Fort. It is a small structure guarding a shallow bay. Today the tower of the fort overlooks the ferry terminal. The wall juts out at this point on a short peninsula, allowing a good view of the entrance to the main city gate.

The main entrance to Dubrovnik is at the Pile Gate. The stone bridge built in 1537, to cross the moat, now crosses over a garden. There was a drawbridge to secure the gate. Above the gate is a statue of the patron saint of Dubrovnik, Saint Blaise. There are three large openings in the curved section of the wall that surrounds the gate. Inside the gate there is a section of the wall to allow viewing from a safe height those who have just stepped inside the city.

The city was heavily fortified on the landward side for good reason. From the twelfth to the twentieth century, successive armies of Normans, Venetians,

Bosnians and French coveted control of Dubrovnik. Solid opposition would meet armies storming the gates.[152]

Just inside the Pile Gate is a plaza, which has in its center the Big Fountain of Onofrio. This large, round, enclosed, dome-topped fountain was the work of Onofrio della Cava, built between 1438 and 1444. There was originally an upper story to the fountain, which was damaged in the earthquake of 1667, to be left instead with the dome on the top of the first level. Della Cava was the architect of the city's water supply system. Water pipes can be seen across the plaza from the fountain. To the left of the gate, against the wall of the Church of Saint Saviour, there is a drainage spout with a whimsical face.

From the vantage point on the wall above the Pile Gate, there is a clear view into the main street of Dubrovnik, the Stradun. The street dates from the twelfth century, when marshland was filled to create a unified city area. The street was paved in 1468. The stone houses along the Stradun were mostly constructed after the earthquake of 1667. At the opposite end of the Stradun is the bell tower. The bells are the work of Croatian master bell-maker Ivan Rabljanin.[153] The bell he forged in 1506, still hangs in the tower.

Just past the Pile Gate is the Franciscan Monastery. Begun in the early part of the fourteenth century, the monastery was completed over the course of one hundred years. The famous pharmacy of Dubrovnik, in use from 1317, was in this building. Today the monastery houses the Franciscan Museum.

The fourth and last defensive tower along the wall is the Minčeta Tower. It was built between 1461 and 1464. The thick-walled, circular tower was built to resist land-based threats from the Ottoman Turks. It has become the symbol of Dubrovnik's invincibility. This tower provides the highest point along the

---

[152] The wall of Dubrovnik rebuffed sieges in 1185, when attacked by the Normans; 1205, when Dandolo, the doge of Venice sacked neighboring Zadar on his way to the fourth crusade, see, The Traveling Horses of Saint Marks, this itinerary; 1451, when attacked by the Bosnian lord Herzeg Stjepan Vukčić Kosača; 1806, by Napoleon; and 1991-1992, during the Croatian War of Independence.

[153] In Italian his name is Johannes Baptista de la Tolle (1470-1540). He was highly regarded as a maker of cannons, with clients in Italy and Spain.

wall. Visitors can climb the stairs to the upper ramparts for an even further view of the surrounding area.

The walk on the wall concludes with a short walk to the starting point. There are four curved vantage point along the wall, which face out to the modern city. Looking inward there are neatly parallel streets running perpendicular to the wall. These streets were laid out after the devastating fire in the thirteenth century.

Just before reaching the starting point, there are three close and short streets perpendicular to the wall, which comprises the Jewish section of Dubrovnik. These streets continue to the Stradun, where there is a synagogue, now also a museum.

It would be easy to spend a few days in Dubrovnik, exploring the streets, examining the museums, lounging in the cafes and strolling along the harbor. When time is short, or when the abundance of cultural attractions is overwhelming, step above the city. Walk the wall of Dubrovnik.

DUBROVNIK
WHERE JEWISH DOCTORS MADE HOUSE CALLS

Dubrovnik is a gem of a walled city on the coast of Croatia. For over a thousand years it was a prosperous trading hub – a stopping point from Venice to numerous ports in the Mediterranean Sea. It remains one of the best-preserved walled cities in the world. As such, Dubrovnik is a popular cruise destination. What is not immediately evident among the well-preserved walls, splendid churches, three monasteries, and four forts is a reason for the success of the city. The credit for part of the visible legacy is owed to the Jewish doctors of Dubrovnik.

The allure of the Jewish doctor is based upon facts that go back 800 years. In Dubrovnik, Jewish doctors expelled from Venice in the thirteenth century were joined by Jewish doctors expelled from Spain in the inquisition of 1492. These doctors made house calls, established a health care system, and built a public health awareness that kept Dubrovnik productive when their source cities and neighbors were decimated by plague.

This is the story of the Jewish doctors of Dubrovnik, the controversies they overcame to build medical systems in the medieval city, and the controversies that persist.

Jewish Doctors Arrive in Dubrovnik

Dubrovnik has always been an international city and its ecumenical population has reflected the extent of its popularity as an open haven. Dominican and Franciscan monasteries dominate key points in the city wall. The presence of a Jewish population dates to the thirteenth century. The first confirmed residence of a doctor in Dubrovnik from Venice is in 1326, when he was offered a job by the city government. By the end of the fourteenth century there were several doctors, in a community that afforded continuity of medical professionals over the generations.

In the thirteenth century, Venice ruled the Adriatic Sea and dominated trade at the ports including Dubrovnik. Jews were tolerated in Venice, but limited to certain professions, that of merchant, teacher, or doctor. For professionals desiring a free climate in which to live, the short sail from Venice to Dubrovnik was easily available. During the fifteenth century when Jews were subject to inquisitions, travel to Dubrovnik was an imperative.

The Dubrovnik city senate passed a law in 1407, making it legal for Jews to settle in Dubrovnik. In 1492, as the Inquisition filtered through Spain and Portugal, in which Jews could either be exiled or worse, boatloads of the Jewish upper classes, those able to afford sea travel, came to Dubrovnik. The host city prospered even as the source cities declined with the loss of their professional class residents.

The success of Jewish doctors and merchants in Dubrovnik was not without resentment. In 1515, the Dubrovnik senate expelled Jews. Trade and health in the city rapidly went into decline. By 1532, the city fathers retracted their expulsion and campaigned for their Jewish residents to return. The synagogue was built at this time. Jews were allowed to come within Dubrovnik and live within the city walls. In 1546, a section of the city was reserved to the Jews, known throughout time as the Ghetto.[154]

The Ghetto is made up of about four parallel streets, just inside the secondary city gate. At the inner edge of these streets, nearest the main boulevard, the Stradun, there is a synagogue, which exists today. It is reputed to be the second oldest synagogue in Europe, second to the old synagogue in Prague.[155]

---

[154] Ghetto is an Italian word, first used in Venice to describe the allowed residential section for Jews.

[155] The synagogue was damaged in the shelling of the Yugoslav War of Independence in 1991-1992. It reopened in 1997.

The number of Jewish residents increased such that by 1587, the ghetto was increased in size. Those who lived in the ghetto paid a special city tax for the privilege of living within the city walls. The ghetto had its own fountain for fresh water. There is also evidence that wealthy Jewish doctors and merchants lived within Dubrovnik, outside of the ghetto, wherever they pleased.

During the sixteenth century, the population of Dubrovnik was five percent Jewish and ninety-five percent Catholic. There were Franciscan, Jesuit, Benedictine, and Dominican monasteries and churches within Dubrovnik, all of which coexisted with each other and the Jews. There were Eastern Orthodox and Vatican Catholic churches as well. Sixteenth-century Dubrovnik was a cosmopolitan city.

Although Jews were a minority of the population, they were a majority of the physicians employed in the city. Since the majority population was Catholic, the city needed to obtain authorization from Rome for the Jewish doctors to treat Catholics. The health care was appreciated, but only to a point.

In times of crisis, the Catholic Archbishop would blame the Jews for whatever problems existed in the city. In 1502, an old woman was found dead in her home and five Jews were convicted and burned at the stake. In 1622, a young girl was found murdered and a member of the Jewish community was convicted. After he served three years in prison, the man was pardoned. Most of the Jewish families left Dubrovnik at this time and headed to Turkey. The Muslim sultans had a history of protecting the Jews.

In 1806, Napoleon entered Dubrovnik and conferred legal equality on the Jewish population for the first time. The population of Jewish families increased. Then, in 1815, the Austrian Empire rescinded all rights.

By the end of the nineteenth century, under Croatian law, equality of rights was reinstated. There were only about 300 people left to celebrate. When the Axis powers took control of Dubrovnik in 1943, there were about 750 Jews in the city.[156] Doctors and nurses worked covertly for the partisans.

---

[156] Encyclopedia Judaica, on line, last visited 12/28/12.

Making House Calls and Innovations in Public Health

The first settlers of Dubrovnik were Greeks. Later inhabitants came from Florence and Venice. All of these source cities had traditions of democratic government, civic institutions, and city planning. City statutes in Dubrovnik go back to 1272, when Roman codes were adapted as the official rule. There was an aristocratic ruling class, whose powers were limited by two city councils.

Within the democratic culture of Dubrovnik, innovation was fostered. Doctors were making house calls as a city institution as early as 1301. The first pharmacy was opened in 1317, which can still be seen today. The first almshouse, the homeless shelter, was opened in 1347. The doctors recognized that some diseases were communicable, so they instituted quarantine hospital facilities.

There are large structures, seen today on the docks of the old Dubrovnik harbor. The doctors knew that they needed to protect their city from unarmed, but deadly intruders, in the form of disease. Since the Dubrovnik economy was based upon world trade, the city could not quarantine itself, so the new arrivals were quarantined outside of the city walls in one of two or three holding hostels.

By a city decree of July 27, 1377, each incoming ship was held as a unit, throwing all classes of people together for thirty days. Later the time was extended to forty days of observation to allow the plague to develop among the passengers, if it existed. At the end of that time, those still healthy could enter the city. Where there was disease, the patients could be treated, remedied or buried, without infecting the city population.

The word quarantine comes from the Latin term of forty, the time the new arrivals were held apart from the population. The holding houses for incoming travelers seen on the docks today began use in 1590. The quarantine practice was effective, as the Black Death that ravaged the medieval world did not enter Dubrovnik.

The leaders of Dubrovnik understood that their city could flourish without the slavery and rampant poverty that kept other cities in the grip of a low producing medieval society. They abolished slavery in 1418, which was a profound step for a sea-trading economy of the time. Slavery did not exist in the city, nor would the city docks allow slave cargo to be part of their business. Dubrovnik shippers refused to be part of the slave trade. An orphanage was opened in 1432, to provide shelter for the young whose parents died at sea and those without family support in the city.

Fresh water came to the city dwellers through an innovative aqueduct system, built in 1436. There were twelve miles of pipe bringing water to the city fountains. The engineers designed the system so as not to lose a drop of water. The most impressive fountain is the one just inside the main gate, Onofrio's Fountain, built between 1438 and 1444. Missing from the top of the large fountain is the statue of a dragon that was lost in the earthquake of 1667. Onofrio della Cava also designed and built a smaller fountain under the bell tower, built from 1440 to 1442. Today, visitors to the city can drink freely from these fountains.

The Controversy that Remains

There are two items of note associated with the Dubrovnik synagogue. One is a thirteenth century Moorish carpet, brought to Dubrovnik from Spain during the Spanish Inquisition. The story surrounding the carpet holds that Queen Isabella of Spain gave the carpet to her Jewish doctor as a parting gift when he was forced to leave. The other item is a Torah, also brought to Dubrovnik from Spain at the time of the inquisition. It is this Torah that is at the center of the recent controversy.

Following the devastation of World War II, there were only thirty-one members of the Dubrovnik Jewish congregation by 1969. The congregation held services irregularly. Then, during the Yugoslav War of Independence, in 1991 through 1992, the congregation grew concerned for the safety of their important artifacts. They sent them to New York, to the Yeshiva University, on loan for an exhibition entitled "Treasures of Dubrovnik." Some of the objects in the museum loan dated to the initial post-inquisition property held by the congregation. Included was the fourteenth century Torah, brought to Dubrovnik at the close of the fifteenth century.

After the War of Independence, a court battle ensued between the Jewish congregation and national interests. Croatia desired that the items on loan to the Yeshiva University, including the Torah, return to the synagogue in Dubrovnik. The items were claimed as state property, to be returned to the museum, where they could be seen by thousands of tourists. Dr. Michael Papo, speaking on behalf of the Dubrovnik Jewish community living in New York, desired to keep the Torah in the control of his family. The new leaders of the Dubrovnik congregation, those living in Dubrovnik, claimed the items as the legacy of their congregation.

It was the position of Dr. Papo that he was a direct descendent of the Tolentino family, that originally brought the Torah from Spain to Dubrovnik. He sued to block the return of the Torah on the basis that neither the Croatian government, nor the remaining Jewish community of Dubrovnik, could guarantee safety of the religious scrolls. The government of Croatia countered in the lawsuit with the claim that Dr. Papo illegally removed the items from Dubrovnik when he took them to New York. The rancor heightened between the present-day members of the Dubrovnik congregation and Dr. Papo, over whether the "new" congregation leaders could rightly claim ancient congregation artifacts. "New" is a relative term in Dubrovnik, meaning several generations of residence there.

The Dubrovnik synagogue presents a unique circumstance in that the size of the congregation grew and receded over time, as members came from diverse continents and left during times of duress. Congregation members sought respite from anti-Semitism and left Dubrovnik when such sentiments erupted there. The artifacts in the synagogue, religious items and furnishings, represent a collection over time as diverse as the congregants who brought them there. The task of disaggregating history, and personal from group ownership of historic artifacts, was a difficult and emotional one.

The World Jewish Congress weighed in with an effort to resolve the dispute.[157] In the end, in 1998, the New York court ruled that the Torah, and the other items that had been part of the museum loan, be returned to Dubrovnik. By this time, the Dubrovnik synagogue was repaired after the damage in the shelling of 1991 and 1992. It was ready to receive the valuable items.

The collection of synagogue artifacts went back as government heritage property in the care of the Dubrovnik Jewish synagogue congregation. The synagogue may hold religious service, but most of its present-day visitors come to see the synagogue as a museum of Jewish history. The museum remains as part of the story of the lives of the Jewish doctors of Dubrovnik.

---

[157] Jim Simon, "Jewish community fights For Its Cultural Heritage," Seattle Times, May 26, 1996.

SPLIT

Retirement Home of the Roman Emperor Diocletian

At the end of the third century of the current era, the Roman emperor Diocletian voluntarily took early retirement. He was the only Roman emperor to have done so. He planned for his retirement by establishing a stable government to continue in his leisure years. Then he built a retirement dream home on the edge of the Adriatic Sea.

Diocletian was forward thinking in other areas besides retirement planning. He came to power from humble beginnings, by means that others would emulate for thousands of years. Although Christians were persecuted during the time of Diocletian, he became the last of the great pagan emperors, laying the groundwork for Christian emperors. He established a path for a grateful Constantine. Diocletian's alterations to Roman government enabled his retirement on his terms, breaking the custom of transfer of power only upon death or banishment. Enjoying active retirement was a novel concept in 305 CE.

For his retirement home, Diocletian chose a sleepy little fishing hamlet, with a commanding view of the Adriatic. Diocletian was able to spend the last six years of his life enjoying retirement, far from Rome and political life. He chose a place then known as Aspalathos, now known as the popular cruise destination port of Split.

This is the story of Diocletian, the last of the great pagan emperors of Rome. Among his successes was the ability to retire while still healthy and to enjoy the palace he built for that purpose. This is also the story of the retirement home of the Roman emperor in Split, Croatia, waiting today to be enjoyed by visitors, retired or not.

Diocletian, From Rise to Retirement

Diocletian was born on December 22, 244, in Solin, a small town in present-day Croatia, then under the empire of Rome. He was born to a family without political connections. It was a free family of low status. Diocletian, then simply called Diocles, began life as a farmhand. Of the few options for advancement open to Diocletian, he chose the military. It was a wise choice.

Three factors contributed to the rise of Diocletian from modest solider to emperor by the time he was forty. First, Rome was constantly at war. A soldier who could survive could also gain experience with which to rise in the ranks of the army. Diocletian rose to become a cavalry commander. Second, Roman emperors stood in battle at the front of their troops. Emperor mortality was a natural consequence of war. The Roman emperor Carus was killed while on a military campaign in Persia, followed shortly thereafter by his son Numerianus. Third, frequent emperor turnover caused leadership vacuums and political instability in Rome. There was great opportunity for a capable and ambitious military leader of suitable rank to become emperor, even without family connections. Diocletian was such a man.

There was some mystery involved in the rise of Diocletian to power and more than a little gossip. At the time of the death of Numerianus, Diocletian was the commander of the emperor's bodyguard. Numerianus died while being carried in his closed personal transport, accompanied by his bodyguard. Someone smelled a foul odor emanating from the emperor's transport. It was opened to disclose a long dead Numerianus. The cause of death was not readily apparent. Diocletian and the bodyguards seemed surprised at the discovery.

Upon the death of Numerianus, the senior military officer, a man named Aper, the boar in Latin, took the helm. He displayed leadership ambitions and some ability. Aper quickly instituted an investigation into the circumstances of the death of the recently crowned emperor.

Diocletian had long been an ambitious man. Years before the death of Numerianus, he had sought insight to his path to greatness from an old druidess fortuneteller. For a fee, she told young Diocles that he would become emperor of Rome once he slayed his boar. For years Diocles mastered the art of war and internal politics as he sought his boar. Diocletian took Aper, the boar, to be the means to greatness that had been foretold.

As Aper assembled the military officers to begin the inquiry into the death of Numerianus, Diocletian seized his opportunity. Diocletian drew his sword and fell upon Aper mortally wounding him. As he fell onto the flailing man, Diocletian called out to the stunned assemblage, "Here is the murderer of Numerianus." As a consequence of the confusion and lack of leadership, and in view of the quick action of Diocletian, the Roman army officers promptly deferred to his leadership. The forty-year-old Diocles became Emperor Gaius Aurelius Valerius Diocletianus.[158]

The abrupt rise to power of Diocletian was not completely unquestioned. Numerianus had a brother, Carinus, who sought the title of emperor of Rome, based upon lineage. Diocletian challenged Carinus in a battle, rather like a duel only with many officers seeking to show their loyalty all engulfed in a melee. Diocletian emerged the victor. His power was firmly established.

Diocletian came to power in a perilous time for a Roman emperor. The Roman Empire's success in conquering territory was also its liability. Germanic tribes to the north of Rome threatened the northern boundary areas. To the east, the Persian Empire threatened Roman conquests. Diocletian's time in the military proved to be an advantageous education for the new emperor. He knew he needed a unified and loyal army to retain power.

Diocletian was also quick to recognize that having a strong unified military depended upon financial and political support from a unified Roman senate. The senators had never liked being dictated to by emperors who gained their position by heredity rather than by vote of the senate. Diocletian embraced ascendance to emperor by vote. Being magnanimous was easier for Diocletian once he controlled the military and pronounced opportunity as a future concept.

---

[158] Wayne Dynes, Palaces of Europe, Hamlyn Publishing Group, Ltd., London, 1968, p. 36.

The hallmark of Diocletian's reign, which enabled him to retire in style while he still had his health, was the institution of sweeping changes to the structure of leadership. Diocletian broke the empire into governing regions. A co-emperor and two vice emperors were each given responsibility for a region. In 285 CE, Diocletian appointed fellow army officer Maximian Augustus the senior co-emperor. Eight years later, two junior emperors were appointed. This tetrarchy made the unwieldy manageable. Roman Empire politics became stable for the first time in decades.[159] The senate could vote their consent to confirm the emperor's actions.

On the military front, Diocletian amassed a series of victories. Each victory secured a border region. Egyptians and Persians were defeated in battles, which were followed by lasting peace in those areas. The military was enlarged with an organizational structure that pleased the numerous loyal officers created by the new system.

Diocletian separated the military regime from the civil structure of his government. He created a massive bureaucracy that only added to his power. The civil government was lumbering and decentralized from Rome, but stable and loyal to its leader.

Diocletian set up regional administrative offices in diverse areas of the realm. The empire had governing offices to administer its laws, and to efficiently collect its taxes, in far flung areas, such as in Turkey and close to the emperor's birthplace in present-day Croatia. In so doing, Diocletian kept power decentralized from Rome, diminishing the effect of the senate, and ensuring his control of the empire. Diocletian never felt comfortable in Rome. For several years his governing palace was in Antioch, Syria.

Debt amassed by the empire in its several wars, runaway inflation in its markets, and unemployment were all problems faced by the now peaceful empire. In these matters, Diocletian sought to involve the senate. Failing to obtain help from their leadership, he was not shy about asserting some dominance as the

---

[159] There is a victory arch dedicated to the tetrarchy in Tunisia. There are remnants of forts built by Diocletian in Budapest, Hungary, in Bulgaria, and in Serbia, giving some idea of the range of the empire.

highest ranking of the emperors. Diocletian established price controls in the markets. He issued a decree that sons would follow into the professions of their fathers and learn their trade. The government took an active role in trade. Taxes were increased, but spread more equitably among the nobles.

To reinforce his authority, Diocletian turned to the people. He took grand steps to move from mortal emperor to deity in the eyes of the populace. It was a bold move for someone in charge of an empire that had seen god-like emperors, such as Nero and Caligula, fall to human proportions and death just centuries before.

Diocletian surrounded his every public appearance in ceremony. People, even relatives, were made to bow low in his presence. He dropped the plain Roman toga for robes decorated with jewels. An elaborate tier system was developed for government officials and courtiers. Rather than such opulence causing his authority to be threatened, the new class of officials and socialites reinforced his authority. The benefits of bureaucracy were shared and appreciated by those included in the bounty.

Not everyone had reason to admire Diocletian. Late in his time as emperor, around 303 CE, the Diocletian tetrarchy began to persecute Christians.[160] The military was idle, with no military foe to engage, so they were instead put to use seeking out and destroying the farms of Christians. Orders were given to raze churches and seize church property. Christian clergy were ordered arrested and decapitated.

The appearance of anti-Christian edicts, which came late in Diocletian's time as emperor, was odd, even for him. From 303 to 305, when the edicts began, Diocletian was on a military campaign north of the Danube. He caught a cold and was very ill. Historians question whether the edicts were of Diocletian's choosing or were the work of the tetrarchy.

The Romans regarded the Christians of this time as more of a cult than a threat to the empire. Diocletian had created a layered economic class of nobles

---

[160] Some historians assert that the persecution was not at Diocletian's urging, but was the work of Co-emperor Galerius, who was more superstitious. Emperor Constantine, the first Christian emperor, places the blame on Galerius, not Diocletian.

in which Christians did not participate. The only other basis for the bloody "Diocletianic Persecution" of Christians would have been their assertion of a kingdom of god, in competition with the self-asserted deity status of the emperor. Constantine later blamed one of the co-emperors for the anti-Christian actions.

The persecution lasted until the time of Diocletian's death in 311 CE. It had the ironic effect of drawing support for the Christians from believers and non-believer sympathizers. The needless bloodshed is often credited with impressing later Emperor Constantine to become Christian and to return all seized property.

At the height of his gilded life, Diocletian chose to retire. He had reigned as emperor, or senior emperor, for twenty-one years. His time in power was marked by gains in peace and economic prosperity, shared with a new class of nobles. No one begrudged him personal compensation for his efforts. He had a daughter, but no sons to vie to succeed him, or to protect his life in later years. In a lifetime of wise decisions, Diocletian made the decision to promote vice-emperors to more senior positions and to retire from the stage while his ratings were still high.

On May 1, 305 CE, Diocletian announced his retirement. He was sixty-one. His health was not the best. He modestly indicated that it was time to enjoy his hobby of gardening, a holdover, no doubt, from his youth as a farmer. He would die in his retirement home five years later, of natural causes.

Diocletian left behind a stable Rome, even though it was an empire with a bloated bureaucracy. The government structure would last for a century. He went into retirement in a time in which there was peace in the empire so that he could enjoy his private life. Most important, he left behind a ruling structure that gave no incentive to anyone to gain by shortening his life. He could live in Split without having to constantly look over his shoulder. Diocletian had carefully planned his retirement. It was a new era in leadership transition.

Diocletian's Palace in Split

Just before retirement, Diocletian became ill while traveling north of the Danube. The cold climate did not agree with him. He regained his health only when he came to Split, his lovely palace on the Adriatic Sea. He lived quietly there until his death in 311 CE.

The palace built by Diocletian exists today. It is often difficult to discern the original palace buildings from the city of Split that has grown within it and just outside the original palace walls. The layered cityscape has been a continuous port city for over 1,700 years.

The original palace was built up against the Adriatic coast. At the time of Diocletian it was the end of the road from his nearby hometown of Solin. The outer palace walls form a rectangle. The three sides not on the sea are thicker than those on the water for defensive purposes.

The entire arrangement has the look of a fort. Despite the palace being occupied by a retired-ruler in peacetime, Diocletian had spent too many years in the military not to value his security. The sea facing wall has a 500-foot long galley from which he could walk along the wall, high above the water, and secure from any errant attack. The palace grounds are entered through a large imposing gate, which opens to an inner courtyard and a second gate. Once inside, the palace area is divided into four rectangles by intersecting streets, much like the Roman forts of the time.

There are two square buildings within the palace walls, each occupying a quarter of the streetscape. The buildings each contain a square inner courtyard. These buildings were used for residences of the emperor and his entourage. Diocletian's architects employed grand use of columns, an elegant backdrop to the emperor's processions. The deeply colored columns were repurposed to this palace, having been imported from ancient structures in Egypt. Diocletian had retired from office, but he had not lost his sense of personal majesty.

The buildings in the residential area would have included baths, a library, and dining areas. The walls were covered with mosaics. Unfortunately, little of the original opulence has survived.

The most notable building within the palace complex is the octagon mausoleum of Diocletian. He directed its construction with care. The eight-sided block and brick structure corresponds to the number eight in late Roman superstition, associated with immortality. The interior is domed with niches in the sidewalls. There is a double row of columns going up the outer walls. The sarcophagus of Diocletian would have rested in the center of the room.

The sarcophagus of Diocletian was removed from the mausoleum in the ninth century or earlier, when the building was turned into a church. It is ironic that Christians were persecuted during the late Diocletian period and his mausoleum served as a model for the construction of churches. The mausoleum has been preserved through medieval times to the present, likely because it was repurposed as a church. The bell tower next to the building was added after its conversion from mausoleum to church.

Another building of note is the temple of Jupiter, Diocletian's patron god. The temple is built of stone, making it look older than any of the other structures. Inside, the temple is small and dark, but the vaulted interior remains intact from the time of its construction.

After the death of Diocletian, the empire claimed ownership of the palace. Since it was far from Rome, the palace made an ideal location to house prisoners and exiles. The army also used it to house seamstresses who made army uniforms. [161]

In 615, barbarian hordes came through the area and sacked Diocletian's childhood hometown. The displaced townspeople came down the road to the palace, where they built refuges within the old palace walls. The elegant palace buildings were altered to accommodate a larger population with a more mundane purpose. Eventually, the new inhabitants transformed the mausoleum into a church. Stones and bricks from older buildings were used to build shops and stalls for evolving village life.

Situated on the water, the growing town of Split became an important trade center in the coming centuries. Evidence of Venetian influence can be seen in Venetian Gothic and later Renaissance era windows, built into the original

---

[161] Dynes, p. 46.

Diocletian structures. In 1764, tourists arrived in Split, including an architect from Scotland, who was so enthralled with the still visible remnants of the palace that he recorded the architectural details. Publication of those drawings increased enthusiasm for travel to Split. Tourism joined trade as economic boosters for the city.

Enjoying Split Today

The original palace was built right to the edge of the water, such that the tides immersed lower walls. Today there is a lovely arcade on the seaside of the palace and a dock for luxury vessels. It is from this side that the length and great size of the original palace can be appreciated. Without losing its place in history, Split has become a more beautiful destination over time.

After the Second World War, tourism supplanted trade, as the medieval town became a major tourist destination. The Yugoslav government and now the Croatian government have carefully maintained Split, restoring those places where restoration can be accomplished without compromising the historic context.

The vaulted basement galley will enthrall the traveler. For years these areas served as refuse pits, until government intervention resulted in clean up and restoration. They exist today, as they would have during the residency of Diocletian, filled at that time with wine and supplies for the palace coming in from the sea.

The dense, marginal living stalls that began in the seventh century, and persisted until the government intervened in the twentieth century, have been removed. Bright shops and restaurants have taken their place. Today walking the town streets in Split, along the original palace grounds, is enjoyed by locals as well as by tourists.

Split is easily recognizable today by its original palace walls, seen by cruise guests as their ships reach the harbor. The interior is a mix of successive Roman, Venetian, and Renaissance touches. It is easy to see how an emperor chose Split as a location for his retirement home.

RAVENNA / ANCONA

Galla Placidia: Mother of the Western World

In the fifth century of the current era, bands of barbarians roamed Europe. The Christian world was in disarray, as the divinity of Christ was debated. Years of war and plague left Rome diminished. The period of antiquity in human existence was on the verge of entering the dark ages.

In the midst of continuing collisions of marauders and civilized folk, court intrigue, and the politics of an evolving church, one young woman became a force of stability. She was beautiful, bright, and wellborn. She was also a savvy diplomat. In her spare time she was a patron of the arts and a mother devoted to her children.

This is the story of Galla Placidia, mother of the western world. As Galla took control of all in her domain, she became Augusta, a female emperor of Rome and Ravenna. Before there was a Vatican in Rome, Galla made Ravenna the center of western Christendom. She endowed churches in Ravenna and embellished them with art in mosaics that endure today. A trip to Ravenna still reveals the Galla Placidia legacy of beauty.

Not to Be a Nun

At the dawn of the fifth century the Christian world spread from Rome to Constantinople, and to cities in northern Africa, such as Alexandria. Bishops of cities were autonomous religious leaders as the Catholic Church was still evolving into a political unit. It was in this environment that the Christian cleric Jerome traveled through Christian cities espousing a role for women in the new order.

Jerome preached that a woman, who could not choose her husband, could choose to remain a virgin. As a virgin she could give her life to Christ. Not only was being a virgin in Christ an attractive option for a high-born woman facing an unattractive wedding partner, the option meant that an emperor could chose virginity for his sisters and avoid potentially troublesome brothers-in-law. Unbetrothed daughters reaching maturity could be kept chaste in the church until needed for a political wedding. Widows could join with Christ instead of a sinful remarriage. Since women had no options outside of the home, Jerome's solution quickly became popular.[162]

One highborn woman resisted Jerome's option at all opportunities. Galla Placidia was as highly pedigreed as a woman could be at the time. She was born in 390, in Constantinople. Her mother, also named Galla, known for her beauty, was the granddaughter of a Roman emperor. Her father, Theodosius I, was a royal, Roman, and Christian. In 380, he outlawed paganism and Arian Christianity in Rome,[163] making Catholic Christianity the state religion. His uncle was married to the granddaughter of Constantine, and was the first Christian emperor of Rome.

In 394, Galla's mother died in childbirth. Her father, Emperor Theodosius I, granted Galla the title of "Most Noble Girl," which entitled her to an independent household, with independent income. This was fortunate as Galla was to witness the death of her father in 395.

As an infant, Galla had been promised in marriage by her parents to the son of her cousin Serena and her husband, the Roman general, Stilicho. Serena and Stilicho lived in Rome. So in 400, Galla again avoided becoming a bride of Christ as she went off to live in Rome.

---

[162] Jerome's model for the pious Christian woman was Helen, the mother of Constantine. In 320, Helen was an old woman who made a pilgrimage from Constantinople through Syria and Palestine to Egypt. Jerome schooled his brides of Christ in the psalms of the Bible, the Old Testament, and Virgil. Hagith Sivan, Galla Placidia: The Last Roman Empress, Oxford University Press, Oxford, 2011, pp. 33-34.

[163] Arian Christians did not accept the divinity of Christ.

Serena headed her household with elegance. She was an intelligent woman, regarded by historians to be the social leader of Rome. Galla was schooled in the womanly arts of embroidery. She was also taught to read and write. Stilicho had a stellar reputation as a general. He ruled almost in tandem with the emperor of Rome. In the home of her adopted siblings, Galla was exposed to the best of social and political statesmanship.

Before she turned twenty, Galla's world again fell apart. The barbarian Visigoths had amassed in the plains and hills north of Italy, under their king Alaric. Ironically, Alaric was a graduate of an imperial military school begun by Galla's father. He was a protégée of Stilicho, who fostered development of his military skills. By 408, Alaric had become the nemesis of his former mentor, Stilicho. Rome was starving under the siege of Alaric.[164]

Rome's best leader in a defense against Alaric was Stilicho. Unfortunately, Alaric had eluded capture by Stilicho in two prior skirmishes. Stilicho's detractors used the incidents to discredit him. In 408, the great general's palace critics succeeded in plotting his murder. A trusted servant killed Stilicho while he was taking a bath.

In 409, devastated by the siege, leading women of Rome rose to suggest that life under Alaric would be better than the death of their children from starvation. Roman civil life and the leadership of the senate were in disarray. As the first among leading woman of Rome, Serena was accused by the senate of conspiring with Alaric to open the gates of Rome. She was executed. Galla was thought to have aided in the death of her guardian by agreeing with the senate or, at least, by not rising to prevent the death sentence. At age nineteen, Galla had title, but she had not yet acquired the power to effectuate justice. Once again she was alone.[165]

Alaric entered Rome in 410. The Visigoth pillage of Rome was short lived, as their army was hungry too. They took all the gold and valuables they could carry and speed off north and to the west, in search of food. With them was

---

[164] Alaric was quite a character, who is deserving of his own story. Unfortunately, as a deconstructionist of civilization, he left no points of interest for a traveler to visit.

[165] The actual conspirator with Alaric in opening the gates of Rome was another noblewoman Proba. Sivan, p. 29.

Galla Placidia as a hostage. Since her half-brother Honorius was emperor in Ravenna, and her nephew Theodosius II was emperor in Constantinople, Galla had value in a future bargain for grain.

A Fifth Century Love Story

Alaric was no longer a young and strong leader as he roamed southern France for the next four years, with his motley army of Visigoths. As soldiers, not farmers, the hoard was incessantly ravaging farmlands in a constant search for food. When he became ill and died, his wife's brother, Athaulf, succeeded Alaric.

Athaulf was good looking, a strong leader, and known to have a great spirit. That may be interpreted as having a fun personality. As the new king of the Goths, he wanted a queen with a strong personality, beauty, and political connections. He needed to look no further than his captive of the prior four years, Galla Placidia.

Alaric had negotiated with Galla's sibling in Ravenna, Honorius, to return Galla in exchange for grain. Honorius sent his trusted friend and general, Constantus, to negotiate. Constantus made several trips to the headquarters of the Goths, but Alaric kept increasing the price. When Athaulf became king, there were further negotiations, but Constantus never sent the agreed-upon grain. Athaulf needed no further excuse. He was more interested in Galla as a life partner, than in her value as a negotiation tool.

In 414, Galla and Athaulf were married in a ceremony in Narbonne, France. Narbonne, a city in southern France, on the western edge of the Mediterranean, was the oldest Roman site in France. In choosing the site of the wedding, Athaulf made a statement about his new connection to the royals of Rome. His wedding attire included a purple robe, of the type worn by Roman generals. It was the type of robe that Constantus would have worn.

Athaulf's wedding gifts to Galla included fifty trays of gold, filled with precious stones. No doubt the gift was booty looted years earlier from Rome. As an additional gift, Athaulf promised his bride that he would not return to attack Rome. If Athaulf was motivated in marriage to spite Galla's brother in Ravenna for failed grain trade deals, the marriage ceremony, gifts, and Athaulf's outward regard for Galla gave the union an aura of true adoration.

Galla historians have long debated whether the bride went willingly into the marriage. She was twenty-four and beautiful. The groom was a few years older, battle-hardened, but still handsome. By comparison, Constantus, the emissary of Honorius, had not ignited a spark, nor had he shown himself dedicated to Galla's return to Ravenna.

Galla had four years to admire the leadership prowess of Athaulf prior to becoming his bride. Their marriage was short-lived; the politics of power being what it was at the time in southern France. Their son Theodosius III, died in infancy. With him died Athaulf's dream of a united Goth and Roman dynasty. As a token of that dream, Galla carried the remains of the infant in a silver coffin wherever she went over the next three decades, until she built a suitable mausoleum for his resting place.

As Galla built her political empire, she would call upon friendships for support made during her time with Athaulf. From what is known of Galla and Athaulf, it is most likely that theirs was a marriage based upon love and mutual respect. It was a marriage most women of the time could only conjure in their dreams, but then Galla Placidia was not like most women.

The marriage of Athaulf and Galla was not well received in Goth or Roman circles. It was not popular in France. The Goths resented Althaulf's emulation of Romans. Honorius was incensed by the marriage of his Catholic half-sister to the barbarian. Worse, Athaulf was part Arian, that branch of Christian loathed by Catholics and outlawed in Rome.

The Goths landed in Narbonne after being pushed out of Marseilles. Narbonne was not the most hospitable site for a Goth headquarters. A few years earlier, Alaric had stormed Narbonne, decapitated city leaders, and sent their heads to Ravenna. The newlyweds did not stay long in Narbonne. By 415, they were living in Barcelona.

Barcelona was a place of beauty and sadness for Galla. In Barcelona Galla was able to visit Centcelles, where the tomb of Constans, the son of Constantine the Great Christian Emperor of Constantinople, was adorned in mosaic tiles.[166] Galla had been able to visit the tomb of Constantina, the daughter of Constantine, when she was in Constantinople as a young child. That tomb was also decorated in mosaics, the beauty of which had a lasting impression on the young Galla.

It was in Barcelona that the infant, Theodosius III, died and was placed in his traveling silver coffin. A few weeks later, Athaulf was dead. He was the victim of a planned assassination, carried out by a trusted servant.

Athaulf's successor saw Galla as a liability. Far from returning her to Ravenna as Athaulf requested as he was dying, the new king forced Galla to walk in front of his horse for twelve miles as she was sent from the city. The act of cruelty so enraged the followers of Athaulf that the successor king had a very short reign. The new king promptly made a deal with Honorius, which allowed the Goths to remain peacefully on Roman land in southern France. In exchange for grain from Italy, Galla was returned to Rome.

Honorius was in his glory. In 416, he held celebrations in Rome to commemorate the revitalization of the city in the aftermath of Alaric's siege. Later that year he welcomed his sister back to civilization. In 417, Honorius forced Galla to marry Constantus. Although second marriages were frowned upon in Catholic Rome, and Jerome was still on the prowl for new brides of note for Christ, Honorius proclaimed that the first marriage to a non-Catholic was not to be recognized. This time he would offer Galla in marriage to an appropriate husband.

There is no doubt that Galla was not pleased to enter into her second marriage. Once again she had the option to become a bride of Christ and live a scholarly, monastic life. Instead, she kept her political options open

---

[166] Constans, the son of Constantine, died in 350. His burial in Centcelles in Tarragona, Spain, south of Barcelona is contested. Tarragona is the site of a large Roman city, at its height in the fourth century. The Mausoleum of Centcelles now sits in the middle of a vineyard. During the time that Galla was in the area there is no doubt that the mausoleum, faced in pink tiles, and with an immense cupola covered in elaborate mosaics, would have been there for her to see. Michelin, The Green Guide: Spain, 2001 edition, p. 366.

and acquiesced to the marriage. As a tribute to Athaulf, Galla invited her Goth in-laws to the wedding.[167]

Galla and Constantus had two children: Honoria, born in late 417, and Valentinian III, born in 419. Constantus was miserable in his marriage to this powerful woman. Galla was agreeable to a divorce in which she could keep her dowry. Honorius stepped in to resolve disharmony between the two people closest to him. In 421, Constantus was made Augustus, co-emperor to Honorius. Galla was then titled Augusta, which assured the rank of her son, Valentinian, as heir to the throne.

Honorius was delighted to have the power couple run affairs of state in Ravenna. He began life with a new bride, the younger sister of his first wife, who had died.[168] Constantus made more enemies than friends in his new role. Within the year he was dead. He was either the victim of another bout of palace intrigue or succumbed to a respiratory disease. Whichever version is more accurate; there is no doubt that he was much diminished in his post-military days.

After the death of Constantus, Honorius and Galla became very close. The populace misinterpreted their affection for each other. Their detractors in the ruling inner circle spread rumors that they were unnaturally close siblings. When in 423 Honorius died, Galla lost her title as Augusta. She quickly fled from Ravenna to Rome, and then to Constantinople with her children. Most of the trip was by ship through stormy seas.

Conquering Popes, Generals, and Huns

Honorius had established Ravenna as his capital of the Christian empire in 402. Ravenna was better fortified than Rome and had a better navy.[169] It was in Ravenna that Galla ruled as Augusta from 417 to 423, when Honorius

---

[167] Sivan, p. 69.
[168] The two sisters were the daughters of Serena and Stilicho. Sivan, p. 61.
[169] In the fifth century Ravenna had a lagoon, like Venice, to connect it to the sea. Bernard Wall, Italian Life and Landscape, Paul Elek, London, 1951, p. 96.

died. Exiled by the senate, she would later return in glory to lead the western Christian world in political, religious, and peacekeeping matters.

In the years 419 and 420, a schism erupted in Rome between two contenders for leadership of the Catholic Church, Eulalius and Boniface. They appealed to Honorius for a decision and he turned the matter over to Galla. Galla was well suited to the task. It was she who is credited with first use of the title "pope" to refer to the father of all bishops.

Galla ordered the two contenders to leave Rome, while the matter was resolved. Eulalius defied the order by sneaking back into the city to conduct Easter mass. Galla then appointed Boniface pope. Honorius confirmed the decision, giving Galla the aura of supreme authority.

Keenly aware of the status of women in the church, Galla did not flaunt her power. When she wished to convene a synod at Spoleto to discuss church matters, she did so under the leadership of a bishop whom she enlisted for the purpose. Through Bishop Paulinus, Galla made certain to include bishops from across Italy and northern Africa. Broader participation of bishops diluted the impact of the warring factions of bishops in Rome. In effect, Galla unified the Catholic Church.

In all church matters, Galla sought and received letters of support from Constantus and Honorius confirming her decisions. This enabled Galla to maintain her appearance of piety. Inside the Galla and Constantus household there was an irreparable rift over one issue. There was no accord on the status of wizards.

As a field general, Constantus often employed wizards, who used their magic to guarantee victory in battle. Galla insisted that soldiers prevailed given their faith in Christ. She felt that mortals should only rely on faith and not mythical gods. She ordered the destruction of pagan statues throughout Italy and Sicily. In doing so, Galla was emulating the actions of her guardian, Serena, who years earlier led the effort to rid Rome of false gods.

When Galla took the next step to outlaw wizardry and order the execution of wizards, Constantus was enraged. He sought to assert his head-of-household status. Galla responded that Constantus could separate from the household.

He relented, angry, but compliant. His place as an inept husband was preferable to loss of all status.

Shortly after the argument over wizardry, Constantus was dead. His surviving generals never forgave Galla for banning a military tradition and for having more power than they in civic affairs. These generals may have played a role in the death of Constantus, but they would deal with Galla in another manner. Rumors were spread that Galla and Honorius had an unnatural relationship. When Honorius died, Galla lost her last male protector in Ravenna. Wisely, she left town. The generals seized all power in the city.

Once Galla and her children were safe in Constantinople, her nephew, Emperor Theodosius II, refused to recognize the usurping generals. He ordered the arrest of their leader, John. First John lost his hands, then his head. The body parts were sent back to the rebellious generals.

Theodosius proclaimed the six-year-old Valentinian III emperor of Italy. His capital would be Ravenna. Galla was restored to the title of Augusta, the regent ruler on behalf of her son. To make certain that his intentions were clearly understood; Theodosius ordered that gold coins be minted in 424, depicting Augusta Galla, imperial mother. So many of these coins were minted that many remain today in museum collections.

Galla understood that the population "associated legitimacy with ritual."[170] She made her return from exile a grand spectacle with a parade through Rome in honor of the mother and son. Galla used the occasion to proclaim a new law that the head bishop of Rome would henceforth be the pope of the Catholic Church.

Always the astute realist, Galla made peace with the Roman generals. She promoted disloyal generals to positions with wonderful titles and assignments in faraway places. Possible conspirators were far apart and easily appeased.

With Galla in charge Rome was secure. Pagan armies were under control. Galla had long-lasting allies among the Goths. The new terror on the doorstep for Goths and Christians was Attila the Hun. Galla used part

---

[170] Sivan, p. 95.

of her considerable wealth to pay the pagans to wage their wars far from Christian cities.

Galla was glorious in her role as the chaste widow. She was a model mother. She said her prayers in conspicuous places like Santa Croce, the church of Helen, who was the mother of Constantine. Galla even paid homage to the senators, with whom she joined in supporting measures that kept the power of the generals in check.

In 437, Valintinian III reached his majority. As emperor he chose to marry Licinia Eudoci, the daughter of his cousin Theodosius II. In deference to the bride's family, the wedding took place in Constantinople. The venue was full of historic significance for Galla. No doubt, the bride was a secondary attraction to her still powerful mother-in-law.

Galla's daughter, Honoria, was the rebellious one in the family. She was unconcerned with how her actions reflected upon the royal family. The siblings were thrown into conflict when Honoria was seen cavorting with men of lower social status, an offense punishable by death. Valentinian's solution was to arrange a marriage between Honoria and a suitably boring senator.

Honoria reacted to the marriage plans by reaching out to Attila, who was camped outside the city walls of Rome. Honoria sent him coins as a bribe to enlist his aide in helping her to escape. She enclosed a ring to prove her identity. Attila interpreted the gesture as a marriage proposal.[171]

The Huns drew their forces together at the gates, threatening the city. By engaging the Huns, his sister undid Valentinian's peaceful reign. Her imprisonment was imminent. For Galla, who had calmed the arguments of popes, generals, and Huns, her children posed the greater challenge.

In the end, Galla paid Attila to go home. Valentinian no doubt threatened Honoria with the appointment of Jerome as her guardian. Honoria dropped out of the public sight, but the damage to Valentinian's leadership was fixed. In 455, five years after Galla's death, an assassin brought an end to Valentinian's reign. Galla's dreams of a long dynasty founded by her grandfather died with him.

---

[171] The Huns were known to be brave, but not too bright.

Galla's Ravenna

Once Galla negotiated peace between her living children, she turned her attention to her first born. For thirty years, from 420, she carried the little silver coffin with the remains of Theodosius III, while she contemplated his suitable final resting place.

In 450, Galla imposed upon Pope Leo to perform a funeral service for the part Arian and barbarian child of Galla and Athaulf. The coffin was placed in the royal mausoleum in Rome, next to the tomb of Saint Peter.[172] This was to be a temporary placement while the mausoleum of Galla Placidia in Ravenna was completed.

The coffin of Theodosius III was removed from Rome. Galla did build a mausoleum in Ravenna. However, it is not known whether the little coffin was brought to Ravenna for permanent placement in the mausoleum that Galla built. It is certain that Galla Placidia is not entombed in the mausoleum that bears her name.

Galla Placidia died in 450, in Rome, at age sixty. Her burial place is unknown. Historians believe the likely place of her tomb would be in the Rotunda of St. Petronilla, adjoining the Basilica of Saint Peter, at the Vatican. It was there that family of Theodosius I were buried and it was there that Galla placed the tomb of Theodosius II, removed from Constantinople, shortly before her death.[173]

In her last decade of life Galla endowed several churches. She adorned them with mosaics such as those she had seen on the tombs of Constan and Constantia in Constantinople and Barcelona. Galla left her greatest legacy in Ravenna, where today there are more churches with fifth-century mosaics than anywhere else in the world.

---

[172] Next to Saint Peter is a vague reference to the burial place. Several places in Rome claim to have held the remains of Saint Peter. None of the present day caretakers of those places will admit to their sacred space also having held the remains of Theodosius III.

[173] Giuseppe Bovini, Ravenna Art and History, Longo Publisher, Ravenna, 1991, p. 12.

One of Galla's earliest commissions in Ravenna is the church of Santa Croce. It was built in 417, about the time of Galla's marriage to Constantus. The building is now in ruins. When standing, it was near the grounds of the mausoleum. A large Byzantine arch through which to enter the city, also built by Galla, was bombed during WWII.[174]

Some of the earliest mosaic commissions were in the church in Ravenna that Galla dedicated to Saint Lawrence. With this structure Galla displayed her appreciation for her safe arrival in Constantinople in 423, when the fleeing Galla and her two young children left Ravenna and Rome. During their flight the little family was caught in a storm at sea. Galla prayed to Saint Lawrence for their safety and the church was her token of gratitude. The church now stands as Saint Giovanni Evangelista (S. John the Evangelist). The mosaics stayed in place from the fifth to the sixteenth century. Today the remaining portraits of the family in exquisite mosaics are in a museum. The church walls are blank white plaster.

The best-preserved structure in Ravenna, with the fifth century mosaics intact, is the Mausoleum of Galla Placidia. The building looks tiny as it sits on the grounds of the imposing Church of Saint Vitale, built in the sixth century.[175] The whole complex was placed on the World Heritage list in 1996.

The mausoleum was built in the Greek style of four equal wings, forming a cross. At the center of the cross is a dome, encased on the exterior by a square tower. The dome sits on eight pillars. The building is red brick with an arcade of doorless, windowless, "blind" arches. The entire building has sunk into the ground about four feet, making it look even smaller. In 1908, Italian King Victor Emanuel III had the fourteen small windows filled with slabs of golden alabaster. The windows give the dark interior a golden glow on sunny days.

---

[174] The German Wehrmacht had their headquarters in Ravenna, causing it to become a substantial target during the war. Many of the historic buildings were repaired, while others are still in ruins. Wall, p. 96.

[175] Saint Vitale was begun in 525 and consecrated as a church in 548, almost 100 years after the death of Galla Placidia. The mosaics are lavish and extensive. The mosaics are clearly influenced by those in the tiny mausoleum.

The mausoleum of Galla Placidia has been used as a church. Whether it was originally built as a church or mausoleum is unknown. Three large sarcophagi in place today are not documented to have been in the structure prior to the fourteenth century.[176] The contents of the center sarcophagus, tucked in an arched niche, were burned beyond recognition in 1577, when two boys threw some lighted candles inside to see the contents. It was reputed to have held a seated person, holding a scepter. That a skull of a woman remained among the ashes set off rumors that it was Galla Placidia. Given that the sarcophagus was not adorned by any Christian symbols, it was most likely the tomb of a pagan person of wealth, set inside the mausoleum to complete the furnishings.

To one side of the mausoleum is a sarcophagus containing the remains of a young, or not very old, not very tall, male, who could be Valentinian III or Honorius.[177] The other sarcophagus holds a larger, older male, who could be Constantus, Galla's second husband. There is no evidence of a tiny silver coffin and the remains of Theodosius III, or even a tiny empty niche where the coffin would have been placed.

The beauty, quality, and preservation of the mosaics inside the mausoleum are astonishing. Saint Lawrence is an easily recognized figure. A smaller, well-defined figure, obviously a saint given the golden halo, holds a book. Some believe this is the figure of Christ holding the book of sins and merits of the people, a prevailing thought in the fifth century.

The decorative mosaic work has been difficult for art historians to place. The ribbons, stars, flowers, and geometric shapes are unique. Since Honorius moved the capital of his kingdom from Milan to Ravenna, historians surmise that the stable of talented court artists also came to Ravenna from Milan. They would have included talent from the far reaches of the empire, whose work was melded into new styles. If so, these styles from the fifth century survive only in Ravenna.

---

[176] Bovini, p. 13.
[177] The identity of the inhabitants of the tombs is tour guide speculation, not science, but they conclude the story nicely. There is great speculation over the identity of the third occupant, the one with the scepter, and the location of Galla's remains.

There is no doubt that the Mausoleum of Galla Placidia was built of quality by a wealthy patron of the arts. It was built to last and to stand in or above the realm of the tombs of the great Emperor Constantine's children. Galla Placidia may not be entombed here, but the handiwork of the notable fifth century woman is present in the walls.

The Cathedral Baptistery in Ravenna was built in the time of Galla Placidia, although she is not often given credit for the commission. The building is red brick, like the mausoleum, and has "blind arches" in the upper level. The interior of the building is covered in breath-taking mosaics. The adjoining Archiepiscopal Museum holds the chapel erected by the Archbishop Peter II, fifty years after Galla's death. The single small room of mosaics is not to be missed. These too reflect the influence of Galla Placidia.

After the death of the Theodosius dynasty, Goths invaded Ravenna. For a while Arian Christians ruled it, before the time of Justinian and his return of Catholic rule. Several churches were built in the century following the death of Galla Placidia. Each became a showplace of mosaics, as though Galla were directing the work. Notable mosaics can be seen in the Basilica of Saint Apollinare Nuovo and, just out of town, the Basilica of Saint Apollinare in Classe.

Post Note: In 1371, Dante came to Ravenna, where he spent the final four years of his life. It was here that he wrote the Divine Comedy. In the work, Dante described the Divine Forest in Ravenna, where the pines extended down to the sea. It was his earthly paradise. The pines are now gone, but paradise remains.

TRIESTE

LAKE BLED: THE ORIGINAL CHOICE FOR DESTINATION WEDDINGS

From the port of Trieste, it is a beautiful drive northeast into Slovenia to the site of the original destination wedding at Lake Bled. The first destination wedding at Lake Bled occurred thousands of years ago, in front of crude stone altars, which have transcended into Slavic mythology. For the last six hundred years, weddings have gone indoors to the jewel-box church, the Pilgrimage Church of the Assumption of Mary. Today, though there are elegant hotels for wedding guests that ring the lake, the beauty of the site remains unspoiled.

This is the story of a small landscape of immense beauty, which has inspired the instigation of matrimonial bliss for thousands of years. Lake Bled, the original choice for destination weddings, remains popular.

The Natural Site for the Wedding of Živa and Siebog

Tiny Lake Bled is a natural glacial lake, which contains the only natural island in Slovenia. A casual stroll around the circumference of the lake takes only about an hour. The island in the center comprises less than an acre of vegetation. The lake is surrounded by dense stands of evergreen trees in a small valley, bounded by steep rock cliffs. Beyond the valley there is the small town of Bled and farmland, then more picturesque mountains.

It is easy to appreciate why the early inhabitants of the area were attracted to Lake Bled. Archaeology places habitation sites around the lake thousands of years in the past. One remnant of early life in the area was a stone altar in the middle of Bled Island. Through time this altar has been associated with the union of Živa and her partner Siebog, the goddess and god of love and fertility. The site of marital joinder was so popular in the ancient world that the altar was expanded into a temple dedicated to Živa.

Slavic mythology contains vivid personalities of immense impact on life in ancient communities across a broad area that includes present-day Poland, Slavic nations, and extending eastward to Iran. Academic study and general knowledge of this mythology has been limited, as Slavs did not have a system of writing until the arrival of Cyril and Methodius in the mid-ninth century.[178] Saint Cyril developed Slavic literacy as a means to preach the Bible, which was not conducive to preserving pagan cultural practices. When Christian monks encountered Slavic mythology, they found it repugnant, uncivilized, and dark. Thus the early written records of the area include the bias of the authors. Pre-Christian, polytheistic practices and stories live on in the archaeological remains of cult images, ancient art-inspired historic art, and pagan festivals that survive today in many regions of Slavic nations.

Although many purported authoritative books on Slavic mythology have been debunked as recent creations, there have been sufficient discoveries of ancient artifacts to indicate that multiple-deity worship was abundant. There have been recurring finds of shrines - platforms surrounded by sacrificial altars. Common at these sites are tall obelisks or carved wooden poles depicting several gods.

Worship of the gods often occurred in the woods, without the benefit of a structure. It is these folk traditions that survive today in local festivals, even if the original meaning is lost. In the Middle Ages of the twelfth to fourteenth centuries, Christianity was accepted throughout the region, although the folk rituals continued.[179]

The Slavic year began in early March, about the time of Christian Easter. This was celebrated with a dark reverence as the time when the spirits of deceased family came to join the living to celebrate the New Year. Spring was, and still

---

[178] See Itinerary IV. Black Sea, Port of Nessebur and the story of Cyril and Methodius.
[179] There is also a rich profusion of fairy tales with demons and heroes, not to be confused with characters of deeper religious significance.

is, ushered in with colored eggs and a feast. The goddess of fertility reigns in spring. In mid-summer the god of thunder brings rain, followed by fall, the time of the harvest. There was a ceremony at the winter solstice, which became the time for Christmas upon the advent of Christianity. In ancient times, Slavic people collected oak branches at the winter solstice, which were decorated with ribbons. The branches were blessed and then an oak log was set on fire.

From what little can be substantiated of Slavic gods, there was, at the least, an all-powerful deity, Perun, who eventually became associated with the Christian god. There was also a god of thunder, a god of the underworld, who was defeated by Perun, and a goddess of fertility. Belief in some of the early gods persists in pagan rituals, while many have slipped into the realm of fairy-tale characters, useful for teaching morals and local customs.

Živa, the goddess of love and fertility, is also known as Siva or Seiba. Her partner, the god of love, is Siebog. The concept of love and devotion between couples has remained unchanged in pagan and Christian times. Imagery of Živa can be found in Slavic poetry and art from medieval times to the present day.

The Bishop of Brixon Moves In

Perched on a rock wall, overlooking Lake Bled, is the Bled Castle. The castle is one of the oldest in Slovenia, dating to the eleventh century. It was home to the Bishops of Brixon. The Bishops of Brixon strengthened the adoption of Christianity in their domain, although they were typically more aligned with their royal brothers, the Holy Roman Emperors of Austria, than with the pope in Rome.

Bled Castle is a sturdy edifice. It has survived through peasant revolts early in its history and through two world wars. The Bishopric of Brixon was dissolved in 1803. Today the castle is open to tourists, affording them a splendid view of the lake and the surrounding mountains.

Under the Bishops of Brixon, Bled was part of the Austria-Hungary domain. Vacationing royals and affluent members of Austrian society had access to Lake Bled. Beautiful homes were built around the lake. Upon the dissolution of Austria-Hungary in 1918, following World War I, Bled came within the kingdom of Yugoslavia. The practice of building large vacation homes around the lake continued. One such house was built for Yugoslavian President Joseph Tito in 1947.

The beautiful scenery and mild climate of Lake Bled made it a prime vacation and recreation destination. Rowing competitions have been held on the lake for over a hundred years. It became a practice site for Olympic hopefuls. Health spas and hotels joined exclusive homes around Lake Bled, enabling more tourism. Although never crowded, Lake Bled is a popular place.

The Pilgrimage Church of the Assumption of Mary

The lovely little island in the middle of Lake Bled has never been ignored. When Christianity replaced pagan practices and the island shrine was replaced with a church, pilgrims flocked to the site. The words of the ceremonies on Bled Island evolved over time, while the purpose of the ceremonies remained constant. Vows of love and matrimony on Bled Island have been continuous for the last two thousand years.

In the fifteenth century, the pink and white Pilgrimage Church of the Assumption of Mary was built on Bled Island. The church looks like the perfect setting for a fairy-tale wedding. It is a small church, with a tall spire that rises 171 feet above the church. A stairway of ninety-nine steps leads from the small dock to the church in a graceful curve. The church was built for happy occasions such as weddings. Sitting in the church it is hard to imagine that a funeral mass was ever held there. To begin the wedding ceremony, it is traditional for the groom to carry the bride up the steps to the church, make a wish, and then ring the church bell together to make the wish come true.

Guests at the wedding arrive at the church on open, gaily decorated boats. There are small boats for the bride and groom that are made of wood in the shape of swans. The whole scene looks like a stage set from a Wagnerian opera wedding.

Still the Choice for Destination Weddings

Živa, or Seiba, and Seibog started a lasting tradition on Bled Island. People no longer come to the island to celebrate pagan rituals. The Virgin Mary has replaced Živa. The Christian altar in a church has replaced the pagan altar in a shrine. Still, the ritual vows made in love persist.

Hotels, small restaurants, coffee bars, shops and a casino that ring Lake Bled today all cater to casual tourists and wedding parties. A web search of Lake Bled weddings will produce about a dozen businesses devoted to arranging weddings for clients from around the world. Health spa patrons and vacationers still come to enjoy swimming, hiking, and boating at the lake, as well as the mineral water springs.[180] Lake Bled provides the setting for a destination wedding and a honeymoon in one place.

---

[180] The huge mineral water swimming pool in the Hotel Golf, one of five swimming choices in the hotel, is all enclosed and looks out over the lake.

VENICE
THE WELL-TRAVELED HORSES OF SAINT MARKS

Sitting above the entrance to the popular tourist site of Saint Marks Cathedral in Venice are the four horses, the Quadriga of Saint Marks. To Venetians, these four horses are emblematic of the enduring spirit of the city. The horses have become the patrimony of Venice, no less than Saint Marks, or the lagoons of the gondoliers.

The larger-than-life-size horses were designed to be viewed from far below their pedestal. However, they were not made for Saint Marks. Before the horses came to Italy, they stood above the Hippodrome of Constantine in Constantinople. Since Constantine was not known for making original commissions, the horses were likely repurposed from some more ancient place.

The design, fabrication, and site of creation of the four horses are mysterious. Their travels of the last two thousand years highlight their importance as a symbol of status and power. This is the story of the four horses, the Quadriga of Saint Marks, their endurance, travels, and position today as a symbol of Venice.

The Enduring Quadriga

A quadriga is a set of four horses, often in full motion pulling a chariot. That they are depicted with raised legs is a sign of power. Standing in the chariot is usually a Greek or Roman god, or an emperor. The horses are set to complement each other, as would a real-life team. They are a classical form, begun in antiquity, which has been much replicated through time. A quadriga sits above a triumphal Brandenburg Gate in Berlin and above the doors to a city theater in Palermo. So often are quadriga used in art and architecture that they may seem ubiquitous to the traveler.

Hector, a son of Troy, is seen on ancient vases, in his chariot pulled by a team of four horses. Likewise, the Greek god Achilles is pictured with his quadriga on vases, plates, and wall art. The Caesar Nero was depicted with his quadriga on Roman coins in 68 CE, and in a sculpture on a victory arch, until his suicide, when all things Nero were dismantled or destroyed.[181]

The Quadriga of Saint Marks is a sculpture of realistic horses, of unknown breed. That their necks and backs are short in relation to their long legs may be artistic license with the physique of the real-life models for the horses by artists who knew the statues would be viewed from below. Until the early nineteenth century the horses each had a bronze bridle.[182]

One of the mysteries of the Quadriga of Saint Marks is their fabrication. The early Etruscans of northwest Italy fabricated statues of bronze when working as craftsmen for the Greeks. The Greeks had a history of chariot racing, long before the Etruscans brought the sport to Rome. The Greek games occurred every four years, while the Romans increased the frequency to annual races.[183] Quadriga easily became a symbol of Roman games, as another art form evolved from Greek styles. Thus, the Quadriga of Saint Marks could have come from an Etruscan artist, commissioned by a Greek or a Roman patron.

---

[181] The quadriga of Nero is so like the quadriga of Saint Marks, that historian's debate whether the horses with Nero are just a quadriga or the quadriga of Venice.

[182] A possible explanation for removal of the bridles is offered as a symbol of unbridled Italy, during the time the Quadriga sat above the entrance to Saint Marks. Charles Freeman, The Horses of St. Marks, The Overlook Press, New York, 2010, p. 11and 127. The poet Lord Byron had belittled Venice in his epic poem, Childe Harold, "Are they not Bridled? – Venice, lost and won, Her thirteen hundred years of freedom done … . Fourth Canto, XIII.

[183] Alcibiades entered the Greek Olympics of 416 BCE with seven teams of quadriga. His teams took first, second, and fourth place, a feat he often touted as he tried to dominate the politics of Athens. True to form, Alcibiades did not actually drive any of the teams himself. See CTH Itinerary III. Athens - Alcibiades: Most Favorite Son.

As art historians of recent times began to examine the Quadriga of Saint Marks to determine the age of the statues, they made a thrilling discovery. The Quadriga of Saint Marks is only gilded bronze. The bodies are made of copper. Copper has a higher melting point than bronze. It is harder to form. The creation of copper statuary is so rarely seen in ancient work, that the fabrication technique is not well known.[184] The Quadriga of Saint Marks could be an original creation, from which similar copies were cast in bronze for two millennia or more.

To place a date on the statues, without destructive testing for chemical analysis, historians look for clues in early reports that may have mentioned them. They also hunt through reports of archaeological excavations and examine ancient pottery and coins. Pure metal is almost impossible to date. There are no artisan signatures on the quadriga.

There are several theories for the origination of the quadriga. One of the most plausible explanations is that when Constantine looted Delphi for statues to decorate his Hippodrome in Constantinople, around 330 CE, the quadriga was part of the booty. There was known to be a chariot and four horses at Delphi. The quadriga was an offering of the citizens of the Greek island of Rhodes for a victory in 304 BCE. If that quadriga is THE Quadriga of Venice, the horses are over 2,300 years old. They have also traveled many miles during that time.

The Traveling Horses

Assuming the Quadriga of Saint Marks began their tour as a gift from the island of Rhodes to the Oracle at Delphi, in northern Greece, it is possible that they were crafted on another of the Greek islands known to be home to prolific sculptors of the time. The horses would have gone island hopping until they reached a suitable port from which to travel overland to Delphi. Once ensconced at the temple at Delphi, the Quadriga would have had a commanding view of the Greek valley leading north to Macedonia and south to the Peloponnese. This was a fitting home for seven centuries.

---

[184] Freeman, p. 175.

As Constantine moved across the civilized world of the time, spreading Orthodox Christianity, he built a Hippodrome, a sports arena, in each city that he conquered. When he came to Rome there was already the Circus Maximus, built by a prior Caesar, so Constantine made it even more glorious. Whole cities were denuded of their statuary to adorn each Constantine arena.

When Constantine reached Constantinople and decided to make it his capital, he reached as far as Delphi for statuary with credentials. The quadriga began their stay in Constantinople perched on top of an arch leading into the field of competition.[185] This became home for another eight centuries.

In 1199, Pope Innocent III launched the Fourth Crusade to the Holy Land, which would eventually have an impact on the quadriga in Constantinople. The contortion of the Fourth Crusade into an assault on the Christian city of Constantinople, and the removal of the quadriga from the Hippodrome of Constantine to their installation in Saint Marks in Venice, has been the subject of heated debate among scholars. Some place the blame on venal acts of the Venetian Doge Enrico Dandolo, while others regard Dandolo as merely a wise strategist, when opportunity presented itself.

In 1201, when the French nobility came to Venice to secure transport for the crusade to the Holy Land, Enrico Dandolo was 95 years old. He was a veteran of skirmishes with the Orthodox Christians of Constantinople, where Venice competed with Pisa for the status of priority trading partner. In 1182, Emperor Andronicus of Constantinople issued an order that all Latins in his city be killed. There were many Venetians in harm's way. Dandolo, then in his sixties, led the defensive. He was injured, although not losing his eyesight at that time. The injury attributed as the cause of his blindness occurred later in

---

[185] One hundred years after Constantine's rule, the Emperor Theodosius II brought gold-gilded bronze quadriga from the Greek island of Chios to Constantinople, thus raising questions of which quadriga eventually went to Venice. Historians generally agree that the earlier horses are the ones that continued their journey. The Venetians may have melted down the second set as part of the razing of Constantinople in 1204.

a blow to the head, although it is often cited as cause for Dandolo to resent the Byzantine city.[186]

From the fifth century, Venice was more closely aligned with Byzantine Constantinople than with Rome. Wealthy Venetians sent their sons to Constantinople to be educated. Venetians prized their collections of Byzantine art. When in 726, Byzantine Emperor Leo decreed that Byzantine churches were to be devoid of images, Venetians actively collected art and artifacts from Constantinople, effectively preserving Byzantine art. Venetian artists began to create art in the Byzantine fashion. Envy of the cultural treasures of Constantinople was still in force while Dandolo was the doge.

The French leaders of the Fourth Crusade greatly overestimated their needs to Dandolo. They ordered ships to transport 30,300 crusading soldiers, plus a large number of armed navy vessels. Dandolo focused all shipbuilding efforts in Venice to meet the needs of the crusade. Merchant vessels, typically engaged in annual shipments of wheat and other profitable items, were booked for transport in support of the crusade. The entire economy of Venice became tied to the crusade. In exchange, Dandolo charged a high price to the French and obtained their agreement to allow Venice a dominant percentage of the spoils of war.

As the time for sailing to the Holy Land approached, the French stalled. Their fund-raising efforts were short of the mark. The number of crusaders was about a third of their expectations. Nobles who could fund their trip and that of several other crusaders were in short supply. Instead, the old, the poor, and the weak dominated the volunteer army. Many volunteers were women without independent support. The pope encouraged the old, the sick, and the women to go home.

---

[186] Donald E. Quellar & Thomas F. Madden, The Fourth Crusade, 2nd ed., U. Penn. Press, 1997, p. 9. Many historians assume that Dandolo's blindness occurred about the time of the incident in Constantinople and not as a result of some subsequent blow to the head. It is further assumed that Dandolo harbored resentment against Constantinople due to the injury, refocusing the Fourth Crusade as a result. These two historians argue for restraint in assumptions. They view Dandolo as a far more complex character.

Dandolo, and all of Venice, was in an economic bind. He offered the French an alternative to enable payment of their debt. Dandolo proposed that the crusaders first go across the Adriatic, to the Christian city of Zara, where they would plunder storehouses to feed the crusaders. Then they would go to Constantinople, where the plunder would be sufficient to repay Venice. Whether Dandolo was motivated by profit, envy of the cultural treasures of Constantinople, or revenge for earlier actions against Venice is unknown. It may have been a combination of all three.

When the army and navy of the Fourth Crusade arrived in Constantinople, it was a vibrant city. The emperor of Constantinople, who was also aging and blind, had been recently and forcibly replaced. Political upheaval in the city was not unusual. The public was unfazed by another of what they regarded as internal family power struggles, of no consequence to their daily lives.

Traveling with the French was the son of the deposed emperor. Dandolo paraded the young heir apparent along the banks of the city, as he threatened an invasion. The city dwellers just laughed at him.

The usurping emperor took Dandolo seriously. He left the city. During his absence pandemonium raged through neighborhoods. While attempting to breach the seawalls, Danodolo's navy started a fire that burned from the docks on the north side of town to the gates of the palace on the south side. Days later the army started a fire that burned across the remainder of the old city. Tens of thousands of people were left homeless. No longer complacent about the effects of the conflict, many more residents left town.

Dandolo did not order or condone the fires. However, he took advantage of their effect. Looting was widespread. The booty was piled high in tents guarded by Venetians. Crusaders, who hoped to become rich in the name of the church, stood by anxiously awaiting their share.

The dreams of riches soon faded for the crusader army. Dandolo made certain that Venice was first to receive over half of the spoils for her part in support of the crusade, in spite of excommunication by the pope for attacking a Christian city. Then Dandolo paid the French debt to Venice from the booty. Next, the French reimbursed themselves for their expenses and received their share of the spoils of war. Very little was left to pay the crusading army.

Mighty Constantinople was left a charred city. Scavengers traversed the city looking for ancient monuments to dismantle for scrap. Dandolo entered the Hippodrome with his crew to "save" the quadriga from the scrap heap. The horses were carefully packed for their voyage to Venice.

By the time the quadriga was installed in Venice, Dandolo was dead. His legacy remained for almost 600 years, as the quadriga stood proudly above the entrance to Saint Marks.[187] Without their chariot the horses stood in a different sequence. In the fifteenth century, the bridles were removed, symbolizing the unbridled power of Venice. The quadriga of Rhodes, Delphi, and Constantinople were regarded as being only Venetian.

Beloved at Home

The quadriga stood looking over Saint Marks Square as it was cleared of trees and clutter, to become the elegant plaza it is today. Fifteenth century painters, such as Gentile Bellini, included the horses as a focal point in pictures of Venice. Sixteenth century tourist guides listed the horses as the site to see in Venice. Copies of the horses were minted as popular souvenirs.

Then, in 1798, the army of Napoleon entered Venice. Napoleon coveted the horses as art and as trophies representing his conquest of Italy. French troops removed the horses from Saint Marks, amid protests from angry Venetians. The horses traveled from Venice to the Tuileries Palace in Paris and then down the avenue to the top of the Arc du Carrousel.[188]

The French quickly became emotionally attached to the quadriga. Napoleon could go into exile, but the horses must stay in Paris. As the victors in the Napoleonic war, the English weighed in on the question of whether the horses

---

[187] During their transit from Constantinople to Venice one of the horses lost a hoof. It was eventually recovered and attached. Freeman, p. 95.

[188] The horses seen today on the Arc du Carrousel are copies of the Venetian Quadriga. They have no chariot. The Arc du Carrousel is at the entrance to the Louvre, before the visitor enters the Tuileries Gardens, walks down the Champs-Élysées, to the Arc de Triomphe.

should stay in Paris or return to Venice. The Duke of Wellington voiced his opinion that the quadriga was better off in France than it would be at home in Venice.

The quadriga might have stayed in Paris but for the champion of Venice, Antonio Canova. Canova was a Venetian sculptor and a celebrity in Europe.[189] He had completed the tomb of Pope Clement XIV in 1788, in the classic style, which brought him a great deal of attention.

When Napoleon collected treasures from Venice, he took with him some of Canova's work. Napoleon tried several times to hire Canova, but the sculptor rebuffed him by saying that he would not work for someone who looted Venice. Finally, under continued pressure from Napoleon, Canova did consent to do a bust and statue of Napoleon. The resulting statue depicts an uncomplimentary rotund and nude Napoleon. After the war, the British purchased the statue of Napoleon and gifted it to Wellington.[190]

Canova was the envoy of the Pope to Paris in the aftermath of the Napoleonic war. He spoke English, which facilitated his work with the British envoy William Hamilton. Together Canova and Hamilton concluded an agreement for the pope to receive back the Vatican statues removed by Napoleon.

With Hamilton and the rest of the British delegation on his side, Canova was able to convince the Austrians, who controlled Venice, to claim the horses for Venice. In 1815, Canova had his own victory for the arts and culture of Venice. Austrian troops were needed to remove the quadriga from the Arc du Carrousel, as crowds of protesting Parisians blocked the streets.

From 1815 to the present, the quadriga has remained in the possession of Venice and at home in Saint Marks. During World Wars I and II, the horses were removed from their perch over the entrance to Saint Marks to safer haven

---

[189] In the dedication to the Childe Harold, his most famous epic poem, Lord Byron pays tribute to Canova, "Italy has great names still, ... and in some the very highest: Europe – the World – has but one Canova." Byron, Childe Harold, American edition, A.C. McClurg and Company, Chicago, 1891, p. 14.

[190] The statue of Napoleon by Canova can be seen on the grounds at Apsley House, London. Freeman, p.215.

between sand bags in a room in the doge's palace. More recently another threat emerged, that of acid rain. To protect the quadriga they have been moved from the outside entrance to a small room under the vaults of a chapel ceiling, where they can still receive visitors. The horses now seen above the great entrance to Saint Marks are stand-ins.

After his efforts on behalf of the quadriga, Antonio Canova went on to be consulted by the British on another matter regarding claims to cultural property. The British sought Canova's opinion on the Parthenon marbles that the British Parliament was considering for purchase from Lord Elgin. That tale leads to another itinerary and another story.

INDEX

A

Achilleion Palace (Corfu) 13, 205-6, 211-12, 214
Achilles 198, 212-14, 310
Agamemnon 198, 322
Agrigento 15, 131, 155, 157, 159-60, 164
Aeneid 45, 48-9, 51, 55
Aquillius, Manus 60, 153-54
Alagiri, Dante 48, 55, 129, 299
Appius, Claudius 17-18, 22, 27
Arc du Carrousel (Paris) 319, 320
Arc de Triomphe (Paris) 100, 319
Arcadia 48
Aristotle 155, 162
Athenion 147, 152-4

B

Baroque 67, 179, 236, 239, 241-2, 245, 246, 254
Bishops of Brixon (Lake Bled) 303, 306, 322
Bled Castle (Lake Bled) 303
Boleyn, Anne 41
Bonaparte 85, 88, 90, 91, 92, 93, 95, 96, 97, 98, 88, 100, 102
    Carlo 33, 89-91
    Caroline 9, 92, 97, 100, 109
    Elisa 92, 95, 97, 99
    Giuseppe (Joseph) 90-3, 246
    Josephine 95, 97
    Letizia 13, 85, 88-93, 95-100, 102, 322
    Louis 95, 97-8, 100, 322
    Lucian 91, 98
    Napoleon 85, 88-93, 95-100, 102, 179, 213-14, 250, 257, 263, 319-20
    Napoleon II 97, 99, 102
    Pauline 95, 97-9
Bourbon Kings and Queens 67, 97, 98, 141, 143
    Amalia, 67
    Beatrice of Provence 125
    Carlo 33, 89-91, 322-3
    Charles of Anjou 123, 125, 127-8, 131
    Charles V 241
    Louis XIV -
    Louis XVIII 97
Bronze Age 115, 118
Byzantium (Byzantine) 126, 127, 129-30, 249, 297

C

Cabrera, Bernardo 171, 173-5
Caesar 47-9, 150, 310, 314
    Augusta (Galla Placidia) 283, 290, 292
    Augustus 49, 51, 273. 290
        Constantus 287-92, 297, 298
        Maximan 206. 254, 273, 314
        Octavius 49
    Caligula 274
    Carus 270
    Gaius Aurelius Valerius 271
        Diocletianus 271
    Julius 47, 150
    Nero 25, 274, 310
    Numerianus 270-1
Canova, Antonio 320-1

Carthage 49, 76, 83, 148, 189, 191-2
Castel del Monte (Puglia) 226
Castel dell' Ovo (Naples) 45, 54
Cava, Onofrio della 254, 257, 265
Cavor, Benso di 137
Charybdis 765, 200
Church 25, 27, 54-5, 109, 128, 173, 221, 234-6, 242, 244-6, 278, 283-4, 293-4, 297-9, 306-7
    Prilgrmage Church of the Assumption of Mary, Lake Bled
        12, 15, 301, 303, 306-7
    St. Apollinare Classe (Basilica), Lecce 299
    St. Apollinare Nuovo (Basilica), Lecce 299
    St. Anna, Lecce 246
    St. Chiara, Lecce 242
    St. Croce (Basilica), Lecce 246, 293, 297
    St. Giovanni Battista (Basilica), Lecce 246
    St. Giovanni Evangelista, Rome 297
    St. Irene, Lecce 244, 245-6
    St. Maria, Lecce 246
    St. Maria en Palmis, Rome (Domine Quo Vadis) 25
    St. Marks, Venice 98, 214, 257, 309-10, 313-4, 319-21
    St. Oronzo, Lecce 244-6
    St. Petronilla, Rome 294
    St. Sebastian, Rome 27
    St. Teresa, Lecce 246
Cicero 128, 159, 186
Cino, Guiseppe 242-3, 246
Circe 200
Collodi, Carlo (nom de plume, Carlo Lorenzini) 30
Constantine 269, 274-5, 284, 288-9, 293, 299, 309, 313-4

Corvaja Palace (Taormina) 173
Croton 71-2, 78-9, 81-2
Crusade 125-6, 218-19, 221, 225, 227, 257, 314-15, 318

D

Damocles 192-3
Dandolo, Enrico 257, 314-15, 318-19
Death ray 182, 186
Delphi, Oracle 82, 160, 192, 313-14, 319, 323
Doric 78, 157, 159
Drogarati Cave
Dumas, Alexandre 70, 104, 133, 137, 144, 159

E

Ecologues (Virgil)
Elba 85, 97-8, 100, 323
Emanuel, Victor 141, 144
Empedocles 4, 12, 155, 157, 159-64

F

Fesch, Cardinal 89, 91, 98, 100, 323
Forster, E.M. 159
Forum (Rome) 22, 78, 99
Fourth Crusade 314-15, 318
France, Anatole 159

G

Galilei, Galileo 43
Garibaldi 3-4, 12, 15, 70, 103-5, 107-11, 129, 133, 135, 137, 139, 141-5
    Anita (Ribeiroda da Silva) 105
    Anita (daughter) 104
    Anna
    Battistina (Ravello) 108
    Clelia 109, 111
    Constance 110, 127, 218, 222
    Francesca (Armosino) 109, 111
    Giuseppe 90-3, 246

Manlio 109-11
　　　Menotti 107
　　　Rosa 109, 111
　　　Teresita 111
Gela 157
Genoa 12, 88, 90, 95, 107, 139, 205
Georgics 48
Ghetto (Dubrovnik) 262-3
Ghibelline 220-1
Giannettino 30
Guelph 220-1

H

Hamilton, William 320, 323
Hannibal (Barca) 72, 83
Heiberg, Johan Ludwig 40
Helios 200
Herodotus 37, 72, 76
Hohenstaufen 125, 127, 226
　　　Conrad IV 125, 218, 222
　　　Enzio 218, 221
　　　Frederick II 125, 215, 217-23, 225-7
　　　Manfred 125, 127, 130, 218, 222
　　　Tancred 218
Holy Roman Empire (Emperors) 217
Homer 48-9, 51, 202
Honorarius
Huns, Attila 292-3

I

Inquisition 261-2, 266
Ionian 71-3, 197, 212
Ithaca 197-8, 201-2

K

Kings and Queens
　　　Blanche I (Aragon and Sicily) 169, 171, 173-4
　　　Charles III (Navarre) 123, 125-31, 322
　　　Christina (Sweden) 40
　　　Edward I (England) 130
　　　Eleanor (Navarre) 175
　　　Ferdinand IV (Naples) 178-9
　　　Gelo (Syracuse) 185
　　　Henry VIII (England) 41
　　　Hiero (Syracuse, Sicily) 181-3,
　　　John II (Aragon) 74
　　　Maria Carolina (Naples) 169, 178-9
　　　Marie Antoinette (France) 178
　　　Martin I (Aragon) 171, 173-4
　　　Martin I (Sicily) 173
　　　Peter (Spain) 25, 127, 129-31
Knights Templar 219

L

Lampedusa, Guiseppe Tomasi di 169, 175
Lancaster, Burt 176
Libro d'Oro 205
Lincoln, Abraham 135
Luther, Martin 41

M

Magna Graecia 73, 82, 84, 239
Manzoni, Alessandro 142
Marmarospilia Cave-Lake 202
Mayerling Incident 210
Mazzini, Guiseppe 103-4, 107, 137, 139, 145
Melena, Elpis (non de plume, Marie Esperance von Brandt) 104, 108-9
Menelaus 198
Melissani Cave
Middle Ages 141, 187, 249, 302
Mount Etna 155, 157, 163-4
Mount Vesuvius 22, 54, 57
Mulini Palace 97, 100

N

Neopolitans 143-4
Nuraghe 113, 115, 117-22

O

Odometer (Archimedes) 184
Odysseus 12-13, 197-8, 200-2, 204
Olympic 18, 306
Oscan 60
Ovid 51

P

Palaeologus, Michael (Emperor) 127
Palatine Library (Heidelberg) 40
Palimpset
Paoli, Pasquale 90-3
Papo, Michael 266
Pappacoda, Luigi 242
Paris 40, 85, 88, 90, 93, 96-8, 100, 102, 209, 212-13, 319-20, 322-5
Paris of Troy 18, 48-9, 82, 147-8, 198, 201-2, 212, 310
Parthenon (Athens) 78, 321
Petrarch, Francesco 43, 55
Philipson, Caroline Gifford 109
Pirandello, Luigi 159
Plague 24, 35, 45, 226, 230, 241, 245, 261, 264, 283
Plato 193
Pliny the Younger 64
Pompeii 21, 57, 60, 64, 66, 70
Pope
    Boniface VIII 131
    Clement XIV 320
    Gregory XVI 220-1
    Honorius IV 131, 287-92, 298
    Innocent III 217, 219-20, 314
    Innocent IV 125, 221
    John XXI 126
    Martin IV 126, 131
    Nicholas III
    Nicholas V 35, 37
    Pius IX 137, 139
    Sixtus IV 38
    Urban IV 125
Puglia 22. 215, 225, 227
Pyrrhus (king Puglia) 22
Pythagoras 72, 79, 325

R

Raimond, Giuseppina 109
Ralph, Elizabeth 84
Red Shirts 105, 110, 142
Renaissance 13, 35, 37-8, 68, 279
Riaro, Girolamo 68
Roberts, Emma 105, 107-8
Rome 11-12, 15, 21-2, 25, 29-30, 35, 37-9, 49, 95-100, 150-1, 153-4, 269-71, 283-4, 286-94, 323
    Catacombs 27
    Circus Maximus 314
    Coliseum 25, 99, 150, 154
    Forum 22, 78, 99

S

Salvius (King Tryphon) 151-4
Sammite 60
Samos 72
Santo Spirito 128
Schonbrunn Palace (Vienna)
Sforza 13, 57, 67-8, 70, 236
    Cardinal Sisto Riario 67
    Catarina 67-8
Slave, slavery 135, 150, 152, 265
Sparta 77, 191
Spartacus 12, 25, 47, 62, 72, 83, 147, 150
St. Croce 323, 325
St. Cyril 302
St. Francis Assisi
St. Helena 85, 98
St. Irene 323
St. Jerome 325
St. Methodius 302

St. Nikolaus 229-30, 233-4
St. Oronzo 245-6
St. Peter 25, 27, 294

T

Telys 79, 82
Temple 78
    Apollo 78, 82, 213
    Asclepius (Agrigento) 157
    Athena 78
    Castor (Agrigento) 157
    Ceres 78
    Concordia (Agrigento) 159
    Hera (Juno) (Agrigento) 78, 159, 161
    Heracles (Hercules) (Agrigento) 61, 82, 89, 157, 201
    Jupiter (Split) 278
    Neptune 78
    Pollux (Agrigento) 157
    Poseidon 78, 200
    Vulcan (Agrigento) 157
    Zeus (Agrigento) 78, 157, 161, 164, 192
Theodosius I 284, 292, 294
Theodosius II 287, 293, 294, 314
Theodosius III 289, 294, 298
Thurii 82, 160
Tito, Joseph General
Treaty of Caltabellotta 131
Troy 18, 48-9, 82, 147-8, 198, 201-2, 212, 310
    Helen 198, 212, 284, 293
    Horse 198
Tuileries Palace (Paris) 319

U

University
    Massachusetts Institute Technology (MIT) 183, 326
    Naples 3, 13, 15, 45, 48, 51, 54-5, 64, 66-7, 70-1, 127, 143-5, 178-9, 326

Yeshiva 266

V

Valentinian III
Vatican 12, 15, 35, 37-40, 43, 68, 88, 133, 135, 139, 141, 283, 294
    Library 3, 35, 37-41, 43
    Sistine Chapel 38, 43
Verdi, Guiseppe 132
Via Appia 17,-8, 21-2, 27
Via Egnatia 18, 21 24
Vigne, Pier delle 221, 223
Villa Aprile (Naples) 67, 70
Villa Miglio D'Ora (Naples) 70
Virgil (Publius Vergilius Marco) 45
Visigoth 286
    Alaric 286-9
    Athaulf 287-90, 294

W

Walters Art Museum (Baltimore) 188
War 35, 40, 49, 66, 79, 81, 97, 123, 129-31, 135, 148, 150-1, 191, 212, 270-1
    Second Servile 151
    Thirty Year 39, 51, 294
    Trojan 13, 197-8, 212
    World War I 176, 306, 326
    World War II 176, 204, 214, 266
    Yugoslav 262, 266, 279
Water screw (Archimedes) 183
Webber, Karl 66
Wellington, Duke (Arthur Wellesley) 320
White, Jesse 104. 107-8
World Heritage Site (ICOMOS) 157, 226, 249-50
World Jewish Congress 267

Z

Zimbalo, Guiseppe 239, 242, 246

www.ingramcontent.com/pod-product-compliance
Lightning Source LLC
Chambersburg PA
CBHW051350070526
44584CB00025B/3704